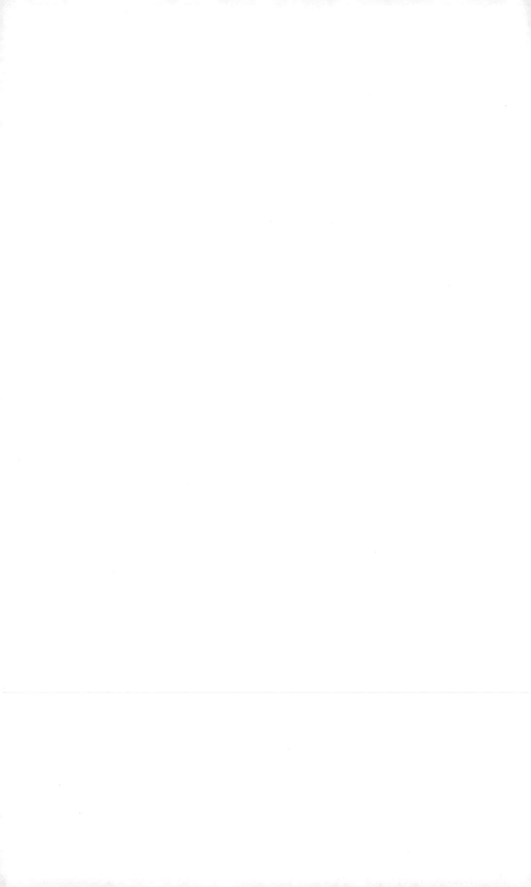

Same-Sex Marriage and Children

Same-Sex Marriage and Children

A Tale of History, Social Science, and Law

Carlos A. Ball

OXFORD
UNIVERSITY PRESS

Oxford University Press is a department of the University of
Oxford. It furthers the University's objective of excellence in research,
scholarship, and education by publishing worldwide.

Oxford   New York
Auckland   Cape Town   Dar es Salaam   Hong Kong   Karachi
Kuala Lumpur   Madrid   Melbourne   Mexico City   Nairobi
New Delhi   Shanghai   Taipei   Toronto

With offices in
Argentina   Austria   Brazil   Chile   Czech Republic   France   Greece
Guatemala   Hungary   Italy   Japan   Poland   Portugal   Singapore
South Korea   Switzerland   Thailand   Turkey   Ukraine   Vietnam

Oxford is a registered trademark of Oxford University Press
in the UK and certain other countries.

Published in the United States of America by
Oxford University Press
198 Madison Avenue, New York, NY 10016

© Oxford University Press 2014

Library of Congress Cataloging-in-Publication Data
Ball, Carlos A.
Same-sex marriage and children: a tale of history, social science, and law / Carlos A. Ball.
pages cm
Includes bibliographical references and index.
ISBN 978–0–19–997787–1
1. Same-sex marriage.   2. Children of same-sex parents.   3. Child rearing—Psychological
aspects.   4. Child psychology.   I. Title.
HQ1033.B35 2014
306.84′8—dc23
2014001942

3 5 7 9 8 6 4 2
Printed in the United States of America
on acid-free paper

To my mother, Elba, and to my sons, Sebastian and Emmanuel

CONTENTS

Acknowledgments ix

Introduction 1

1. A Historical Review 11

2. Responsible Procreation 37

3. Family Optimality 69

4. Sexual Orientation and Parenting 83

5. Same-Sex Marriage before the Supreme Court 111

Conclusion: Lessons for the Future 129

Notes 137
Index 169

ACKNOWLEDGMENTS

I would like to thank Jyl Josephson, Courtney Joslin, Douglas NeJaime, and Clifford Rosky for reading sections of the manuscript and providing me with extremely helpful suggestions that encouraged me to make this a better book. I presented an earlier version of chapter 1 at faculty workshops at the Loyola University School of Law (Chicago) and at the University of Minnesota School of Law. I thank the participants for their superb comments and suggestions. I have also benefited immensely from having a life partner, Richard Storrow, who happens to be a law professor and who has given much thought to many of the issues I discuss in this book. And thank you to the anonymous reviewers for both expressing enthusiasm for the project and suggesting ways to improve it.

Lee Sims, a librarian at the Rutgers University School of Law, was of great assistance in tracking down research materials. Sean Dickson provided crucial research assistance, especially on the empirical studies following the welfare reform legislation of the 1990s. A warm thank you as well to Sarah Harrington of Oxford University Press for believing in the project and expertly guiding it to publication.

The content of this book is part history, part social science, and part law. It seems appropriate, therefore, to recognize one member of each of these disciplines whose work has been particularly instrumental in inspiring my own. George Chauncey, through his revelations of gay history; Charlotte Patterson, through her pioneering work studying lesbian and gay families; and Mary Bonauto, through her indefatigable efforts to use the law to promote the interests of the LGBT community, have contributed in crucial ways to whatever wisdom can be found in these pages.

An earlier version of the section of chapter 1 that discusses antimiscegenation regulations in colonial Virginia appeared as Carlos A. Ball, "The Blurring of the Lines: Children and Bans on Interracial Unions and Same-Sex Marriages," 76 *Fordham Law Review* 2733 (2008). And chapter 4 is a modified version of Carlos A. Ball, "Social Science Studies and the Children of Lesbians and Gay Men: The Rational Basis Perspective," 21 *William & Mary Bill of Rights Journal* 691 (2013). I thank both journals for permitting me to build on the earlier material.

Introduction

When Jack Baker, in the spring of 1967, asked Michael McConnell to join him in committing themselves to be a couple for life, McConnell agreed on the condition that they would some day marry. The two men, both in their midtwenties, had met six months earlier at a Halloween barn party near the University of Oklahoma, where McConnell was pursuing a degree in library sciences. Shortly after they met, Baker, who was an engineer and Air Force veteran, took a civilian job at the Tinker Air Force Base in Oklahoma City, only to be quickly fired for being openly gay.[1]

In 1969, Baker moved to Minneapolis to start attending the University of Minnesota Law School. McConnell followed several months later after the University of Minnesota offered him a librarian position. (The University's Board of Regents later rescinded the job offer because of McConnell's open support of gay rights, a decision eventually upheld by a federal appellate court.)[2] Shortly after arriving in Minneapolis, Baker joined the student group Fight Repression of Erotic Expression (FREE), Minnesota's first (and only three-month-old) gay rights organization, quickly becoming one of its most visible leaders.

While FREE focused most of its advocacy on relatively modest steps such as trying to get large companies in the Twin Cities to agree not to discriminate on the basis of sexual orientation, Baker kept thinking about his promise to marry McConnell and how gay people would not be able to attain true equality if they were denied the opportunity to marry. After persuading some of his more cautious comrades at FREE that a push for marriage would force the media and the public to take gay issues more seriously, the organization distributed a press release announcing that Baker and McConnell planned to request a marriage license.

The gay couple held a press conference on May 18, 1970, and then walked to the Hennepin County courthouse in Minneapolis accompanied by a throng of reporters. A few minutes later, the two men stood together before the court clerk raising their right hands and swearing to answer his questions truthfully. At that moment, a photographer with United Press International took a picture of the two clean-cut men, wearing suits and ties, which appeared the following day in newspapers across the country. The clerk's office accepted their marriage application (and the $10 filing fee), only to deny it four days later because there were "sufficient legal impediment[s] ... prohibiting the marriage of two male persons."[3]

Baker and McConnell appear to have been the first same-sex couple to seek a marriage license in the United States.[4] They were also the first gay couple to legally challenge the prohibition against same-sex marriage. After a trial judge dismissed their lawsuit, they appealed to the Minnesota Supreme Court, raising a series of constitutional claims.

1

One of their main arguments was that gay childless couples were similarly situated to straight childless couples and that since the government did not require that heterosexuals procreate as a condition of marrying, the state had an equality-based constitutional obligation to permit same-sex couples to marry. The plaintiffs, after noting that Minnesota law did not explicitly disqualify gay people from adopting, also argued that the prohibition against same-sex marriages denied the children of gay adoptive parents the benefits of marriage made available to the children of heterosexuals.[5]

Although procreative and child welfare considerations eventually came to play prominent roles in policy and legal debates over same-sex marriage, the state, in responding to Baker and McConnell's lawsuit, did not deem it necessary to argue that the purpose of marriage was to promote procreation or that maintaining marriage as the union of a man and a woman was best for children. This appears to have been because, as the Hennepin County attorney's office explained in its brief to the state supreme court, the plaintiffs' lawsuit gave rise to one of those "rare instances wherein to merely raise the question is to answer it."[6] The government's position, in other words, was that the plaintiffs' legal request—that they be allowed to marry—was so illogical and outlandish that it barely merited a response.

In September 1971, a month before the Minnesota Supreme Court rejected Baker and McConnell's constitutional claims, Paul Barwick and John Singer submitted a marriage license application in Seattle.[7] After the marriage clerk's office turned down their application, the two men sued, and their case eventually reached the Washington Court of Appeals. Barwick and Singer's lawyer essentially made the same arguments that Baker and McConnell had raised in their case, emphasizing the similarities between gay and straight childless couples and that procreation was not a required component of marriage.[8] As in the Minnesota lawsuit, the government prevailed without raising arguments related to procreation or child welfare. Although the state did note that marriage was the foundation of the family and that without the family "there can be no civilization," it did not rely on either the importance of promoting procreation within the institution of marriage or the need to protect the well-being of children as justifications for denying same-sex couples the opportunity to marry.[9] Instead, the government asserted that the plaintiffs' lawsuit should be dismissed because the very definition of marriage required a union between a man and a woman. This meant that the gay couple was seeking a legal remedy that, according to the government, was simply impossible to grant.[10]

It is in many ways not surprising that the government defendants in the early same-sex marriage cases did not rely on procreative and child welfare considerations to justify same-sex marriage bans. At the time, the idea that openly gay and lesbian individuals could be parents was as foreign to most people as the notion that two individuals of the same sex could marry. For most Americans, it was so obvious that parenting, like marriage, was for heterosexuals only that to suggest otherwise seemed hardly worth discussing.

After a flurry of marriage lawsuits filed in the early 1970s, the issue of same-sex marriage largely receded from public view for the next two decades. Rather than emphasizing marriage, most gay rights organizations and activists, in the years following the

Stonewall riots, focused on other issues such as repealing sodomy laws and protecting lesbians and gay men from police harassment and employment discrimination. Although the movement during this time paid relatively little attention to the question of whether same-sex couples had the right to marry, it could not so easily ignore the growing number of open lesbians and gay men (in particular the former) who, around the middle of the 1970s, started raising children.

At first, the vast majority of these children were born to heterosexual marriages that later dissolved after one of the spouses came out as lesbian or gay. Some of these parents ended up in court fighting over custody and visitation rights and, in the process, trying to persuade courts not to hold their same-sex sexual orientation and relationships against them.[11] By the mid-1980s, a growing number of lesbians were deciding, either by themselves or with their partners, to have children through alternative insemination. These so-called planned lesbian families raised the question of whether it was appropriate for children to be raised in homes without fathers from birth.[12] In addition, by the early 1990s, a growing number of lesbians and gay men in some parts of the country (primarily in urban areas outside the South) began adopting children, while others started serving as foster parents. This phenomenon raised the question of whether the state should approve of (and license) parenting by lesbians and gay men who were open about their sexual orientation.[13]

Many social conservatives reacted with great concern at every stage of this evolution in parenting by lesbians and gay men. Those concerns only intensified after the Hawai'i Supreme Court in 1993 unexpectedly questioned the constitutionality of denying same-sex couples the opportunity to marry.[14] Following the Hawai'i court's decision, many states adopted statutes explicitly prohibiting the recognition of same-sex marriages. For its part, Congress responded by enacting the Defense of Marriage Act of 1996 (DOMA).

Opponents of gay rights in Congress did not mince words about what they perceived to be the urgent need to prevent the recognition of same-sex marriages—in their view, gay marriages threatened the very future of society by weakening the nation's families. This concern led one congressman, Representative Bob Barr (R-Ga), to remind his colleagues that "as Rome burned, Nero fiddled" and "the very foundations of our society are in danger of being burned. The flames of hedonism, the flames of narcissism, the flames of self-centered morality are licking at the very foundations of our society: the family unit."[15]

In addition to these kinds of generalized, and rather hysterical, fears about the future of American families, legislators expressed more specific concerns about the impact of same-sex marriage on procreation and child welfare. The statute's legislative history contains repeated references to the fact that human reproduction requires the contributions of a man and a woman, a biological fact that for DOMA's supporters justified the privileging of heterosexual marriage. That privileging was also justified by child welfare considerations, in particular the notion that families headed by married opposite-sex couples constituted the optimal way of raising children. Representative Charles Canady (R-Fl), one of the bill's main sponsors, made both of these points at a House committee hearing, arguing that marriage is inherently and necessarily reserved for unions between one man and one woman. This is because our society recognizes that heterosexual marriage provides the ideal structure within which to beget and raise children. This fundamental, unavoidable fact of our human nature belies any attempt to betray this bill as a defense of some archaic social construct. Marriage exists so that men and women will come together in the type of committed relationships that are uniquely capable of producing and nurturing children.[16]

For his part, Representative Cliff Stearns (R-Fl) claimed that "if traditional marriage is thrown by the wayside, brought down by [the] manipulation of the definition [of marriage] that has been accepted since the beginning of civilized society, children will suffer because family will lose its very essence. Instead of trying to ruin families we should be preserving them for future generations."[17] A report supporting the legislation issued by the Judiciary Committee of the House of Representatives also tied the proposed bill to children and their well-being: "were it not for the possibility of begetting children inherent in heterosexual unions, society would have no particular interest in encouraging citizens to come together in a committed relationship. But because America, like nearly every known human society, is concerned about its children, our government has a special obligation to ensure that we preserve and protect the institution of marriage."[18]

Concerns about human procreation and child welfare were not the only reasons why Congress enacted DOMA. The statute's supporters also relied on considerations of morality (as understood by conservative Christians), and on the (mistaken) view that without DOMA, the Constitution's Full Faith and Credit Clause would require the other forty-nine states to recognize the same-sex marriages that might take place in Hawai'i, to argue in favor of enacting the law.[19] It is clear, however, that concerns about the proper exercise of human procreation, the well-being of children, and the future of American families were crucial in justifying a federal statute defining marriage, a definition that had up until then been almost exclusively a matter of state law.

On the same day in September 1996 that the Senate, by an overwhelming margin (85 to 14) joined the House of Representatives (342 to 67) in voting for DOMA, a trial began in Honolulu that considered the legality, as determined by the state constitution, of denying same-sex couples the opportunity to marry. The trial became necessary after the Hawai'i Supreme Court ruled that the government had the burden of demonstrating the existence of a compelling state interest that justified using gender to determine marriage eligibility. In stark contrast to the same-sex marriage cases of the early 1970s, in which the government defendants had not raised arguments related to procreation or child welfare, the state in the Hawai'i trial relied exclusively on such claims to defend the exclusion of same-sex couples from marriage. In fact, the opening statement given by the assistant attorney general, Rick Eichor, encompassed all of the procreation and child-related arguments that government lawyers and conservative advocates have repeatedly raised since then to defend same-sex marriage bans.

Eichor made several different points during the trial's opening. First, and most fundamentally, he noted that only different-sex couples are able to procreate. Second, he emphasized that the government seeks to promote procreation within marriage because it encourages men and women to take responsibility for their children. Third, he framed the question of child welfare as one of "optimality," that is, of promoting and privileging those families (headed by married men and women who are biologically related to their children) that he argued led to the best child outcomes. Fourth, Eichor claimed that men and women have distinct and complementary parenting styles that benefit children in crucial ways. Fifth, he contended that other types of familial arrangements, including those led by lesbians and gay men, "burden child development" because the children who are part of them "are more vulnerable to adjustment difficulties." Finally, he dismissed the growing number of social science studies showing that the sexual orientation of lesbian and gay parents did not harm their children, claiming that these studies were biased and methodologically unsound.[20]

Although the presiding judge, after hearing the evidence introduced during the nine-day trial, disagreed with the proposition that it was better for children to be raised by straight parents than by lesbian/gay ones, as well as with the other procreative and child welfare arguments made by the state, those who defended marriage as an exclusively heterosexual institution continued to raise similar claims.[21] A few months after the trial ended, the law professor Lynn Wardle published a law review article in which he argued against "the legalization of same-sex marriage and homosexual parenting" by contending that when lesbians and gay men serve as parents, they threaten their children with "potential harm." According to Wardle, these harms included a greater chance that the children of lesbian mothers and gay fathers would themselves turn out to be lesbian or gay, which would, he claimed, lead to higher incidences of "suicidal behavior, prostitution, running away from home, substance abuse, HIV infection, highly promiscuous behavior with multiple sex partners, and premature sexual activity."[22]

Many who defended the marriage bans also worried that the legal recognition of same-sex unions as marital would significantly undermine the government's interest in promoting "responsible procreation." The responsible procreation claim was centered around the idea that the primary social function of marriage is to encourage those who conceive children to take responsibility for them. The recognition of same-sex marriage, it was claimed, would inevitably and irrevocably delink marriage from procreation, thus leading more heterosexuals to procreate irresponsibly. For example, the state of Maryland, in a brief filed in 2006 defending its then existing same-sex marriage ban, explained that "governments recognize marriage to encourage potentially procreative couples to bind themselves together for the good of their natural offspring, a circumstance that does not arise with same-sex couples."[23] Or, as a group of Washington state legislators opposed to same-sex marriage succinctly explained in a 2004 brief, "the institution of marriage brings order to heterosexual intercourse."[24]

Opponents of marriage equality, in addition to claiming that the recognition of same-sex marriage would make the promotion of responsible procreation more difficult, also contended that married heterosexual couples constituted the "optimal" familial arrangement for the raising of children. From this perspective, it was entirely legitimate for the government to refuse to recognize (and thus to encourage) the formation of same-sex couple households, which—because of the absence of a mother and a father who were both biologically related to their offspring—were incapable of providing children with the type of care, nurture, and guidance that opponents of marriage equality claimed led to the best child outcomes. At the same time, the opponents brushed aside as unreliable the growing number of social science studies concluding that parental sexual orientation was not associated with the welfare of children, claiming that the studies were biased and methodologically flawed.

Opponents of same-sex marriage have continued to raise similar kinds of procreative and child welfare objections. Indeed, these arguments played crucial roles in the 2010 federal trial that was held to assess the constitutionality of Proposition 8, California's constitutional amendment prohibiting the recognition of same-sex marriages. These arguments were also critical to the defense of that amendment, and of DOMA, before the Supreme Court in 2013.

The purpose of this book is to bring together historical, social science, and legal considerations and analyses to explore the role that procreative and child welfare claims have played in policy and legal debates involving same-sex marriage. The book seeks to comprehensively address and refute social conservatives' often-repeated claims that same-sex marriage bans promote responsible procreation and children's welfare. In doing so, the book adopts an explicitly interdisciplinary approach, one demanded by the questions at stake. In order to fully assess the consequentialist claims made by those who contend that the recognition of same-sex marriage harms families and children, it is necessary, as this book does, to grapple with questions of history, social science, and law.

Some marriage equality proponents have contended that the procreative and child-based objections raised by their opponents mask more deeply seated prejudices against lesbians, gay men, and bisexuals. I do not in this book explore the possible motivations of opponents of marriage equality. Instead, I seek to determine whether their claims are historically accurate, empirically supportable, and constitutionally valid.

Chapter 1 provides a historical perspective, explaining how supporters of earlier class-based marital regulations (such as interracial marriage bans, disability marriage prohibitions, and the differential treatment of nonmarital children), like opponents of same-sex marriage today, defended their policy positions by relying on particular understandings of how individuals should exercise their procreative capacities and how they should form families and rear children in order to promote the social good. The chapter explains that these highly problematic precedents in American marital policy history should make policymakers, courts, and the general public highly skeptical of efforts to impose or maintain class-based marital disqualifications or limitations in order to (ostensibly) promote the social good in matters related to procreation and child-rearing.

Opponents of marriage equality have claimed that the most important social function of marriage is to encourage mothers and fathers to take responsibility for their offspring and that allowing same-sex couples to marry dangerously undermines that function because it delinks marriage from procreation. Chapter 2 examines the development, nature, and scope of the responsible procreation claims that conservatives have used to defend same-sex marriage bans. In doing so, it pays particular attention to the way these claims are grounded in many of the same arguments conservatives have raised in attacking the federal government's welfare policies. In both instances, critics have promoted their understanding of responsible procreation through arguments that reject or ignore the interests of a highly stigmatized segment of the population: single mothers in the case of welfare reform, and lesbians, gay men, and bisexuals in that of marriage.

Furthermore, in examining the historical context of the responsible procreation objections to same-sex marriage, chapter 2 explains that it was the legal and cultural changes that took place during the twentieth century affecting *heterosexual* relationships, rather than the push for lesbian, gay, bisexual, and transgender (LGBT) rights in general and same-sex marriage in particular, that significantly diminished the procreative channeling function of marriage. Indeed, the link between marriage and procreation began to fray long before the first same-sex marriages were recognized in this country.

Chapter 2 also points to the lack of empirical support for the claim, raised by opponents of same-sex marriage, that the recognition of gay marriages has deleterious effects on heterosexual marriage and procreation. The chapter ends by explaining why the effort to promote responsible procreation among heterosexuals by denying same-sex couples the opportunity to marry is morally objectionable because it uses lesbians, gay men, and bisexuals (and their children) instrumentally in order to advance the interests of others.

Many conservatives have also reasoned that same-sex marriage bans are justified because households headed by married mothers and fathers who are biologically related to their children are the optimal family structure for children. Chapter 3 explores why family optimality is not an appropriate standard for the state to use in determining which individuals should be encouraged to marry and to parent. It also explains why the social science evidence that opponents of marriage equality rely on to defend same-sex marriage bans does not support their child-rearing optimality claims. In particular, the chapter points out that there is little evidence that marital status (by itself), or biological status, or parental gender is associated with better child outcomes.

Chapter 4 explores the relevance of the social science literature on the children of lesbians and gay men to the question of whether same-sex marriages bans are constitutional. In doing so, the chapter distinguishes between three different areas of study: (1) psychological adjustment and social functioning, (2) gender role development, and (3) sexual orientation of the children of lesbians and gay men. The social science studies have consistently and uniformly failed to find associations between parental sexual orientation and the psychological adjustment and social functioning of children. The chapter explains why it is therefore constitutionally untenable to defend same-sex marriage bans based on concerns about the psychological adjustment and social functioning of the children of lesbians and gay men, even when applying the most deferential (to the government) form of judicial scrutiny (known as the rational basis test).

Although most studies have also concluded that there is no association between parental sexual orientation and the gender role development and sexual orientation of children, a minority of studies have suggested the possibility that some differences may exist in these measures between the children of lesbian/gay parents and those of heterosexual parents. However, even if these differences could be shown to exist conclusively, they would be constitutionally irrelevant in defending same-sex marriage bans because the state does not have a legitimate interest in promoting particular forms of gender role development and sexual orientation.

After two decades of hard-fought lawsuits and intense debates in Congress and on the floors of state legislatures, the Internet, and the streets, the issue of same-sex marriage arrived before the Supreme Court in 2013 in the form of two cases, one challenging California's constitutional ban on same-sex marriage (Proposition 8) and the other DOMA. Chapter 5 explores the role that procreative and child welfare considerations played in the political campaign in favor of Proposition 8, as well as in the constitutional litigation that followed its approval by voters. The chapter also looks at the role that the same considerations played in the constitutional defense of DOMA, as well as in the Supreme Court's decision striking down that statute in *United States v. Windsor*.[25]

As we will see, the Court in *Windsor* dealt a major blow to the child welfare justifications behind same-sex marriage bans by concluding that children are harmed not by same-sex marriages, but by the failure of the government—in this case, the federal government—to recognize the relationships of same-sex couples as marital. Child welfare considerations, in other words, played an important role in the Court's reasoning, but in ways that significantly undermined rather than supported the constitutionality of same-sex marriage bans.

The conclusion sets forth five important lessons the nation can learn from the role that procreative and child welfare considerations have played in policy and legal debates involving same-sex marriage. These lessons are as follows: (1) legislators and other policymakers should not promote class-based relationship-recognition exclusionary policies that are linked to procreative and child welfare considerations; (2) legislators and other policymakers should not adopt family policies grounded in the "facts of nature"; (3) there are no quick fixes in promoting responsible procreation; (4) the advancement of child welfare requires a focus on well-being rather than on differences; and (5) gender in parenting should matter less, not more.

A growing percentage of Americans live in states that recognize same-sex marriages. Given that young Americans overwhelmingly support the idea that same-sex couples should be provided with the opportunity to marry, it seems inevitable that lesbians and gay men, regardless of where they live, will eventually be permitted to marry those whom they love. Although there is a great deal of truth to the saying that "justice delayed is justice denied," it is also the case that the protracted debates over same-sex marriage, while often heated and not always illuminating, have had the positive effect of encouraging the nation to focus on several crucial questions of family law and policy, including what is the purpose of marriage and what constitutes good parenting.

It is likely that when Americans fifty or one hundred years from now look back at our contemporary disagreements over same-sex marriage, they will see them as constituting the beginning rather than the end of difficult but important conversations about how society should go about supporting and recognizing the multiplicity and diversity that characterize American families.

1

A HISTORICAL REVIEW

The ongoing attempt to deny same-sex couples the opportunity to marry is not the first effort in American history to defend exclusionary, class-based marital policies grounded in particular understandings of how individuals should be encouraged to exercise their procreative capacities and how best to form families and rear children. Those who supported laws aimed at (1) prohibiting interracial couples from marrying, (2) restricting the ability of individuals with mental disabilities from marrying, and (3) denying rights and benefits to nonmarital children also defended the use of state authority to define marriage and its attendant benefits in ways that promoted what they believed were socially optimal goals in matters related to procreation, family formation, and child welfare.

Although almost everyone today agrees that these earlier efforts to impose marital disqualifications or benefits limitations were deeply misguided, more attention needs to be paid to how supporters of the earlier laws, like many who defend same-sex marriage bans today, turned to procreative and child welfare considerations to defend class-based marital policies aimed at promoting social stability and progress. These troubling precedents in American marital policy history should lead us to be skeptical of efforts to impose or maintain class-based marital disqualifications or limitations in order to achieve particular understandings of so-called optimality in matters related to procreation and child-rearing.

Most of this chapter explores the role that concerns about procreation and children played in the defense of antimiscegenation laws, disability marital bans, and the differential treatment of nonmarital children. The remainder of the chapter discusses the role that those considerations played (or did not play) in justifying two marital bans that still enjoy wide support today: the bans on incestuous marriages and on polygamous unions.

ANTIMISCEGENATION LAWS

For the last two decades, many marriage equality proponents have sought to draw an analogy between the same-sex marriage bans of today and the interracial marriage prohibitions of yesterday. The gist of the argument is that using gender to determine who can marry whom is as improper (and as unconstitutional) as using race. There is another connection, however, between antimiscegenation laws and same-sex marriage bans that has gone largely unnoticed: in both instances, procreative and child welfare considerations played crucial roles in justifying these laws' enactment and enforcement.

I explore this connection here by tracing the role that procreative and child welfare considerations played in the implementation and defense of antimiscegenation laws. I begin with a look at interracial marriage bans in colonial Virginia, which implemented the earliest and most comprehensive regulation of interracial intimacy and the children that resulted from it. I then proceed to discuss the ways antimiscegenation proponents, following the Civil War, turned to science in general and eugenics in particular to support their views. I finish with an exploration of the role that consequentialist arguments based on the need to channel human reproduction and to promote child welfare in ways that were perceived to be socially optimal played in constitutional litigation involving antimiscegenation laws in the twentieth century.

Slavery and Miscegenation in Colonial Virginia

In Virginia, prior to the 1660s, there was no explicit regulation of interracial intimacy. Fornication (that is, sex outside of marriage) was a crime, but before the 1660s, black-white fornication was legally regulated in the same way as white-white fornication.[1]

Interracial intimacy as such became problematic when it led to the births of a growing number of interracial children. It was important, in a society where slavery was increasingly becoming entrenched, to determine the status of those children. The regulation of interracial relationships in colonial Virginia, therefore, began with a law addressing not interracial *marriage*, but the legal status of interracial *children*. In 1662, the Virginia Assembly enacted a law that made the status of interracial children dependent on the status of their mothers.[2] If the mother was a slave, then her children would also be slaves, regardless of the father's race. If the mother was a free woman—whether white, of mixed race, or black—then her children would be free as well.

The Virginia statute was a departure from English law, which made the children's status dependent on that of their fathers. Although precise numbers are difficult to establish, it is likely that a majority of interracial children born in seventeenth-century Virginia were conceived by white fathers and black mothers, most of whom were slaves.[3] If the colony had followed the English rule, interracial children conceived by white fathers would have been deemed free even if their mothers had been slaves. This was problematic for white Virginians, both because it would have significantly increased the number of free blacks (who might forge alliances with slaves) and because it would deny an additional supply of labor to the owners of female slaves. In contrast, a rule that assigned interracial children the status of their mothers aided in the entrenchment and expansion of slavery.

The second step the Virginia Assembly took with respect to miscegenation—through the same 1662 statute—was to address, for the first time, the issue of interracial sex by doubling the punishment for interracial fornication compared to same-race fornication. The fact that the new interracial fornication provision was part of the statute that assigned to children the status of their mothers shows that the legislators were particularly concerned with the possibility that interracial sex would lead to the creation of racially mixed children.

Although most interracial children born in the seventeenth century in Virginia were likely conceived by white men and black women, not all were. Some resulted from sexual contact between white women and black men. This second category of interracial children challenged slavery and racial supremacy in two ways. First, these children, as the offspring of white women, were not categorized as slaves regardless of how dark the color of their skin might be. These children, therefore, eroded the seemingly natural link between blackness and slavery. Second, while white Virginians were largely indifferent to the issue of black women having interracial children (as long as the children of slaves were also deemed slaves, as called for by the 1662 law), they were deeply troubled by the notion of white women having interracial children. It was white women (rather than white men) who were charged with the responsibility of keeping the white race "pure." White women were understood, in effect, to be the guarantors of racial purity and therefore had to be punished when they transgressed by engaging in sexual relationships that crossed racial lines.

For three decades after the enactment of the 1662 statute, the only legal disincentive for white women to engage in sexual relationships with black men was the existence of the fornication statute that doubled the punishment for interracial sex. By definition, however, the crime of fornication did not apply to married couples. Indeed, cases are reported of white women marrying black men in seventeenth-century Virginia.[4]

As a result, the Virginia Assembly concluded that there was a need for additional regulation further discouraging interracial unions and the children that might result from them. In 1691, the assembly enacted its first interracial marriage law, a descendant of which was struck down by the Supreme Court almost three hundred years later in *Loving v. Virginia*.[5] The new law was particularly critical of interracial marriages between white women and nonwhite men. In expressing its disapproval of that category of relationship, the legislature noted that the statutory proscription was required to "prevent...that abominable mixture and spurious issue which hereafter may encrease in this dominion, as well by negroes, mulattoes, and Indians intermarrying with English, or other white women, as by their unlawfull accompanying with one another."[6] The language of the statute shows that what motivated the legislators to condemn interracial marriages was an objection to the offspring (i.e., the "abominable mixture and spurious issue") that resulted from the unions of white women and nonwhite men.

Although the possibility of white women having children fathered by nonwhite men led to the strong language contained in the law's text, the statute called for the lifetime banishment from the colony of any white person who married a nonwhite individual, regardless of whether that white person was a man or a woman. Despite the fact that the statute, in theory, applied to all whites, it was women who were likely to be prosecuted for violating antimiscegenation laws.[7] Furthermore, also as a practical matter, the lifetime banishment of the white mother meant the lifetime (or at least the long) banishment of the interracial children born to her. While legislators dealt with the interracial children of slave mothers by enslaving them, they dealt with the interracial children of white mothers by banishing them from the colony.

Concerns other than white women having interracial children also led colonial leaders to strongly condemn white women's interracial relationships. One of these was the unique revulsion many white Virginians felt at the very idea of sexual intimacy between white women and black men (regardless of whether it led to procreation), a revulsion that was not present when white men (usually owners) had sexual relationships with black women (usually slaves). Sexual relationships between white women and black men reinforced two related stereotypes: black men as "savagely sexual" creatures and white women as sexually vulnerable beings who needed the protection afforded by white men. Some historians have argued that the restrictions on white female sexuality were also motivated by the perceived need to keep the relatively small number of white women sexually available to the much larger number of white men who lived in the colony at the time.[8] It does appear, however, that the concern about white women giving birth to interracial children was the primary motivation behind Virginia's first interracial marriage law.

That this motivation was primary in the passage of the 1691 antimiscegenation law is supported not only by the statutory language already noted, but also by two other provisions in the same statute that dealt with interracial children. The first provision required white women who had biracial children—all of whom were now, by definition, illegitimate—to pay church wardens 15 pounds in one month of the baby's birth.[9] (The law did not punish black women who bore racially mixed children, suggesting once again that white Virginians were not particularly troubled by the idea of sexual intimacy between white men and black women.) If the mother did not have the money, then the law authorized church wardens to auction off her services for five years. As if that was not enough of a disincentive for white women to have interracial children, a second provision authorized church wardens to take the children away from their mothers and auction them off as servants until they attained the age of thirty.

In short, the 1691 statute prohibited interracial marriages because they could lead to the creation of "abominable mixture and spurius issue." And if some white women insisted in having children with black men, then the law imposed draconian penalties on them and their children. It is clear, then, that the prohibition against interracial marriage in colonial Virginia was one component of a complex, interlocking set of regulations that were intended to cope with the growing number of biracial children.

By the end of the seventeenth century, Virginia's colonial leaders felt it necessary to enact a comprehensive regulatory regime to try to bring order to the racial confusion created by interracial children, whose existence challenged the idea of racial categories as God-given, natural, static, and unchanging. Virginia's law barring interracial marriages was thus part of a broader regulatory mechanism aimed at maintaining clear boundaries between the races, boundaries that were threatened by the growing number of individuals who were neither entirely white nor entirely black.

Virginia was by no means alone in enacting antimiscegenation laws. In 1664, Maryland became the first colony to adopt a law condemning interracial marriage, although that initial provision applied only to unions between white women and black men. The statute expressed the legislature's disapproval of "freeborne Englishwomen [who were] forgettful of their free Condition and to the disgrace of our Nation doe intermarry with Negro slaves."[10] The law decreed that a white woman who married a slave had to become a servant of her husband's owner and that her children "shall be slaves as their fathers were."[11] In 1692, the Maryland legislature enacted a provision also prohibiting marriages between white men and black women and requiring that white women who had interracial children be indentured as servants for seven years. As for the interracial children of white women, Maryland law called for their indenture until the age of thirty-one.

It was not just southern colonies that enacted such laws. Under a Pennsylvania statute dating to the 1720s, for example, a free black man who married a white woman could be sentenced to serve as a slave for the rest of his life. As in Virginia and Maryland, interracial children in Pennsylvania could be sold as servants for the first three decades of their lives.[12] In addition, Massachusetts's 1705 antimiscegenation law echoed the language used by the Virginia statute of 1691, calling for the prevention of "a Spurious and Mixt Issue."

Following independence, all the states (except for Pennsylvania) kept their antimiscegenation statutes. After the turn of the nineteenth century, new states like Arkansas, Indiana, Missouri, and Texas enacted bans on interracial marriages.[13] During the antebellum period, few questioned the states' authority to impose such bans. That changed with the end of slavery and the adoption of post–Civil War laws aimed at promoting racial equality.

The Turn to Science and Eugenics

The end of the Civil War brought uncertainty about the validity of antimiscegenation laws. One of the consequences of emancipation was that antimiscegenation statutes could no longer be justified as means to protect and promote the institution of slavery. Additional uncertainty resulted from the enactment of the Civil Rights Act of 1866 and the adoption, two years later, of the Fourteenth Amendment, both of which aimed to prohibit states from discriminating on the basis of race.

The uncertainty regarding the states' authority to ban interracial unions encouraged legal challenges of antimiscegenation laws. These lawsuits raised two main issues. The first question was whether the state's involvement with marriage primarily entailed the recognition and enforcement of a private contract or instead constituted a more vigorous exercise of its police power (i.e., regulatory) authority. If it was the former, then marital regulations were more likely to be subject to constitutional and statutory provisions aimed at protecting the rights of individuals to contract freely regardless of race. The second question was whether the equal application of antimiscegenation laws to whites and blacks immunized them from equality-based challenges.

Courts in the second half of the nineteenth century consistently upheld interracial marriage bans by adopting a public rather than a private/contractual understanding of marriage, making the issue one of societal well-being rather than individual rights.[14] The courts also uniformly held that the equality protections afforded by the Fourteenth Amendment and the Civil Rights Act of 1866 did not apply to marriage restrictions that treated whites and blacks equally.[15]

However, there was more to postbellum interracial marriage judicial opinions than these questions of legal doctrine. These rulings also reflected a growing "scientific" understanding of antimiscegenation laws that was particularly concerned with the hereditary implications of interracial procreation. The Kentucky Court of Appeals in 1867, for example, worried that the legalization of interracial marriage would lead to the "deteriorat[ion of] the Caucasian blood."[16] Two years later, the Georgia Supreme Court, in upholding the criminal conviction of a black woman for marrying a white man, proclaimed:

> the amalgamation of the races is not only unnatural, but is always productive of deplorable results. Our daily observation shows us, *that the offspring of these unnatural connections are generally sickly and effeminate, and that they are inferior in physical development and strength, to the full-blood of either race.* It is sometimes urged that such marriages should be encouraged, for the purpose of elevating the inferior race. The reply is, that such connections never elevate the inferior race to the position of the superior, but they bring down the superior to that of the inferior. They are productive of evil, and evil only, without any corresponding good.[17]

Tennessee's attorney general expressed a similar view in 1871 when he compared antimiscegenation laws to ancient "Mosaic laws" that forbade Jews from intermixing different animals, as in the breeding of horses with donkeys to create mules. According to the attorney general, a law against "breeding mulattoes" was not any more problematic, since it was also aimed at "prevent[ing] the production of [a] hybrid race."[18] For its part, the Missouri Supreme Court in 1883 was troubled by what it took to be the purported inability of biracial individuals to procreate—in its view a sufficient basis upon which to uphold the constitutionality of antimiscegenation laws. As the court put it, "it is stated as a well authenticated fact that if the issue of a black man and a white woman and a white man and a black woman intermarry, they cannot possibly have any progeny, and such a fact sufficiently justifies those laws which forbid the intermarriage of blacks and whites."[19]

Many Americans, since the colonial days, had understood interracial procreation to be unnatural. But the views expressed by these postbellum courts and officials reflected new concerns related to reproductive barrenness, hereditary deterioration, and the physical and psychological weaknesses and deficiencies of interracial offspring. The arguments in favor of interracial marriage bans, in other words, grew to include sociobiological considerations grounded in empirical claims about procreation and the well-being of children. Indeed, it is interesting to note that the very word "miscegenation" was coined by opponents of racial equality in 1864 who thought that the new word, which combined *miscere* (mix) and *genus* (race), was a more scientific-sounding term for interracial sex and marriage than "amalgamation," the word that had been commonly used until then.[20]

The historian Peggy Pascoe has detailed how defenders of antimiscegenation laws, starting in the second half of the nineteenth century, turned to science in general, and eugenics in particular, to justify prohibitions of interracial unions.[21] The growing number of scientists and policymakers who enthusiastically embraced eugenics believed it was possible to improve the human race and its social conditions by controlling and channeling procreation.[22] Many of those who called for "race regeneration" and the avoidance of "race suicide" came to see antimiscegenation laws as important tools in the promotion of procreative optimality.

The science of eugenics started in England in the 1880s under the auspices of the biologist Sir Francis Galton, who was Charles Darwin's first cousin. Galton believed that high intelligence ran in families; "eugenics," the term he coined, derives from the Greek root meaning "well-born." This view, combined with his cousin's theory of natural selection, led Galton to claim that the human race could be improved if those of "higher stock" reproduced in greater numbers. Galton and his fellow English eugenicists focused largely on so-called positive eugenics, that is, on the need to increase the number of offspring among those who were highly intelligent and successful, paying little attention to those of "lower stock" (i.e., the lower classes and those perceived to be less mentally competent). In contrast, American eugenicists—spurred by the rediscovery of Gregor Mendel's laws of genetic heredity around the turn of the twentieth century—focused on negative eugenic policy measures, aimed at discouraging reproduction among individuals deemed physically, psychologically, or socially inferior.

Not surprisingly, eugenic ideas were happily embraced by many who believed that America's European heritage was threatened by the potential racial intermixing of whites with blacks and Asians.[23] The idea that science could prove—in seemingly objective and conclusive ways—(1) that nonwhite races were biologically inferior to whites, and (2) that whites put themselves at risk by genetically intermixing with nonwhites, proved irresistible to many who believed that the strict separation of the races was essential to moral progress, economic prosperity, and social peace.

The political scientist Julie Novkov has explained how a scientific discourse on race in the early twentieth century changed many people's understandings of the differences between the races. Although many white Americans had always believed that blacks were inferior, the race discourse was now "couched in normative scientific and social scientific language. The legal system would incorporate these new 'breakthroughs' in the social sciences, believing that the scientific method would lead to rationalized legal results."[24] One particular manifestation of this shift was a change in racial categorization—while individuals throughout the nineteenth century had been deemed white or black depending largely on their appearance, after the turn of the century the belief grew that it was blood that biologically determined race. As Novkov explains,

> blood was [now] the bearer of blackness, the means through which its dangerous and backward characteristics were conveyed from generation to generation. Ultimately, many [authors] (both scientific and popular) saw only two options regarding blood: either complete amalgamation would take place, producing one race in the United States combining white and black, or a complete separation would have to be enforced, with the current mixed-race people being permanently and irrevocably defined as black.[25]

The toxic combination of eugenics and racism in the United States reached its apogee in 1924 with the enactment of Virginia's Racial Integrity Act.[26] That statute was the first to codify the so-called one-drop rule, rendering individuals with any traceable nonwhite ancestry (or blood), no matter how tenuous or far removed, ineligible to marry a "pure" Caucasian person.[27] In a 1923 article in a Richmond newspaper, "Is White America to Become a Negroid Nation?," two of the law's leading supporters claimed that "the development of eugenical science" showed that "in crossing two varieties [races], the more primitive, the less highly specialized always dominates" the other.[28] For his part, the physician Walter Plecker, Virginia's first registrar of vital statistics and the most visible and outspoken defender of the Racial Integrity Act on explicitly eugenic grounds, claimed in a 1924 speech at the annual convention of the American Public Health Association that

> two races as materially divergent as the white and the negro, in morals, mental powers, and cultural fitness, cannot live in close contact without injury to the higher [race], amounting in many cases to absolute ruin. The lower [race] never has been and never can be raised to the level of the higher. *This statement is not an opinion based on sentiment or prejudice, but is an unquestionable scientific fact....* It is evident that in the hybrid mixture the traits of the more primitive will dominate those of the more specialized or civilized race. It is equally obvious that these culturally destructive characteristics are hereditary, carried in the germ plasm, and hence they cannot be influenced by environmental factors such as improved economic, social and educational opportunities.[29]

Starting in the early 1930s, views such Plecker's came under increasingly stronger attacks, first because they were grounded in unsupportable scientific claims and later due to the horrors perpetrated by Nazi Germany in the name of eugenics. Yet it is clear from the constitutional litigation that challenged antimiscegenation statutes in the decades after World War II that supporters continued to raise notions related to eugenics and procreative optimality in defending interracial marriage bans. In addition, that litigation showed that defenders also sought to justify the marital bans on the ground that they promoted the welfare of children.

Constitutional Litigation in the Twentieth Century

When Andrea Perez, a Mexican American deemed a white person under California law, and Sylvester Davis, an African American, attempted to marry in 1947, the Los Angeles County's marriage license bureau relied on the state's nearly century-old antimiscegenation law to turn them away. After the couple challenged the statute's constitutionality, the state raised several medical/eugenic and sociological arguments in its defense.

The government first claimed that whites were superior to the other races and the progeny of racially mixed couples were inferior to whites. According to the state, the prohibition of interracial marriages "prevents the Caucasian race from being

contaminated by races whose members are by nature physically and mentally inferior to Caucasians."[30] California also contended that "biological data" showed that "the
crossing of widely different races has undesirable biological results" and that "the parties who enter into miscegenetic marriages have proved generally to be the dregs of
both races," making it likely "that the offspring of such marriages will turn out to be
inferior to both of their parents."[31]

In addition to such medical/eugenic claims, California defended its antimiscegenation law on sociological grounds, contending that interracial marriages led to greater
social tension because most people disapproved of them. Furthermore, the state
claimed that blacks were "socially inferior" and, as a result, "the progeny of a marriage
between a Negro and a Caucasian suffer not only the stigma of such inferiority but the
fear of rejection by members of both races."[32] In other words, antimiscegenation laws
promoted child welfare because they aimed to protect children from the social inferiority and stigma that accompanied interracial marriages.

The California Supreme Court's opinion in *Perez v. Sharp*, issued six years before the
U.S. Supreme Court's ruling in *Brown v. Board of Education*, is frequently praised today
for its relatively early recognition of the constitutional impermissibility of relying on
racial categories in the setting of government policies. Little attention has been paid,
however, to the California Supreme Court's explicit rejection of the state's empirical
justifications for its antimiscegenation law. As such, the *Perez* court took a different
approach from that of the U.S. Supreme Court in *Loving v. Virginia*, which as we will
see refused to grapple with the state's empirical claims regarding the alleged harm to
society and to children caused by interracial marriages.

The *Perez* court explicitly rejected the contention that the children of interracial
unions were somehow defective or deficient by noting that "modern experts are agreed
that the progeny of marriages between persons of different races are not inferior to
both parents." The court also explained that whites' greater success in society was not
the result of their mental superiority, but of the social advantages attached to their
skin color. Furthermore, in addressing the state's claim that children of interracial
couples suffered social disadvantages, the court reasoned that the large number of
"persons in the United States of mixed ancestry" showed "that the tensions upon them
are . . . diminishing and are bound to diminish even more in time. Already many of the
progeny of mixed marriages have made important contributions to the community."[33]

Several years after *Perez*, a Virginia couple—Ham Naim, a Chinese man, and Ruth
Lamberth, a white woman—traveled to North Carolina to get married. After the cer-
emony, the couple returned to Virginia, later acknowledging that they had traveled to
the neighboring state to evade the Racial Integration Act of 1924. Although the couple
was happy at first, Mrs. Naim eventually filed for a divorce or, alternatively, an annul-
ment. The trial court annulled the marriage, claiming that Virginia's antimiscegenation
law rendered it void from the beginning. Mr. Naim then appealed, contending that the
Racial Integration Act was unconstitutional.

In challenging the statute, Mr. Naim's lawyer chose not to question the medical/
eugenic and sociological bases for the Racial Integration Act.[34] The attorney reasoned
that doing so would be expensive, requiring the calling of many expert witnesses, which

would then only "invite counter testimony by state witnesses to the effect that the off-spring of interracial marriage were unhappy and had difficulty adjusting to a hostile world."[35] Mr. Naim's failure to dispute the antimiscegenation law's medical/eugenic and sociological bases left the Virginia Supreme Court of Appeals free to uphold the statute on the basis of its views regarding the legitimacy of the state's pursuit of eugenic and racial purity objectives. As that court saw it, the Fourteenth Amendment did not

> prohibit the State from enacting legislation to preserve the racial integrity of its citizens, or...deny [it] the power...to regulate the marriage relation so that it shall not have a mongrel breed of citizens. We find [in the Constitution] no requirement that the State shall not legislate to prevent the obliteration of racial pride, but must permit the corruption of blood even though it weaken or destroy the quality of its citizenship. Both sacred and secular history teach that nations and races have better advanced in human progress when they cultivated their own distinctive characteristics and culture and developed their own peculiar genius.[36]

The U.S. Supreme Court eventually refused to hear the case on the highly questionable ground that it failed to raise an issue of federal law.[37] In reality, it is likely that the justices did not want to tackle the question of interracial marriage at a time when the Court was facing increasing southern hostility and backlash to its school desegregation ruling in *Brown*.[38] In any event, the Court's refusal to hear the *Naim* case meant that Virginia's Racial Integration Act—along with the antimiscegenation laws of sixteen other states—remained in place for another decade.

Three years before the Supreme Court held in *Loving* that antimiscegenation laws were unconstitutional, it agreed, in *McLaughlin v. Florida*, to hear a challenge to a Florida statute that criminalized interracial cohabitation. In 1962, the police knocked on the door of Dewey McLaughlin and Connie Hoffman's Miami Beach apartment to investigate the landlady's complaint that an interracial couple was living on the premises. After identifying McLaughlin as a black man and Hoffman as a white woman, the police charged the two with violating Florida's ban on interracial cohabitation.[39]

McLaughlin and Hoffman contended that they had a common law marriage and therefore could not have violated the cohabitation statute. The problem with this claim was that Florida also had an antimiscegenation law that prohibited all interracial marriages, including common law ones. Following their conviction by a jury, the couple served eighteen days in jail. After the Florida Supreme Court rejected their constitutional challenge to the interracial cohabitation statute because it applied equally to whites and blacks, the U.S. Supreme Court agreed to hear their appeal.[40]

The state, in defending the constitutionality of its law before the U.S. Supreme Court, relied heavily on child welfare considerations, claiming that the statute was needed in order to prevent the infliction of psychological and social harm on children born from interracial sexual intimacy. Florida argued that its interest in avoiding such harm was enough to justify the enactment of antimiscegenation laws and, as a result, was also enough to justify the interracial cohabitation ban. The state's brief explained that it is well known that both the white and the negro race tend to shun the offspring of interracial marriages....The need of offspring to identify with others is a well understood psychological factor in present times. The interracial offspring are not fully accepted by either race. There is therefore a clear psychological handicap problem among interracial offspring....Interracial offspring will not have the same psychological or social standing that such offspring would have if they were descendants of sexual partners of the same race.[41]

According to the state, the "psychological handicaps of children born of negro-white parentage" were enough to uphold the constitutionality of its statute.[42]

Although the state attempted to link the validity of its interracial cohabitation law to that of its antimiscegenation statute, the Supreme Court refused to rule on the constitutionality of the latter. The Court in *McLaughlin*—as it did in *Loving* several years later—also refused to address the state's contention that its law was justified on child welfare grounds. Rather than analyzing the statute through the lens of children's well-being, the Court viewed it as part of a broader regulatory effort that also included prohibitions on adultery and fornication, aimed at reducing promiscuity. The goal of discouraging promiscuity, the Court pointed out, could be achieved without targeting individuals for special punishment on the basis of their race.[43]

The Supreme Court finally got around to assessing the constitutional validity of antimiscegenation laws after authorities arrested and convicted Richard and Mildred Loving, an interracial couple living in Virginia, for traveling to Washington, D.C., to get married. The state in *Loving*, like California in *Perez* and Florida in *McLaughlin*, attempted to defend its racial law on consequentialist and empirical grounds, primarily by raising concerns about procreative and child welfare optimality. Regarding the latter, the state's brief quoted extensively from a recently published book by Albert I. Gordon, a rabbi trained as a sociologist, who worried about the impact of interracial marriages on children.[44] Claiming that such marriages were more likely to end in divorce than same-race ones, Gordon argued that interracial unions should be avoided because they harmed children. He explained that "persons anticipating cross-marriages, however much in love they may be, have an important obligation to unborn children. It is not enough to say that such children will have to solve their own problems 'when the time comes.' Intermarriage frequently produces major psychological problems that are not readily solvable for the children of the intermarried.... It is not likely that the child will come through the maze of road blocks without doing some damage to himself."[45] Gordon added that "when we make it difficult and sometimes quite impossible for children to identify with us and our way of life, or our people, we have created a threat to their welfare and to the welfare of society as well because highly charged emotional experiences often leave such children disturbed, frustrated and unable to believe that they can live normal, happy lives."[46]

In addition to pointing to Gordon's claims of harm arising from interracial unions, the state of Virginia, in a deeply ironic move, defended its antimiscegenation law by making an analogy between the psychological harm to children it contended was caused by the social stigma that accompanied interracial marriages and the ways segregated schools harmed black children as recognized by the Supreme Court in *Brown*.[47] Virginia took the position, rather implausibly, that the goal of promoting (what it believed) was in children's best interests allowed it to rely on the Court's landmark racial equality case to defend a law grounded in the perceived racial inferiority of blacks.

Finally, the state also raised medical/eugenic justifications for its antimiscegenation law. The state's brief in *Loving*, quoting from a 1959 opinion by the Louisiana Supreme Court, claimed that "a state statute which prohibits intermarriage or cohabitation between members of different races…falls squarely within the police power of the state, which has an interest in maintaining the purity of the races and in preventing the propagation of half-breed children."[48]

The Supreme Court in *Loving*, as it had in *McLaughlin*, refused to address the state's effort to defend its law based on consequentialist and empirical claims grounded in considerations of harm to society and children. Instead, the Court, after rejecting the state's claim that the statute should be upheld because it applied equally to blacks and whites, struck it down as an invidious form of discrimination aimed at promoting white supremacy.[49]

Although the Supreme Court in *Loving* found it unnecessary to address the state's claims regarding procreative optimality and the promotion of child welfare, those who sought to justify racial marital bans—from the colonial period until the 1960s—repeatedly raised such claims. Antimiscegenation laws, in other words, were not only about racial hierarchy and subordination; they were also about specific understandings of what constituted appropriate—and socially useful—forms of human reproduction and of how best to promote the well-being of children.

MARITAL BANS AND THE "FEEBLEMINDED"

Antimiscegenation statutes were not the only marriage disqualification laws in American history that were justified on procreative and child welfare grounds. Supporters of statutes prohibiting so-called feebleminded individuals from marrying, which were first enacted at the end of the nineteenth century, also defended them on the grounds that they optimized human reproduction and minimized the chances that children would develop physical and psychological deficiencies.

A combination of statutes and common law principles had made it possible, during the first half of the nineteenth century, to challenge the marriages of mentally disabled individuals, but only if they were so mentally incompetent that they could not understand the implications of marriage. This approach was consistent with the prevailing understanding that mentally disabled individuals, through treatment and care in specialized institutions (i.e., asylums), could lead happy and productive lives. As the legal historian Michael Grossberg has noted, "a society which resisted biological determinism and which busily constructed asylums with the optimistic faith that even the hereditarily insane could be rehabilitated easily accepted a loose nuptial standard of mental capacity."[50]

This understanding of mental disability began to change around the middle of the century, as a stronger hereditary and more deterministic conception of mental illness, coupled with a growing confidence in the ability of scientific learning and knowledge to solve social problems, began to take a firmer hold among both experts and the general public. These changes led to a shift in emphasis from treating mental illness to preventing it. Correspondingly, marriage bans came to be seen by some as an important tool in avoiding the social costs associated with the birth of mentally disabled individuals. As one constitutional scholar starkly put it in 1886, "if the blood of either of the parties to a marriage is tainted with insanity there is imminent danger of its transmission to the offspring, and through the procreation of imbecile children the welfare of the state is more or less threatened."[51]

It was around this time that a new term, the "feebleminded," began to be used as a catchall label to designate a wide category of individuals who were deemed mentally inferior. With time, officials and commentators began blaming the "feebleminded" for a long list of social ills. As the superintendent of the Massachusetts School for the Feeble-Minded explained in an 1893 speech,

> The adult [feebleminded] males become the town loafers and incapables, the irresponsible pests of the neighborhood, petty thieves, purposeless destroyers of property, incendiaries, and very frequently violators of women and little girls. It is [also] well known that feeble-minded women and girls are very liable to become sources of unspeakable debauchery and licentiousness which pollutes the whole life of the young boys and youth of the community. They frequently disseminate in wholesale way the most loathsome and deadly diseases, permanently poisoning the minds and bodies of thoughtless youths at the very threshold of manhood. Almost every country town has one or more of these defective women having from one to four illegitimate children, every one of whom is predestined to be defective mentally, criminal, or an outcast of some sort.[52]

Two decades later, a zoologist and eugenicist who taught at the University of Wisconsin would make the same points more succinctly: "a considerable amount of crime, gross immorality and degeneracy is due at bottom to feeblemindedness."[53]

The first law specifically aimed at excluding the "feebleminded" from marriage was a criminal statute enacted by the Connecticut legislature in 1896. That law called for prison sentences of up to three years for a couple who attempted to marry if one or both of them was "epileptic, imbecile or feeble-minded."[54] The legislation only applied if the female partner was under the age of forty-five, making it clear that it was driven by procreative concerns. In the years that followed, several states, including Kansas, Michigan, New Jersey, and Wisconsin, adopted similar statutes.[55] Two states, South Dakota and Nebraska, went even further by requiring that all mentally disabled individuals register with the state and prohibiting them from marrying unless one of the wedding partners was infertile.[56] A supporter of these legal restrictions wrote in the *ABA Journal* in 1923 that they were "based not on historical rules...but on scientific facts. [They are] directed against two evils, the bringing into the world of children with hereditary taints and the protection of the public health by preventing the spread of disease through marriage."[57]

Eugenicists generally supported laws that prohibited so-called feebleminded individuals from marrying.[58] Many eugenicists were also aware, however, of the laws' limitations—the bans, after all, did not prevent the feebleminded from procreating outside of marriage. For this reason, eugenicists looked to other regulatory measures aimed at promoting negative eugenics, including the sexual segregation of the feebleminded in state institutions, restrictions on the influx of immigrants from eastern and southern European countries (who were viewed by many Americans of northern European descent as socially and mentally inferior), and the sterilization of criminals, the feebleminded, and epileptics. Eugenicists came to see these additional measures as more effective in achieving their goals than marriage bans.[59] With time, sterilization became the policy of choice in these matters among eugenicists, especially after the Supreme Court in 1927 upheld the constitutionality of sterilization laws in *Buck v. Bell*.[60]

Although the Supreme Court never ruled on the constitutionality of statutes denying mentally disabled individuals the opportunity to marry, lower courts upheld them on the ground that the state had a legitimate interest in preventing the births of individuals with certain kinds of illnesses. For example, the Connecticut Supreme Court, in a 1905 case involving the application of the marital ban to an epileptic man who attempted to marry, explained "that epilepsy is a disease of a peculiarly serious and revolting character, tending to weaken mental force, and often descending from parent to child, or entailing upon the offspring of the sufferer some other grave form of nervous malady, is a matter of common knowledge, of which courts will take judicial notice." The court concluded that the statute's objectives were reasonable since the law applied to "a class [of individuals] capable of endangering the health of families and adding greatly to the sum of human suffering." Although the court acknowledged that the question of who could marry whom might have been understood in the past as one of individual rights, the more modern view was to see it from the perspective of preventing harm to society.[61]

Many legal commentators in the first decades of the twentieth century agreed that the state had an expansive authority to impose marital restrictions in order to promote the safety and health of the public. As one author explained in the *Yale Law Journal* in 1915, marriage was "a matter of general or common right, [and as such] is so firmly bound up with the very life of the state and with its social, moral and economic welfare as to be distinctively and preëminently within the police power." In addition, that power unquestionably permitted the government to legislate for "the protection of the public or posterity through the prevention of diseased or degenerate offspring."[62] Laws such as Connecticut's marriage ban, therefore, did not raise questions of constitutional or individual rights; instead, the important point was that the state should be permitted to promote its understandings of the public good through marital restrictions and regulations.

Some states still have laws on the books prohibiting individuals with mental disabilities from marrying, though they are admittedly almost never enforced.[63] These laws are another troubling example of the ways consequentialist arguments regarding procreative optimality, child welfare, and the social good were deployed in the past to justify imposing class-based restrictions on the ability of individuals to marry.

ILLEGITIMACY AND THE PROMOTION
OF OPTIMAL FAMILIES

Marital laws intended to promote the social good by accounting for procreative and child welfare considerations have not been limited to outright bans. Those considerations also played crucial roles in defending laws that disadvantaged children born outside of marriage.

The American colonies followed English law in distinguishing between children born in wedlock, who were "legitimate" and could inherit property from their parents, and children born outside of marriage, who were "illegitimate" and could not inherit from anyone. Children born out of wedlock were considered *filius nullius*, "the child and the heir of no one." In colonial America, as in England, the parents of illegitimate children (in particular mothers) were subject to punishment, including fines, imprisonment, and even public whippings, for what society deemed their sexual sins.[64]

The dawn of the nineteenth century saw the introduction of legal reforms aimed at reducing the number of so-called illegitimate children and mitigating some of their legal disabilities. Although English law did not allow for the legitimization of children through the parents' subsequent marriage or the fathers' acknowledgment of paternity, some American states beginning in the early 1800s enacted laws providing for one or both of these avenues to legitimization. The advent of common law marriages and the judicial application of a strong presumption that the children of married women were also the children of their husbands contributed to further reducing the number of so-called illegitimate children. In addition, some states began allowing illegitimate children to inherit from their mothers (but not their fathers).[65]

The move to reform laws affecting so-called illegitimate children stalled during the second half of the nineteenth century. As Michael Grossberg explains, "the post-1850 American obsession with improving family life reinvigorated the use of the law to separate illegitimate from legitimate offspring…. The belief that discriminatory laws reinforced legitimate families and deterred spurious birth inhibited [additional] reform efforts."[66]

By the turn of the twentieth century, eugenic ideas began to be reflected in prevailing understandings of illegitimacy, in particular the notion that the phenomenon was largely caused by the mental defectiveness and feeblemindedness of single mothers.[67] In 1918, Percy Kammerer, an Episcopalian minister and Harvard Ph.D. student, sought to provide an empirical account of the causes of illegitimacy by publishing the first comprehensive study of nonmarital births in the United States. After collecting five hundred case records detailing the history and traits of mothers who gave birth to children outside of wedlock in Massachusetts, Kammerer identified several factors that led to single women having children. One of the most important of these was "bad home conditions," that is, home environments in which the girls who later became unwed mothers were subject to abuse, neglect, and inadequate supervision due to the parents' "illness or low mentality."[68] Improved home environments, Kammerer believed, would lead to fewer cases of child illegitimacy.

Another principal cause of out-of-wedlock births was the "mental abnormalities" of unwed mothers. According to Kammerer, two kinds were particularly relevant. First, "feeblemindedness" rendered some young women "in constant danger of becoming pregnant...[because of] an inherent incapacity to adjust sexually to the life of the community." Second, "an abnormal lack of [sexual] self-control" was often found in "ordinarily intelligent women." For Kammerer, the link between illegitimacy and mental deficiencies meant that the prevention of the former required, first, identifying "the mentally abnormal individual" and then, second, "segregating or controlling her in some way during her child-bearing period."[69]

Other studies conducted in the early twentieth century reached similar conclusions. A report published by the Department of Labor's Child Bureau in 1921, for example, explained that illegitimacy was the result of maladjustment during adolescence, immorality caused by poor home environments, defective mental capacities, and poor job training and opportunities.[70] This report, as one commentator has noted, "happily combined eugenic, psychological, and sociological" theories of illegitimacy.[71]

Not all those who sought to provide scientific and sociological explanations for illegitimacy were unsympathetic to the challenges faced by children born outside of marriage. Indeed, Kammerer urged his readers to view the question of illegitimacy not from a moral perspective, but as "an unfortunate indication of social and biological maladjustment" on the part of the mothers.[72] Kammerer therefore joined reformers who argued that children should not be punished for their mothers' actions.

Many remained firmly opposed to legal reforms, however, believing that nonmarital children represented a social threat that justified their second-class status. This view was unapologetically reflected in the writings of the sociologist Kingsley Davis. Davis, who eventually became a leading expert on the causes and consequences of population growth, and whose defense of a traditional understanding of marriage was later relied on by supporters of same-sex marriage bans, claimed in a 1939 article in the *American Sociological Review* that "the bastard, like the prostitute, thief, and beggar, belongs to that motley crowd of disreputable social types which society has generally resented, always endured."[73] For Davis, the social repudiation of illegitimacy was explained empirically and justified normatively by viewing human reproduction from a functional or institutional perspective, which required that the procreative capacities of individuals be harnessed in socially useful ways. As he explained,

> the function of reproduction can be carried out in a socially useful manner only if it is performed in conformity with institutional patterns, because only by means of an institutional system can individuals be organized and taught to co-operate in the performance of this long-range function, and the function be integrated with other social functions. The reproductive or familial institutions constitute the social machinery in terms of which the creation of new members is supposed to take place. The birth of children in ways that do not fit into this machinery must necessarily receive the disapproval of society, else the institutional system itself, which depends upon favorable attitudes in individuals, would not be approved or sustained.[74]

From Davis's deeply consequentialist perspective, therefore, the legal disabilities imposed on illegitimate children, such as their ineligibility to inherit from their fathers, played an entirely appropriate "institutional function" in protecting the interests of "the legitimate family." Although procreation was obviously indispensable to the survival of the human race, the more relevant point was that social survival and progress depended on the condemnation of procreation outside of marriage. Even if it might be possible to end illegitimacy by eliminating marriage and the family, doing so would also "abolish society...because...reproductive institutions...are necessary for societal existence."[75]

Although some states, around the middle of the twentieth century, enacted additional reforms aimed at reducing the number and impact of legal disabilities on nonmarital children (by, for example, permitting them to inherit from both their mothers and fathers), there were still, by the 1960s, many laws on the books that denied benefits to children born outside of marriage. In 1967, the Supreme Court agreed to hear a challenge to one of those laws: Louisiana's refusal to allow nonmarital children the opportunity to sue in tort for the wrongful deaths of their mothers, a right the state made available to legitimate children. The Louisiana Court of Appeal in *Levy v. Louisiana* had upheld the law, after concluding that the state had legitimate interests, based on considerations of morality and general welfare, in discouraging out-of-wedlock births.[76]

In its brief to the U.S. Supreme Court in *Levy*, the government pursued a consequentialist defense of its differential treatment of nonmarital children. The brief began by noting that "Bolshevik Russia" had eliminated illegitimacy legislatively in 1918, with the nefarious purpose of having the state replace the family as the social institution that deserved the most fealty and respect. The brief added that Nazi Germany had encouraged illegitimacy as a way of increasing the number of births. In contrast to the unwillingness of these totalitarian regimes to account for the social costs of illegitimacy, the state of Louisiana aimed to discourage such births by promoting "marriage as one of the most important institutions known to law" and by "preserving the legitimate family."[77]

According to the state, "marriage was the preferred social institution for civilizing...children." Specifically, Louisiana contended that "the stable family socializes the child and invests him with the values required in Western civilization. Marriage provides the preferred method of assuring the stable family. Marriage has been found to be an extremely useful social requirement for the preservation of the family and stabilizing the primary group in which children are reared." The brief then pointed to data showing that the United States had the highest marriage rate of any Western country and that the number of marriages entered into for the purpose of avoiding illegitimacy was increasing nationally. As for the fact that the number of nonmarital children was also growing nationally, that was the result not of "the failure of the marriage laws, but [of] the fact that society now does more to help unmarried mothers." Society encourages illegitimacy, the state claimed, when it "grants almost as much respect for non-marriage as for marriage." In contrast, "superior rights of legitimate offspring are inducements or incentives to parties to contract marriage, which is preferred by Louisiana as the setting for producing offspring."[78]

The Supreme Court in *Levy*, as it had done recently in *Loving*, refused to address the consequentialist and empirical arguments raised by the state in defending the constitutionality of a law aimed at advancing its understanding of optimality in family formation and child-rearing. In a short opinion that did not refer to any of the state's claims related to social progress and familial optimality, the Court concluded simply that treating nonmarital children differently because of the circumstances of their births was a form of invidious discrimination. The Court pointed out that those children, when they became adults, were subject to the same legal obligations as everyone else, yet the state denied them rights and benefits enjoyed by their fellow citizens. Such differential treatment was prohibited by the constitutional mandate requiring equal protection for all.[79]

Three years after *Levy*, the constitutionality of another Louisiana statute, which precluded nonmarital children from inheriting from their fathers if legitimate children also claimed an inheritance, reached the Court in *Labine v. Vincent*. The state once again argued that the differential treatment of so-called illegitimate children was a necessary means to achieve the end of promoting marriage and the nuclear family. Laws that denied benefits to nonmarital children, the state explained, "are based on the proposition that the family is a critical unit of society." The government added that the statutes in question "encourage marriage and family ties."[80] Although the Court upheld the law on the ground that the state had the authority "to make rules to establish, protect, and strengthen family life," as well as the power to manage the disposition of property following death, *Labine* turned out to represent the last gasp of the long-standing effort to justify the differential treatment of nonmarital children on the basis of considerations of family optimality.[81]

The year after *Labine*, the Court in *Weber v. Aetna Casualty & Surety Company* addressed the constitutionality of a statute that denied workers' compensation benefits to the nonmarital children of employees. The *Weber* Court held that whatever interests the government might have in promoting marriage and discouraging the birth of nonmarital children, they were not advanced by denying workers' compensation benefits to those children. This was because, the Court explained, it was irrational to believe that individuals would "shun illicit relationships" simply because their children might someday be denied access to particular benefits.[82]

After *Weber*, governments ceased defending the differential treatment of nonmarital children based on the need to encourage procreation within marital families and to discourage other family forms. Instead, government defendants focused on narrower justifications for the differential treatment, including the administrative difficulties of establishing paternity in the absence of marriage and the need to discourage spurious claims for government benefits. Although these arguments sometimes prevailed, the Court since *Levy* has been consistently skeptical of efforts to deny individuals benefits because of the circumstances of their births.[83]

HISTORICAL LESSONS

The ongoing effort to deny lesbians and gay men the opportunity to marry is only the most recent instantiation of status-based marital classifications grounded in the perceived need to promote procreation and the raising of children in ways that are deemed socially optimal. The troubling nature of earlier manifestations of this phenomenon—as reflected in interracial marriages bans, disability marriage prohibitions, and the differential treatment of nonmarital children—should make policymakers, judges, and the general public skeptical of efforts to impose or maintain class-based marital distinctions on the ground that they lead to the most socially useful procreative and child welfare outcomes.

Later, I assess the strength and merits of the specific procreative and child welfare arguments raised by same-sex marriages opponents, such as the need to promote responsible procreation (chapter 2) and the purportedly unique benefits to children of being raised by their biological mothers and fathers (chapter 3). For now, I want to highlight four similarities between the consequentialist reasoning of contemporary opponents of marriage equality and the arguments made by earlier supporters of interracial marriage bans, marital disability restrictions, and the differential treatment of nonmarital children.

The first similarity is that the consequentialist reasoning in all four instances begins with a status-based classification. The threshold problem with same-sex marriage, in the eyes of some, is the sexual orientation (or gender) of the prospective spouses, in the same way that the race, disability, or legitimacy status of the parties triggered the other regulatory regimes.

Second, the laws' supporters, in all four instances, have shared a highly functional understanding of marriage that has sought to justify the differential treatment of particular classes of individuals in matters related to marriage based on the need to promote the social good. As a result, in all four instances, the regulations' supporters have dismissed objections to the unequal or unfair treatment of individuals based on their status by pointing to (what they have argued constitute) provable social gains arising from those regulations.

Third, these social gains have been understood in all four cases to be dependent on the (dis)incentives associated with the ways that individuals exercise their procreative capacities. From this perspective, the legal restrictions related to marriage have been necessary to prevent or discourage certain classes of individuals from making procreative decisions that are deemed harmful to society. As a result, in the same way that the opposition to same-sex marriage today is driven in important ways by the perceived social need to maximize the chances that children will be brought into this world and raised by married heterosexual couples, the opposition to interracial marriages was driven in important ways by the perceived social need to maximize the chances that children would be brought into this world and raised by racially homogenous couples. In addition, some opponents of same-sex marriage argue that it is better for society if lesbians and gay men do not raise children, in the same way that supporters of marriage bans by the feebleminded contended that society was better off if those with mental disabilities did not have children. Same-sex marriage bans are also frequently defended as justifiable means to attain the end of encouraging heterosexuals to procreate within marriage, in the same way that the imposition of legal disabilities on nonmarital children were defended as legitimate means to achieve the same objective.

Finally, proponents of the regulations, in all four instances, have asserted that the family forms they favor promote the social good by protecting the welfare of children. Opponents of same-sex marriage, as I explore in some detail in chapter 3, frequently describe households headed by married heterosexuals who are biologically related to their children as the "optimal" setting for the raising of children. As a result, they argue that other types of households—including ones headed by same-sex couples or by single parents regardless of their sexual orientation—put children at greater risk of suffering psychological and social harm.

The defenders of the laws explored in this chapter relied on the same type of reasoning. Supporters of antimiscegenation laws, prohibitions on marriages by the mentally disabled, and the differential treatment of nonmarital children argued that the regulations in question were needed in order to promote the best possible child outcomes. From the perspective of these supporters, children were harmed in tangible ways when raised by racially heterogeneous parents or by mentally disabled parents or by unmarried parents, outcomes that, in their view, justified the laws in question.

To support allegations of harm to children, proponents of all four regulatory regimes turned to the social science evidence. For example, the states of Virginia and Louisiana, in defending their antimiscegenation and illegitimacy laws, pointed to sociological and psychological literatures to claim that the equal treatment demanded by the laws' critics threatened the well-being of children. Similarly, marriage equality opponents, as we will see in chapter 3, rely on social science studies to claim that same-sex couples should be precluded from marrying because doing so promotes the welfare of children.

In short, efforts to prohibit same-sex couples from marrying is only the latest instantiation of a recurring phenomenon in American history: the move to prohibit certain individuals from enjoying the benefits of marriage in order to promote (what are taken to be) socially useful ways of procreating and of raising children. Note that in order to make this point, it is not necessary to claim that those who oppose same-sex marriage on procreative and child welfare grounds are motivated by homophobia or other forms of irrational biases that are analogous to the kinds of deeply disturbing prejudices shown by those who supported marital bans on the grounds of race and disability, as well as by many who defended the differential treatment of nonmarital children. The analogy I am drawing here does not depend on defending the moral equivalence between, for example, the ideologies of racism and eugenics of yesterday and the opposition to same-sex marriage today. Instead, the relevant question is whether the consequentialist reasoning of those who seek to promote heterosexual procreation and parenting within marriage by denying lesbians and gay men the opportunity to marry individuals of their choice is analogous to the consequentialist reasoning of those who defended antimiscegenation laws, marital bans on the basis of mental disabilities, and the differential treatment of nonmarital children. For the reasons noted here, I believe the answer to that question is yes.

The mere fact that consequentialist arguments based on procreative and child welfare optimality have been deployed in highly problematic ways in the past when justifying marital policies grounded in status-based distinctions does not necessarily mean that all such efforts should be deemed per se impermissible. (As we will see in the next section, for example, those arguments may have a legitimate role in defending narrow bans on incestuous marriages.) It does mean, however, that decisionmakers in this area should proceed with great caution in order to avoid repeating the mistakes of the past. At the very least, the nation's troubling history in these matters means that the moral and legal burden should be placed on those who seek to deny marital benefits to entire classes of individuals in order to promote particular understandings of the social good in matters related to procreation and child welfare.

Finally, I should note that my argument here is not against all consequentialist reasoning in the setting of marital and family policies. Such reasoning can sometimes play an appropriate role in determining how the state should use its authority and resources to promote and protect the well-being of families and children. Thus, my argument is not against consequentialist reasoning writ large in matters related to marriage and families. Instead, my brief is against one particular type of consequentialist argument (one based on procreative and child-rearing considerations) to justify a particular kind of policy (class-based restrictions on marriage or marital benefits). It is this subset of consequentialist arguments that has been deployed in deeply troubling ways in our nation's past. That history shows that marital class-based regulations based on the social dangers of disfavored forms of procreation and child-rearing have almost always turned out to be either empirically groundless or normatively problematic (or both). An understanding of this historical record should lead contemporary policymakers, courts, and the public to be highly skeptical of efforts to rely on consequentialist claims based on procreative and child welfare considerations to justify denying same-sex couples the opportunity to marry.

It may be argued that by considering three regulatory regimes (antimiscegenation laws, disability marital bans, and the differential treatment of nonmarital children) that are largely discredited today, I am stacking the deck against the use of procreative and child-based considerations in justifying restrictions on marital rights and benefits. In order to address this possible criticism, I next explore the role such considerations played (or did not play) in justifying two marital bans that still enjoy wide support today: the bans on incestuous marriages and on polygamous unions.

INCEST

Early American statutes generally followed English canon law in prohibiting marriages between individuals related by blood or marriage. There was, however, considerable disagreement among jurisdictions on how close an intrafamily relationship had to be in order to preclude marriage.[84] The fact that most of the early statutes included relations of affinity within the definition of incest (by, for example, prohibiting a man from marrying his dead wife's sister), shows that they were concerned with more than just procreative matters. It has been suggested, for example, that early American incest marriage bans were aimed at preventing the deleterious effects of sexual competition within families while helping to maintain clarity in the lines of succession to property.[85] It is undoubtedly the case, however, that concerns about degenerative physical effects resulting from intrafamily procreation played an important role in the enactment of incest marriage laws, even before much was known about genetics and the workings of heredity.

The political writer and lexicographer Noah Webster, for example, wrote in 1790 that consanguineous marriages would have "fatal consequences to society" and would lead "men [to] soon become a race of pygmies."[86] Almost a century later, Joel Bishop, a leading family law scholar who wrote at a time when knowledge about genetics and heredity was still extremely limited, explained that the principal reason for banning incestuous marriages was that "persons closely allied in blood are apt to produce an offspring feeble in body, and tending to insanity of the mind." Bishop noted that the fact that prior generations had defended the bans on other grounds—such as the need to protect families and promote favorable alliances outside families—"shows how in the world's history, the promptings of the nature of man frequently carry him in the right direction even where his mere intellect fails to discern the path."[87]

Concerns about the sociobiological implications of reproduction by consanguineous relatives explains the two major changes in incest marriage laws following the Civil War: the move to prohibit, for the first time in American history, marriages between first cousins and the gradual lifting of affinity marital bans. As with efforts to defend antimiscegenation laws and the enactment of disability marital bans in the second half of the nineteenth century, concerns about social survival and progress were the primary reasons for these changes in incest marriage law. As the anthropologist Martin Ottenheimer explains, "by the middle of the nineteenth century, marriage was widely viewed in terms of social evolution and as a mechanism necessary to society's survival and progress. Marriage between 'natural' relatives (i.e., cousins) became the concern now rather than marriage between 'contractual' relatives (i.e., in-laws). The former now were seen to harbor potential dangers to society and had to be carefully regulated."[88]

The move in the United States to prohibit first cousins from marrying was inconsistent with the practices of many Western countries, most of which permitted cousins to marry.[89] Furthermore, scientific studies eventually showed that the offspring of first cousins had little increased risk of genetic abnormalities.[90] Nonetheless, about half of the states today still prohibit first cousins from marrying.[91] It would seem that this ban is an additional example of a marital restriction imposed on questionable empirical grounds.

As for bans on marriage between closer relatives (for example, between parents and their children or between siblings), some studies suggest that the biological offspring of these unions are at some increased risk of developing physiological abnormalities.[92] Some experts, however, have noted that the question of whether incest bans can be justified on genetic grounds needs further scientific study.[93]

Aside from the uncertainty regarding the genetic consequences of close-relative procreation, incestuous marriages raise legitimate concerns about society's interest in maintaining the family sphere free of sexual coercion and tension.[94] Thus, valid consequentialist grounds may very well exist for enacting narrow bans on incestuous marriages (for example, bans that do not include first cousins within their ambit). This view is reflected in the contemporary enforcement of criminal incest laws in cases where there is no biological connection between the parties. As a federal appellate court explained in upholding the criminal conviction of a stepfather for having consensual sex with his adult stepdaughter, "unlike sexual relationships between unrelated…adults, the stepparent-stepchild relationship is the kind of relationship in which a person might be injured or coerced or where consent might not easily be refused, regardless of age, because of the inherent influence of the stepparent over the stepchild."[95]

Even if there are legitimate reasons for prohibiting marriages between close relatives, those restrictions are, at most, one apparent exception to an otherwise consistent and troubling pattern in American history of defending class-based marital restrictions on the basis of procreative and child welfare considerations in ways that have been either empirically misguided or normatively problematic (or both).

POLYGAMY

Unlike in the case of incest, concerns about procreation and the well-being of children did not play a role in the adoption of the most important and hotly debated antipolygamy laws in the nation's history—the federal antipolygamy statutes enacted during the second half of the nineteenth century. Polygamous marriages first appeared openly in this country after Joseph Smith, the founder of the Church of Jesus Christ of Latter-day Saints, claimed shortly before he died in 1844 that he had received a revelation from God encouraging Mormon men to enter into plural marriages. After some initial resistance, the Mormon church leaders who succeeded Smith embraced polygamy as a necessary step toward eternal salvation. By the time the Mormons, fleeing persecution in the Midwest, arrived in what soon thereafter became the Utah Territory, the holiness of polygamy was established church doctrine.[96]

One of the first acts of the Mormon-controlled territorial legislature in Utah was to award corporate status to the church, granting it extensive powers, including the authority to control unlimited amounts of property and wealth, and to govern the marriages of its members. The economic, social, and political power of the church in Utah, having no parallels in American society, eventually led to significant tension with the federal government and with the growing number of Americans (especially in the North) who began to criticize the Mormon practice of polygamy.

By the end of the 1850s, antipolygamists were demanding that Congress enact federal laws prohibiting plural marriages in Utah. Initially, such demands went unheeded, primarily because of opposition from Democrats who, in wanting to protect the institution of slavery from federal intervention, were loath to support an expansion of federal power in the territories.[97] Not until halfway through the Civil War did the Republican-controlled Congress enact a statute—the Morrill Act for the Suppression of Polygamy—prohibiting plural marriages in the territories.

The Morrill Act was wholly ineffective in ending polygamy in Utah, both because the federal government lacked the means to enforce it and the Mormons were united in their resistance to it.[98] Twelve years later, Congress enacted the Poland Act of 1874, which sought to make the Morrill Act enforceable by granting federal courts in the territories exclusive jurisdiction over most criminal and civil matters. As a result of the new law, federal authorities began prosecuting Mormon polygamists for the first time. But Congress was not done. Eight years later, it enacted the Edmunds Act of 1882, which criminalized cohabitation with more than one woman (making it no longer necessary for prosecutors to establish the existence of an actual polygamous marriage) and deprived those who practiced polygamy or cohabitation of the right to vote and to hold public office. Finally, the mortal wound to polygamy in Utah—and to the absolute economic, social, and political power of the Mormon church in that territory—was inflicted by the Edmunds-Tucker Act of 1887. That statute included provisions (1) repealing the act of incorporation of the Church of Jesus Christ of Latter-day Saints, (2) authorizing the seizure of church property, and (3) abolishing spousal privileges in the prosecution of polygamy cases. Three years later, the church officially disavowed polygamy, paving the way for Utah to achieve statehood in 1896.[99]

It is important to note that antipolygamists, unlike the supporters of the other marital polices discussed in this chapter, during the second half of the nineteenth century did not rely on considerations related to procreation and child welfare to support the prohibition of polygamous marriages. Instead, antipolygamists began their campaign in the 1850s by trying to link plural marriages to slavery. The platform of the Republican national convention of 1856—the party's first—called for the abolition of both slavery and polygamy, deeming them the "twin relics of barbarism." As the legal historian Sarah Barringer Gordon explains, this link was crafted "in explicitly political terms, connecting patriarchy (in the South as well as in Utah) to barbarism, and voluntarism (in labor as in marriage) to civilization."[100]

This political understanding of polygamy led to the linking of plural marriage, which was understood as lacking the free consent of the women involved, with despotism and authoritarianism, while monogamous marriage, which was understood to be freely chosen by its participants, was linked to republican democracy. Antipolygamists were also concerned about the well-being of women who found themselves participating in polygamous marriages.[101] In addition, antipolygamists railed against the dangers of religious sectarianism and of granting economic and political power to a church.[102] Finally, antipolygamists came to associate monogamy with their northern European ancestry while connecting polygamy with dangerous Asian and African cultures, a perspective that led to the widely shared view that white Mormons were somehow not actually white.[103]

Most of these antipolygamist claims were reflected in the Supreme Court's 1878 ruling in *Reynolds v. United States* upholding the constitutionality of the Morrill Act's ban on polygamy in the territories. The Court explained that "polygamy has always been odious among the northern and western nations of Europe, and, until the establishment of the Mormon Church, was almost exclusively a feature of the life of Asiatic and of African people."[104] The Court added that the way a society decided to structure and rule itself depended on its preference for monogamous or polygamous marriages. Agreeing with Francis Lieber, a nineteenth-century political theorist and a committed foe of plural marriages, the Court claimed that "polygamy leads to the patriarchal principle,... which, when applied to large communities, fetters the people in stationary despotism, while that principle cannot long exist in connection with monogamy."[105]

What is notably absent from all of these arguments is any attention to either the procreative or child-welfare consequences of polygamous marriages.[106] In stark contrast to the claims made in favor of interracial, disability, and same-sex marriage marital bans, the most protracted and important campaign in favor of antipolygamy laws in the nation's history was not grounded in considerations related to procreation and child welfare. This means that those who today defend same-sex marriage bans cannot use the federal response to Mormon polygamy as a historical example of regulations aimed at discouraging certain kinds of marriages on the basis of the need to promote particular procreative and child welfare goals.

It is in many ways not surprising that same-sex marriage opponents have consistently turned to procreative and child welfare considerations to defend their positions. Concerns about social survival and progress, to say nothing about protecting the well-being of children, seem to be, on their face, appropriate and legitimate. However, the historical record on the use of these concerns to defend class-based marital restrictions and benefits limitations in the United States reveals several examples of their being deployed in deeply problematic ways. It is likely that in the not-too-distant future, society will judge the procreative and child-welfare arguments currently raised by same-sex marriage opponents with the same deep skepticism and incredulity with which it now views the use of those claims by large segments of prior generations to defend antimiscegenation laws, disability marital bans, and the differential treatment of nonmarital children. The odds are quite good that, when it comes to these issues, today's opponents of same-sex marriage will tomorrow be on the wrong side of history.

2

RESPONSIBLE PROCREATION

It was to a great extent predictable that LGBT rights opponents chose to focus so intently on procreation-related considerations in their fight against the legal recognition of same-sex marriages. The characteristic that most clearly distinguishes different-sex couples from same-sex ones, after all, is that only the former are capable of creating new human beings through sexual intimacy. This "fact of nature," from the very beginning of policy and legal debates over same-sex marriage, became the foundation for defending the law's use of gender as a marriage eligibility criterion.

Supporters of same-sex marriage bans also made clear early on that their concern was not so much with procreation for its own sake as with the promotion of *responsible* procreation. These supporters have claimed that marriage's most important social function is to encourage biological parents to commit to each other and to their children. The primary reason why society provides married couples with the structure and benefits of marriage is to encourage parents, especially men, to take responsibility for their offspring. The recognition of same-sex unions as marital undermines the institution's primary social function because it awards marital status to couples who cannot procreate. Indeed, allowing same-sex couples to marry sends the message that marriage and procreation should be thought of as two entirely different spheres of human conduct. A society that recognizes same-sex marriages, the argument goes, is conceding that the state can issue marriage licenses without concerning itself with how individuals exercise their procreative capacities. It is therefore necessary to deny same-sex couples the right to marry in order to preserve the historically and socially beneficial link between marriage and procreation.

This chapter explores the responsible procreation defense of same-sex marriage bans. The first half of the chapter is largely descriptive, explaining the nature and scope of the procreative claims that have been raised in support of same-sex marriage bans. In doing so, the discussion pays particular attention to how the responsible procreation claims that opponents of marriage equality have made are grounded in many of the same arguments conservatives previously raised in attacking the federal government's welfare policies.

The chapter's second half proceeds to assess the responsible procreation claims. It begins by explaining that it was the legal and cultural changes that took place during the twentieth century affecting *heterosexual* relationships, rather than the push for LGBT rights in general and same-sex marriage in particular, that significantly diminished the procreative channeling function of marriage. Indeed, the link between marriage and procreation began to fray long before the first same-sex marriages were recognized in this country.

The question then arises why social conservatives, starting around the mid-1990s, focused so intently on maintaining the prohibition on same-sex marriage as an essential bulwark in the promotion of so-called responsible procreation. I suggest that they did so because gay marriage, unlike other policy issues as such as contraception and divorce, provided them with a hotly contested question of family law and policy that, for the first time in several decades, offered the enticing possibility of actually defeating the forces of liberalization. Their chances of success were a direct result of the fact that lesbians, gay men, and bisexuals, like single-mother welfare recipients, were a highly stigmatized segment of the population, whose proclaimed interests could seemingly be easily rejected or ignored in the name of promoting the well-being of society and children.

The second half of the chapter also explains that there is no empirical support for the claim, repeatedly made by opponents of same-sex marriage, that the recognition of gay marriages has deleterious effects on heterosexual marriage and procreation. The chapter ends by arguing that the effort to promote responsible procreation among heterosexuals by denying same-sex couples the opportunity to marry is morally objectionable because it uses lesbians, gay men, and bisexuals (and their children) instrumentally in order to advance the interests of others.

THE FACTS OF NATURE

American constitutional law has generally followed the Aristotelian principle that the government's obligation to treat citizens equally applies only when the individuals in question are similarly situated. When the state, in other words, affords a benefit to a certain class of individuals, it is not constitutionally required to make it available to another class if the latter is not similarly situated to the former.

In the 1990s, as LGBT rights supporters increasingly began pushing for the recognition of same-sex marriages, social conservatives responded by claiming that lesbian and gay couples were not similarly situated to different-sex couples in relation to the institution of marriage. Some conservatives argued, for example, that the former were not as committed to each other or to raising children together as were the latter. These claims, however, became increasingly untenable in the face of the greater social visibility of LGBT people and their relationships. Indeed, (1) the care and love gay men showed for their partners during the early days of the AIDS epidemic, (2) the growing number of lesbians and gay men who were seeking to become parents, and (3) the very push by (committed and loving) same-sex couples (many of whom were raising children together) to be permitted to marry largely dispensed with the argument that same-sex couples were somehow incapable of or uninterested in forming lasting intimate and familial relationships.

One claim, however, could not be factually disputed, no matter how much lesbians and gay men loved their partners and their children: the sexual intimacy of same-sex couples could not lead to the formation of a new life. This biological reality was, in turn, reflected in the reproductive differences between men and women, differences that in the view of marriage equality opponents justified limiting marriage to opposite-sex couples.

This perspective was advanced in a series of law review articles written in the mid-1990s by natural law theorists. The articles contended that the distinct procreative sexual organs of men and women allowed them to create real, true, and unique marital unions. It was claimed, on the other hand, that the sexual intimacy of same-sex couples "has nothing to do with their having children by each other, and their reproductive organs cannot make them a biological (and therefore personal) unit," which, in turn, meant that they could not, regardless of their intent, participate in a true marriage.[1] These natural law proponents, in responding to the objection that infertile different-sex couples were incapable of procreating yet were permitted to marry, responded by emphasizing that such couples nonetheless still engaged in the same physical act (i.e., penile-vaginal intercourse) that, but for their infertility, could lead to the creation of a new being. As one article explained,

> the difference between sterile and fertile married couples is not a difference in what they do. Rather, it is a difference in a distinct condition which affects what may result from what they do. However, the difference between any heterosexual couple engaging in penile-vaginal intercourse and a homosexual couple is much more than that. The lack of complementarity in homosexual couples is a condition which renders it impossible for them to perform the kind of act which makes them organically one.[2]

Opponents of marriage equality also argued that there was a prudential (and perhaps even constitutional) reason why the government allowed infertile opposite-sex couples to marry: any effort by the state to try to determine which different-sex couples were infertile, in order to exclude them from marriage, would be highly intrusive and violate privacy rights. Furthermore, as the law professor Douglas Kmiec reasoned, the fact that a small minority of married heterosexual couples were not able to procreate did not constitute a social threat. In contrast, "it is far more questionable whether any state can rationally be indifferent to sustaining its population by giving public marital sanction to individuals who, because of physical reality and the nature of their sexual relationship, cannot procreate."[3]

Critics raised similar kinds of arguments against same-sex marriage outside law reviews. For example, in a statement given during a 1996 congressional hearing on DOMA, the political science professor Hadley Arkes claimed that the meaning of marriage could not be separated from "certain bodily acts" and from "the N-word (nature)." Arkes explained that sexuality is

> imprinted in our very natures—in the obdurate fact that we are all, as the saying goes, "engendered." We are, each of us, born a man or a woman. The committee needs no testimony from an expert witness to decode this point: Our engendered existence, as men and women, offers the most unmistakable, natural signs of the meaning and purpose of sexuality. And that is the function and purpose of

begetting. At its core, it is hard to detach marriage from what may be called the "natural teleology of the body": namely, the inescapable fact that only two people, not three, only a man and a woman, can beget a child.[4]

The same reasoning was reflected in appellate briefs defending the constitutionality of same-sex marriage bans. A government brief filed with the Indiana Court of Appeals in 2003, for example, pointed out that every child has a biological father and mother and that, as a result, it was appropriate for the state to limit the institution of marriage to the "only union that can produce children."[5] Similarly, in an amicus brief filed with the New York Court of Appeals a few years later, the Family Research Council, a conservative advocacy organization deeply opposed to LGBT rights, emphasized that, as a matter of biological necessity, all same-sex couples had to rely on third parties (either sperm donors, surrogate mothers, or biological parents who later gave up their children for adoption) in order to have children.[6]

Marriage equality opponents were drawn to biological arguments based on the "facts of nature" for several reasons. First, as noted, the empirical cornerstone of the argument (that the reproductive organs of different-sex couples generally allow them to procreate while those of same-sex couples *never* do) was indisputable. Second, the natural law and universalist component of the argument dovetailed nicely with the fact that marriage in most countries for most of history had been limited to unions between men and women.[7]

Ultimately, however, defending same-sex marriage bans on the sole basis of the "facts of nature" proved inadequate. Despite the best efforts of natural law proponents and others to distinguish between infertile heterosexual couples and same-sex ones, the view that penile-vaginal intercourse was uniquely valuable (and thus somehow uniquely marital) regardless of whether it led to procreation did not resonate with many Americans. Indeed, even the conservative Supreme Court Justice Antonin Scalia pointed out in a 2003 dissenting opinion that the purpose of marriage could not possibly be procreation, given that infertile and elderly heterosexual couples were permitted to marry.[8] Opponents of marriage equality, therefore, were forced to go beyond the "facts of nature" to make their case. They did so by claiming that the sine qua non of marriage was not to encourage procreation for its own sake (that is, by maximizing the total number of new lives created), but to promote *responsible* procreation. This contention still left room to highlight the different and complementary procreative capabilities of men and women. At the same time, emphasizing the difference between responsible and irresponsible procreation permitted marriage equality opponents to situate the question of same-sex marriage within a broader cultural debate over how our society and its laws should go about encouraging (heterosexual) Americans to exercise their procreative capacities.

RESPONSIBLE PROCREATION IN THE EARLIER CONTEXT OF WELFARE REFORM

By the time the debate over same-sex marriage heated up in the mid-1990s, the post–World War II conservative political movement was about to achieve one of its most significant policy victories: persuading Congress to fundamentally alter the federal government's policies aimed at assisting families living in poverty. As they were starting to do with same-sex marriage, conservatives had for decades attacked welfare policies for undermining the institution of marriage and promoting irresponsible procreation.

When Congress in 1935 enacted the Social Security Act, it created a small program, the Aid to Dependent Children (ADC), modeled on the "mothers' pensions"—cash aid programs for widowed mothers—adopted by some states and municipalities during the 1910s and 1920s.[9] The ADC program, like the mothers' pensions that preceded it, was intended to encourage mothers without husbands—in particular widows—to forgo the labor market in order to stay at home caring for their children. Four years after the federal government created the ADC, almost two-thirds of the beneficiaries were widows, and a quarter were women who were divorced, separated, or had been abandoned by their husbands; only 2 percent were never-married single mothers. In addition, during its first years of existence, the ADC program, like the earlier mothers' pensions, was limited almost exclusively to white households.[10]

In 1939, Congress amended the Social Security Act in order to render widows whose husbands had contributed to the social security system eligible for survival benefits under the Old Age Insurance program (today commonly referred to as "social security") rather than through the ADC. This change emptied the ADC rolls of the women whom society deemed most deserving of government assistance, that is, women whose need for aid was not the result of (what were thought to be) questionable personal decisions, but of a circumstance (i.e., the death of their husbands) beyond their control. After 1939, ADC beneficiaries were primarily mothers who were thought less deserving of aid than widows, either because they had chosen the wrong men to marry (as reflected, for example, in the fact that their husbands later abandoned them) or, even worse, they had never married at all.[11]

The Social Security Act called on states to administer the ADC program with little federal supervision. Starting in the 1940s, many states began implementing a wide variety of administrative regulations aimed at making sure that the cash aid went only to so-called suitable households. These measures were used to monitor, regulate, and penalize the reproductive choices of women with limited economic means. State welfare officials, for example, routinely excluded from the program mothers who took on male boarders, cohabited with a man, or failed to identify the father of children born out of wedlock. State officials also routinely conducted so-called midnight raids looking for any evidence (in closets, bureaus, bathrooms, and so on) that there might be "a man-in-the-house," rendering the household ineligible for ADC funds.[12]

Welfare officials were much more likely to characterize the homes of black women as "unsuitable" than those of white ones. But even in the face of often blatantly discriminatory enforcement of welfare suitability rules, the percentage of black women on ADC grew, increasing from 31 percent in 1950 to 48 percent in 1961. One of the reasons for this increase was that black women, after 1957, had higher fertility rates than white ones. But other factors also accounted for the rise, including the fact that black women were more likely to be separated, divorced, or widowed. In addition, by 1955, the rate of unemployment of black men was twice that of white men, and many of them had moved to northern cities after losing agricultural jobs in the South. This economic marginalization and displacement, as one historian of welfare policies has noted, rendered "black men less available for marriage and family support."[13]

As critics of government welfare saw it, however, the increase in the number of women receiving aid, and of black women in particular, was largely the result of their promiscuity and irresponsible procreative decisions. These were no longer the "deserving" (i.e., white) widows whose circumstances had led to the creation of the ADC program in the first place. Instead, these were "undeserving" (largely black) single mothers whose poverty was the result of their irresponsible procreative choices.[14]

The 1950s saw the introduction of several bills in state legislatures calling for the forced sterilization of women on welfare. One of these was sponsored in 1957 by the North Carolina state senator Wilbur Jolly. In pushing for his bill, Jolly claimed that illegitimacy and welfare dependency were "Negro problems" and that the solution to black poverty was the sterilization of women on welfare.[15] A year later, the Mississippi state representative David Glass introduced a bill authorizing courts to order the sterilization of women who had children while on welfare if judges determined that the women's moral character threatened the community. Glass focused his attention almost exclusively on black women, contending that his bill was essential to reducing the rate of illegitimacy in the black community.[16]

The sterilization bills, none of which was enacted into law, were not the only efforts by officials to target what they claimed were the irresponsible procreative choices of black women on welfare. In 1960, Louisiana moved to drop twenty-three thousand children, 95 percent of whom were black, from the program on the ostensible basis that their unmarried mothers had had additional children while receiving welfare benefits. This brazen attempt to prevent thousands of children from receiving welfare assistance proved too much for the federal government, which issued a directive prohibiting states from denying ADC benefits on the basis of home suitability.[17] Later that decade, the Supreme Court struck down Alabama's "substitute father rule," under which benefits had been denied to sixteen thousand children (90 percent of whom were black) because their unmarried mothers were sexually intimate with able-bodied men who were presumed under state regulations to be capable of providing for the children's financial needs.[18] A few years later, the Court voided a New Jersey statute that limited the receipt of welfare benefits to married households and therefore entirely excluded single mothers from the program.[19]

These new limits on the ability of states to exclude certain households from (what was now called) the Aid to Families with Dependent Children program (AFDC), coupled with the growing political activism of welfare rights groups, led to a steady increase in the number of families participating in the program. In 1971, 11 million children received AFDC aid, almost three times the number who had a decade earlier.[20]

Rising enrollments, of course, led to rising government expenditures, which in turn fueled sharper political and ideological attacks on single mothers and their procreative choices. For welfare critics, the increase in the assistance rolls was not due to economic and social factors such as the steady drop in urban industrial jobs across the country or the growing incarceration rates of black men or the stark disparities in the quality of education provided by suburban (mostly white) school systems and their urban (mostly minority) counterparts. Instead, welfare critics contended that the increase in the number of families participating in AFDC was largely the result of the growing irresponsibility of poor women, in particular black ones, in deciding to have children outside of marriage. It was claimed that these women, rather than choosing to work and to make sure that the fathers helped support the children, were instead irresponsibly relying on government handouts to pay for the costs of raising their children. The perception of mothers on welfare as both lazy and opportunistic became increasingly prevalent, despite the fact that the average annual AFDC payment to a family of four in 1966, for example, was $1,728, barely half of the official poverty line of $3,355.[21]

In 1967, Ronald Reagan, the newly elected governor of California, promised in his inauguration speech that "we are not going to perpetuate poverty by substituting a permanent dole for a paycheck."[22] For his part, Senator Russell Long of Louisiana described mothers on welfare as "brood mares" who chose to stay at home to have more children and raise them in a culture of dependency.[23] These political attacks on welfare recipients came on the heels of a controversial report issued by the Department of Labor, written by the assistant secretary of labor (and future senator) Patrick Moynihan, claiming that nonmarital childbearing among urban blacks was the most important contributor to long-term poverty in the cities, the growth in the AFDC program, and the "steady disintegration of the Negro family over the past generation."[24]

Although Congress took some steps in 1967 to address the purported irresponsibility of unmarried mothers on welfare, more than twenty years would pass before it enacted significant changes to federal welfare policy.[25] In the meantime, conservative critics continued their attacks on welfare programs. In 1984, the political scientist Charles Murray wrote an influential book, Losing Ground, in which he claimed that AFDC's financial incentives encouraged single women to choose to have out-of-wedlock children.[26] Murray and other conservative authors reasoned that the existence of a growing number of families headed by single women was not an *effect* of poverty, but a primary *cause* of it. These critics called for a fundamental rethinking of welfare policies in order to encourage poor women to find paid work and to only have children within marriage.

The call for the reform (read: retrenchment) of welfare policies became a cornerstone of the Reagan administration's domestic policy. Indeed, welfare reform was a priority for two of the Reagan coalition's most important groups: those who believed that the free market offered the most effective solutions to the nation's ills and those calling for a return to so-called traditional family values. This promotion of family values was also soon deployed to try to keep lesbians, gay men, and bisexuals outside of the institution of marriage.

In 1986, an interdepartmental working group formed by President Reagan issued a report accusing government assistance programs of threatening the well-being of American families. The report, largely written by undersecretary of education Gary Bauer, claimed that "the fabric of family life has been frayed by the abrasive experiments of two liberal decades."[27] According to the report, those experiments had led to increases in crime, illegitimate births, drug use, teen pregnancy, divorce, sexually transmitted diseases, and poverty. The document added that the "easy availability of welfare in all of its forms has become a powerful force for destruction of family life through perpetuation of the welfare culture."[28]

Conservatives were particularly alarmed by the growing number of children raised without fathers in the home. For these critics, the absence of male parental figures deprived children of the opportunity to thrive and created a cycle of poverty and dependency on government handouts. As the Reagan working group's report explained,

> raised in an environment in which fathers don't provide for their young and [in which] dependency on the government is assumed, few children will develop the skills of self-sufficiency or even the concept of personal responsibility. Young men will not strive to be good providers and young women will not expect it of their men. Family breakdown becomes cyclical, out-of-wedlock births become cyclical, and poverty and dependency become cyclical.[29]

Congress, responding in 1988 to these claims of procreative irresponsibility, enacted the Family Support Act, a law that required most single mothers on AFDC to find work or enroll in a training program. The statute also demanded that states meet strict federal standards for establishing the paternity of children born out of wedlock and to set up procedures for automatic attachment of fathers' wages.[30] The objective behind these mandates was to transfer the public's support for children in the AFDC program to private hands.[31]

The steady conservative drumbeat about the social ills caused by single-mother households continued into the 1990s. During the 1992 presidential campaign, Vice President Dan Quayle condemned the popular television show *Murphy Brown* for its positive portrayal of the main character's decision to raise a child without a father. Quayle criticized Murphy Brown for "mocking the importance of fathers, by bearing a child alone, and calling it just another 'life style choice.'" Quayle added that "ultimately, marriage is a moral issue that requires cultural consensus and the use of social sanctions. Bearing babies irresponsibly is, simply, wrong. Failing to support children one has fathered is wrong. We must be unequivocal about this."[32]

Writing in the *Atlantic* the following year and claiming that "Dan Quayle was right," the conservative journalist Barbara Dafoe Whitehead decried the nation's growing embrace of family diversity (as represented by single-parent and stepparent families following divorce), which she argued was dramatically weakening and undermining society. Whitehead traced the problem back to the 1970s, when social and cultural mores shifted from a focus on child well-being to that of adult happiness.[33] For his part, Charles Murray published an essay in the *Wall Street Journal* in 1993 claiming that "illegitimacy is the single most important social problem of our time—more important than crime, drugs, poverty, illiteracy, welfare or homelessness because it drives everything else." Like Patrick Moynihan twenty-five years earlier, Murray despaired about the culture of the "black inner city," dominated by "the values of unsocialized male adolescents made norms—physical violence, immediate gratification and predatory sex." According to Murray, however, this was "old news"; what now truly worried him was the growing rate of illegitimacy among the white lower classes, a phenomenon he claimed was the greatest threat facing the nation.[34]

To solve the crisis, Murray recommended that single mothers be deprived of all welfare benefits. Doing so would transfer the maintenance responsibilities for these women-led families from the government to their extended families and to local communities, which would in turn restigmatize out-of-wedlock births. Murray also recommended that parental rights and benefits only be made available to married individuals. This would teach young boys that if they wanted to be fathers when they grew up, they would have to marry. And it would teach "young girls from their earliest memories that if they want to have any legal claims whatsoever on the father of their children, they must marry."[35]

Murray's article was followed by the publication of two books that contributed to the growing sense of alarm about the absence of fathers in many children's lives. In one, the sociologist David Popenoe despaired about "the human carnage of fatherlessness."[36] In the other, David Blankenhorn, the president of the Institute for American Values, and a future defender of same-sex marriage bans, decried what he took to be the cultural attack on traditional fatherhood and masculinity, an attack he claimed was inflicting great harm on children.[37]

In another influential book published in the mid-1990s, the sociologists Sara McLanahan and Gary Sandefur reported on the results of research showing that "growing up with only one biological parent frequently deprives children of important economic, parental, and community resources, and that these deprivations ultimately undermine their chances of future success."[38] Specifically, the authors found that children raised by single parents dropped out of high school and out of the job market, and had children as teenagers, at higher rates than children raised in intact (i.e., never-divorced) married households.

Although conservative critics who blamed the growing rates of single parenting and illegitimacy for most of the nation's social problems embraced the book's findings, they paid little attention to the fact that McLanahan and Sandefur concluded that as many as half of the differences in the child outcomes they reported were explained by the fact that married-parent households had higher incomes than single-parent ones. Conservatives also ignored the authors' recognition "that poverty is not just a consequence of family disruption; it is also a cause." Furthermore, McLanahan and Sandefur never claimed that female single parenting, and the corresponding absence of fathers, was the primary cause of poverty in the United States. In fact, as the authors noted, it was quite telling that "black children in two-parent families have much higher poverty rates than white children in single-parent families."[39] This finding suggested not only that two-parent families were not a panacea for solving social problems associated with poverty, but also that economic and social forces, such as discrimination and unequal opportunities in education and employment, were crucial factors in accounting for the higher poverty rates among blacks.

Those who contended that irresponsible procreation was the main cause of most of America's social ills, however, did not seem interested in discussing racial discrimination or the absence of meaningful employment opportunities for young people in urban areas or the drop in real wages experienced by many working-class Americans or the globalization of the labor market or the growing income gap between the haves and the have-nots. To talk about those subjects required uncomfortable conversations about the history of racism in America and the social dislocation engendered by a largely unfettered and unregulated free market. It was much easier to place the blame for social problems such as poverty, drug abuse, and homelessness on the choices—in particular the *procreative* choices—of women who had children outside of marriage. More particularly, it was simpler to argue that urban poverty was largely the result of the purported "parental irresponsibility" of black men and the supposed "sexual irresponsibility" of black women.[40]

In the early 1990s, it seemed that no welfare reform proposal was too outlandish to be taken seriously. Some welfare critics, including Charles Murray and the Georgia representative Newt Gingrich (later Speaker of the U.S. House), called for bringing back government-funded orphanages, which they claimed would help diminish welfare rolls.[41] There was also considerable discussion of offering mothers on welfare additional money if they agreed to have the contraceptive Norplant implanted in their bodies.[42] Legislators in Mississippi and South Carolina introduced bills that would have required women to agree to the contraceptive implant as a condition for receiving future welfare payments.[43] In addition, bills were introduced in Ohio and Washington that would have offered cash payments to women on welfare who agreed to be sterilized for life.[44]

The relentless conservative attack on single mother welfare recipients succeeded in convincing many Americans that government assistance was the primary cause of poverty, leading the Democratic presidential candidate Bill Clinton to promise during the 1992 campaign to "put an end to welfare as we know it." The mainstream media contributed to the antiwelfare frenzy by repeatedly profiling young single mothers with large numbers of children who seemed to care more about sex, drugs, and cashing their government checks than providing a nurturing, safe home environment for their offspring.[45] These sensationalist stories provided the public with a grossly inaccurate picture of the lives of most women on welfare, while contributing greatly to the stereotyping of single mothers who received government assistance as oversexualized, lazy, and dysfunctional.

Although the women portrayed in these media stories were almost all members of racial minorities (most were black, some were Latina), African-American families in the early 1990s constituted less than 40 percent of families on welfare.[46] Furthermore, 72 percent of women on welfare had no more than two children, 90 percent had three or fewer, and *almost two-thirds of recipient mothers did not have children while on welfare.*[47] In fact, single mothers on AFDC had an average of 1.9 children, essentially identical to the average number of children (1.88) in two-parent families.[48] While out-of-wedlock births were increasing among poor women, this increase was hardly unique to women on welfare.[49] In addition, the average monthly welfare payment for a family of four in 1995 was a paltry $377 (or $4,524 a year), and the average increase in AFDC benefits for an additional child was $60 a month, which, as one commentator put it, was "barely enough to pay for milk and diapers."[50] These were hardly the kind of financial incentives that would lead single mothers to have additional children. As one welfare official explained, "anyone who thinks that a woman goes through nine months of pregnancy, the pain of childbirth and eighteen years of rearing a child for $45 more a month...has got to be a man."[51]

In 1994, seventy-nine social scientists issued a statement explaining that there was no evidence of an association between the availability of welfare and decisions by single women to have children.[52] The lack of empirical support, however, did not prevent Republican congressional leaders that same year from making welfare reform a main component of their "Contract with America" platform. Their proposed bill, the "Personal Responsibility Act," called for denying AFDC benefits to all mothers under the age of eighteen who had children outside of marriage and authorized states, if they so chose, to deny welfare benefits (as well as housing subsidies) to single mothers between the ages of eighteen and twenty.[53] The bill also contained a mandatory "family cap," a measure prohibiting states from increasing payments to single mothers who had additional nonmarital children while on welfare. This provision was intended to remove the financial rewards that conservative critics claimed were contributing to the growing rate of nonmarital births.

The welfare reform bill that was ultimately adopted into law in 1996, known as the Personal Responsibility and Work Opportunity Reconciliation Act (PRWORA), softened some of these provisions by, for example, allowing unmarried mothers under eighteen to continue receiving benefits as long as they attended high school or enrolled in training programs while living with their parents or guardians.[54] In addition, as a result of a technical violation of legislative process rules, the final version of the bill was stripped of the mandatory family cap provision, leaving the question of whether to adopt one up to the discretion of the states. (Several states had already implemented family caps on their own after receiving the necessary waivers from the federal government.)

Nonetheless, the new law fundamentally changed welfare policy in the United States by (1) abolishing the AFDC program in favor of block grants to the states, (2) requiring single-parent recipients (the vast majority of whom were women) to work, and (3) placing limits on the period during which individuals could receive benefits.[55] The statute, in other words, essentially eliminated federal support guarantees for poor families headed by unmarried mothers.

The welfare reform law also required states, in return for the block grants, to submit specific plans aimed at reducing nonmarital pregnancies and births.[56] In addition, it offered monetary incentives to the states that were most successful in increasing their marriage rates and decreasing their nonmarital births rates. Finally, the statute provided federal funds for educational programs to teach welfare recipients about the benefits of "abstaining from sexual activity."[57]

It is clear, therefore, that the promotion of marriage and the discouragement of non-marital births were among PRWORA's principal aims. In fact, the statute's first three provisions stated as follows: "(1) marriage is the foundation of a successful society; (2) marriage is an essential institution of a successful society which promotes the interests of children; (3) promotion of responsible fatherhood and motherhood is integral to successful child rearing and the well-being of children."[58]

It is not a coincidence that three weeks after Congress enacted the welfare reform statute, it adopted DOMA. Indeed, a report issued by the House Judiciary Committee in support of DOMA used language mirroring that of PRWORA, explaining that "at bottom, civil society has an interest in maintaining and protecting the institution of heterosexual marriage because it has a deep and abiding interest in encouraging responsible procreation and child-rearing. Simply put, government has an interest in marriage because it has an interest in children."[59]

In many ways, DOMA and PRWORA were two sides of the same coin. The same understandings of the proper relationship between social well-being and procreation that conservative critics had for decades raised in welfare reform debates were now becoming part of the effort to defend the idea that marriage had to remain an exclusively heterosexual institution. According to these critics, society's well-being depended on individuals' ability to take responsibility for the consequences of their procreative acts. It was therefore essential that government policies, in particular those involving welfare and marriage, create the incentives and communicate the messages that would encourage mothers and fathers to take responsibility for their offspring and for each other.

RESPONSIBLE PROCREATION AND SAME-SEX MARRIAGE

As the discussion of welfare policy and reform shows, by the time Americans began grappling with the question of same-sex marriage in the mid-1990s, conservatives had spent decades claiming that irresponsible procreation by unmarried individuals was to blame for many of the nation's social ills. For conservative critics, the push for same-sex marriage became the latest—and in many ways the most—alarming indicator that growing segments of society no longer believed in traditional marriage and the importance of having children only within marriage. Conservatives worried that if the government offered same-sex couples the opportunity to marry, it would devalue marriage and promote irresponsible procreation—the same consequences, according to right-wing critics, that the federal government had encouraged through its welfare policies prior to the adoption of PRWORA.

Many leading conservative figures were active in both the welfare reform and same-sex marriage debates. One was Gary Bauer, who pushed for welfare reform as the undersecretary of education in the Reagan administration and who later became one of the most prominent foes of marriage equality as president of the Family Research Council. Another conservative leader on both fronts was William Bennett, a former secretary of education under President Reagan and a self-described defender of traditional values. In testimony he gave before Congress in 1995, Bennett urged legislators to reform welfare as a means to reducing nonmarital birth rates because they represented "the single most destructive social pathology in modern American society." He warned Congress that the nation was "headed for ruin if these numbers on illegitimacy continue."[60]

In particular, Bennett was a strong supporter of denying single mothers on welfare additional monies if they had children while on government assistance. When critics raised concerns that family caps might have the perverse effect of encouraging women to have abortions, Bennett pushed back, claiming that such unsubstantiated fears should not prevent Congress from addressing the national emergency represented by the growing rates of nonmarital births.[61] (A later study of New Jersey's family cap program, the nation's first, found an association between the program and an increase in abortions among some women on welfare.)[62]

Bennett also claimed that the well-being of society was at risk if the state recognized same-sex marriages. He argued in a 1996 *Washington Post* op-ed that "recognizing the legal union of gay and lesbian couples would…be the most radical step ever taken in the deconstruction of society's most important institution." He added that "the institution of marriage is already reeling because of the effects of the sexual revolution, no-fault divorce and out-of-wedlock births. We have reaped the consequences of its devaluation. It is exceedingly imprudent to conduct a radical, untested and inherently flawed social experiment on an institution that is the keystone in the arch of civilization."[63] A few years later, Bennett published a book decrying the state of the American family and arguing that same-sex marriage, by detaching marriage "from the natural, complementary teleology of the sexes," would lead to social, intellectual, and moral chaos.[64]

For Bennett and other critics, the fundamental problem of the AFDC program had been that it conveyed the dangerous message that the government did not care whether individuals married or had children outside of marriage. Opponents of same-sex marriage were similarly concerned about the message that the recognition of such marriages would send regarding the connection between marriage and procreation. In particular, opponents claimed that the lifting of same-sex marriage bans would communicate the message that marriage was no longer the socially preferred way of having children and that it did not matter whether children were raised by both their mothers and fathers. As explained in a brief filed in 1998 by Vermont in that state's same-sex marriage litigation, "providing legal sanction to same-sex unions through marriage licenses would diminish society's perception of the link between procreation and child rearing. By encouraging the formation of same-sex unions, such a policy could be seen to advance the notion that fathers or mothers, as the case may be, are mere surplusage to the functions of procreation and child rearing."[65] An amicus brief filed in the Massachusetts same-sex marriage case a few years later made a similar point when it warned that "including same-sex couples in civil marriage would be counterproductive to the purpose of the marriage laws by diluting the distinctive character of marriage as a procreative institution, and by undermining the state's ability to draw principled boundaries around the institution of civil marriage."[66]

Many marriage equality opponents, like many proponents of welfare reform, also despaired about the diminished role fathers were playing in the lives of growing numbers of children, a phenomenon they blamed on the nation's failure to socialize men as fathers. According to many conservative critics, while women became mothers through extended biological processes (gestation, giving birth, and lactation) that essentially channeled and determined their social roles as mothers, men provided only one quick (and rather pleasurable) biological contribution months before the child's birth. Critics argued that fatherhood, much more than motherhood, was a socially constructed category, which meant that its attributes and responsibilities depended almost entirely on society's expectations of men. It was therefore crucial that the country's laws and policies send the appropriate messages and provide the necessary incentives that would encourage procreative men to assume the role of fathers.[67]

As noted, the concern about the state of fatherhood in America had played a crucial role in the push for welfare reform. The same concern was present in the effort to thwart the legal recognition of same-sex marriages. Indeed, the authors of books on the importance of fathers in the lives of children testified in two trials held to assess the constitutionality of same-sex marriage bans. In 1996, the state of Hawai'i, while defending its same-sex marriage ban from a constitutional challenge, called on the sociologist Kyle Pruett, the author of *The Nurturing Father: Journey Toward the Complete Man*, to testify about the impact on children of being raised without fathers.[68] Fourteen years later, supporters of California's Proposition 8 called on David Blankenhorn, the president of the Institute of American Values and author of *Fatherless America: Confronting Our Most Urgent Social Problem*, to testify that children do better when raised by their biological mothers and fathers.[69]

The concern about the impact of same-sex marriage on fatherhood was also addressed by the conservative law professor Lynn Wardle in an influential law review article published in 2001. Wardle worried that the recognition of same-sex marriages would make the meaning of fatherhood

> even more ambiguous. The paternal role...would be loosed from its social and moral moorings. That is especially dangerous for absent biological fathers, whose parental position after three decades of easy divorce has been severely eroded. The further separation of procreation from marriage implicit in legalization of same-sex marriage would send a cultural message of parental disconnection from family duties that could further diminish the level of responsibility of absent parents [i.e., fathers].[70]

From the perspective of Wardle and other traditionalists, there was a pressing need for the nation's laws to communicate to men that society's future and well-being depended on their willingness to assume the role of responsible procreators. The state would muddle that message, perhaps irrevocably so, if it allowed same-sex couples to marry.

Another component of the responsible procreation argument found in both welfare reform and same-sex marriage debates was the criticism that the adults who were seeking the benefits in question (single mothers in the case of welfare recipients and same-sex couples in the case of gay marriage) were acting in socially detrimental ways by placing their needs ahead of those of children. As noted, many welfare critics had for decades claimed that single mothers on welfare were out to benefit themselves and their so-called irresponsible lifestyles at the expense of society and their children. Similarly, opponents of marriage equality claimed that LGBT rights activists, by pushing for same-sex marriage, were promoting the sexual and privacy rights of lesbians and gay men over the interests of society and the needs of children. Wardle, for example, warned that

> the bill for the exciting adult adventure of opening new frontiers of sexual liberation and experiencing the thrill of social endorsement of new relations would be paid by the next generation. Advocates of same-sex marriage would balance the accounts on the backs of children—not just those who would grow up in same-sex homes, but all children who would grow up in a society in which social support for responsible procreation, dual gender parenting, and the linkage between procreation and child rearing had diminished.[71]

A similar point was made by a conservative organization in an amicus brief filed in the same-sex marriage litigation in Connecticut when it noted that "many of society's ills are rooted in adult alternative lifestyle choices in which children are the chief victims."[72]

In short, the need to promote responsible procreation, an already well-established battle cry among conservatives in the context of welfare reform, quickly became a crucial argument deployed against the recognition of same-sex marriages. Allowing same-sex couples to marry, it was claimed, would delink marriage from procreation in ways that would have pernicious consequences for the nation. A society that was already grappling with the problems of reduced marital rates and significant increases in nonmarital births could ill afford to remove gender as an eligibility requirement for marriage. To codify into law the proposition that the gender of prospective spouses was irrelevant would only push the country further into procreative anarchy and the privileging of adult gratification over the advancement of society's and children's well-being.

ACCIDENTAL PROCREATION

A few years into the new century, opponents of marriage equality began raising a modified version of the responsible procreation claim that focused more specifically on the differences between different-sex and same-sex couples on the question of *accidental* procreation. This version of the argument emphasized the fact that different-sex couples frequently conceive children unintentionally and that since lesbian and gay couples cannot make the same mistake, the former need marriage more than the latter. According to this (rather circumscribed) understanding of what traditionalists otherwise claimed was the exalted institution of marriage, the principal purpose of the institution was to provide special assistance and support for heterosexuals who have children without intending to do so.

Law review commentators who have written about the genealogy of the responsible procreation defense of same-sex marriage bans have not distinguished between the "responsible procreation" claim and the "accidental procreation" argument, treating the two as essentially fungible.[73] I view the genealogy differently, because the concern about heterosexuals having children outside of marriage is not exactly the same as worrying that heterosexuals might have children accidentally, though of course there is overlap between the two concerns, since many heterosexuals who procreate outside of marriage do not intend to have children when they engage in sexual intercourse. But the responsible procreation claim, as discussed, was based on the perceived dangers of the supposed delinking of marriage from procreation that accompanied the recognition of same-sex marriages and the message that such a delinking sent to heterosexuals. What was new about the "accidental procreation" version of the claim was a threefold emphasis: first, on how easy it was for heterosexuals to have children accidentally; second, on how impossible it was for same-sex couples to have children unintentionally; and third, on how same-sex couples, since they usually have children through the use of reproductive technologies or adoption, had to plan methodically and responsibly before bringing children into their homes.

Law review commentators have traced the accidental procreation claim to justice Robert Cordy's dissenting opinion from the Massachusetts Supreme Judicial Court's ruling in 2003 holding that the ban against same-sex marriages violated the state constitution.[74] There is, however, little in Cordy's opinion that discusses either how easy it is for different sex partners to have children unintentionally or how much planning same-sex couples must engage in before they can have children. Rather than articulating the accidental procreation claim, Cordy essentially endorsed the wider responsible procreation reasoning of Wardle and others.

Thus, for example, Cordy claimed that "paramount among its many important functions, the institution of marriage has systematically provided for the regulation of heterosexual behavior, brought order to the resulting procreation, and ensured a stable family structure in which children will be reared, educated, and socialized." He added that "the institution of marriage provides the important legal and normative link between heterosexual intercourse and procreation on the one hand and family responsibilities on the other" and fills a void "by formally binding the husband-father to his wife and child, and imposing on him the responsibilities of fatherhood." Cordy then warned that "a society without the institution of marriage, in which heterosexual intercourse, procreation, and child care are largely disconnected processes, would be chaotic."[75]

Although it is true that Cordy's opinion became the most explicit and elaborate judicial articulation of the responsible procreation defense of same-sex marriage bans, little in his reasoning addressed what I am here referring to as the accidental procreation version of that claim, by which I mean the justification for same-sex marriage bans that focuses on how easy it is for heterosexuals to procreate accidentally and explicitly distinguishes between the irresponsibility of many heterosexuals who procreate and the responsibility shown by same-sex couples who have children.

It was the Indiana Court of Appeals in the 2005 case of *Morrison v. Sadler* that first articulated the accidental procreation argument. In doing so, the *Morrison* court emphasized both the fact that heterosexuals often conceive unintentionally (and thus irresponsibly) and the fact that same-sex couples are less likely to act irresponsibly because of the extensive planning that is required in order to become parents through assisted reproduction or adoption. The Indiana court reasoned that since same-sex couples have to engage in considerable planning in order to become parents, they are more likely to be better prepared to meet parental responsibilities than heterosexuals, who can become parents as a result of, in effect, a one-night stand. As the court explained, same-sex couples "who have invested the significant time, effort, and expense associated with assisted reproduction or adoption may be seen as very likely to be able to provide [stable] environment[s], with or without the 'protections' of marriage, because of the high level of financial and emotional commitment exerted in conceiving or adopting a child or children in the first place." In contrast, for different-sex couples, "procreation...may occur...with no foresight or planning. All that is required is one instance of sexual intercourse with a man for a woman to become pregnant."[76] For the court, this distinction between different-sex and same-sex couples meant that the state could constitutionally limit marriage to the former because they, in effect, were in greater need of the structure and support provided by marriage.

The accidental procreation version of the responsible procreation claim quickly caught the attention of those defending same-sex marriage bans, especially after New York's highest court adopted its reasoning in upholding the state's then-existing ban on same-sex marriages.[77] Part of the appeal of the accidental procreation claim may have been that it did not require a denigration of same-sex relationships.[78] In fact, the claim, at least as conceived by the Indiana court in *Morrison*, suggested that same-sex couples who decided to have children were *better* prepared to parent, and were more likely to be responsible parents, than heterosexuals who became parents unintentionally.

It bears emphasizing, however, that conservative advocates, while adopting the first half of the *Morrison* formulation (that it is unfortunately too easy for opposite-sex couples to have children accidentally), did not embrace the second (that same-sex couples are more likely to provide a stable environment for children because of the amount of planning they must engage in before having children). The reason for this selective incorporation of the *Morrison* formulation was obvious—such reasoning was inconsistent with another frequent justification for maintaining marriage exclusively for heterosexuals, namely that parenting by different-sex couples is better for children than parenting by same-sex ones (a contention I explore in chapters 3 and 4).

Another appealing aspect of the accidental procreation claim for marriage equality opponents may have been that it was less abstract than the wider responsible procreation argument. In addition to relying on generalized links between marriage and procreation, conservative advocates and government lawyers now found a way of defending same-sex marriage bans in a manner that was both more concrete and factually irrefutable by emphasizing the fact that different-sex couples can procreate accidentally while same-sex couples cannot.

At the same time, however, marriage equality opponents' embrace of the accidental procreation claim exposed their strategic expediency. After all, no one, not even social conservatives, had ever claimed that seeking to prevent *accidental* procreation was the sine qua non of marriage. It seems clear that marriage equality opponents adopted the accidental procreation claim, which represented a somewhat sanitized and easier-to-defend version of the responsible procreation argument, because it maximized their chances of winning in court.[79]

HETEROSEXUAL MARRIAGE BEFORE SAME-SEX MARRIAGE: THE HISTORICAL RECORD

Opponents of marriage equality have repeatedly articulated what is at best an incomplete, and at worst a highly skewed, account of the relationship between marriage and procreation in our nation's history. In order to provide a fuller and more accurate historical description of that relationship, this section explores some of the legal and cultural changes that took place during the twentieth century that, quite independently of the issue of same-sex marriage, significantly diminished the procreative channeling function of marriage. As we will see, the link between marriage and procreation began to fray long before the first same-sex marriages were recognized in this country.

At the beginning of the twentieth century, marriage in the United States had a virtual monopoly on how and when heterosexuals exercised their procreative capacities. As time progressed, legal and cultural changes began to chip away at that monopoly so that by the end of the century, marriage played a significantly diminished role in regulating and channeling the procreative capabilities of different-sex couples. A synopsis follows of how this came to be—a process that had little to do with LGBT individuals or same-sex relationships.

Birth Control

In 1873, Congress enacted the Comstock Act, a law criminalizing the use of the mails to distribute "obscene, lewd or lascivious" material. Under this statute, neither contraceptives nor information related to their use could be sent via the mails.[80] In the decades that followed, more than half the states adopted so-called mini-Comstock laws, which banned the distribution or sale of contraceptives.[81] Some states, like Connecticut, went even further and criminalized their use, a prohibition that applied to married couples.

The legal barriers to contraceptives, of course, significantly increased the chances that sexual contact would lead to pregnancies. To put it another way, the legal barriers helped to maintain a somewhat predictable link between sex and reproduction. If couples were sufficiently young and healthy, their engaging in sexual intercourse without contraception would in most cases eventually lead to pregnancy. As a result, it was prudent for couples to wait until they were married to have sexual relations, a fact that helped to reinforce the traditional religious and moral link between marriage and procreation.

During the 1910s, a political movement led by the feminist nurse and sex educator Margaret Sanger began to agitate for the easing of restrictions on the distribution of contraceptives.[82] Sanger, who was arrested several times for violating anticontraception laws, opened the nation's first birth control clinic and worked assiduously to find influential allies in the medical profession.

In 1936, the U.S. Court of Appeals for the Second Circuit held that the Comstock Act did not limit the ability of physicians to promote public health by mailing contraceptives, a ruling that effectively ended the federal government's ability to prevent the distribution of birth control devices.[83] A year later, the American Medical Association issued a report recognizing the use of contraceptives as a proper medical practice and urging that medical schools instruct students about their use.

The number of birth control clinics in the United States grew from fifty-five in 1930 to more than eight hundred by 1942.[84] The concerted political and legal challenges to contraceptive bans were so successful that by the 1950s, only Connecticut and Massachusetts still had them in place. In 1965, the Supreme Court ruled that anticontraceptive laws violated the constitutional right of married couples to decide how best to exercise their sexual intimacy.[85] Seven years later, the Court held that unmarried individuals also had the right to determine, without state interference, whether their sexual intimacy should result in procreation.[86] Several years after that, the Court struck down a statute restricting the ability of minors to gain access to contraceptives.[87]

In the course of about fifty years, then, access to birth control in the United States went from extremely limited to largely unfettered. It is now estimated that 98 percent of contemporary women who have had heterosexual intercourse have used some form of contraception.[88]

The wide availability of birth control has delinked sex from marriage and procreation. A century ago, many heterosexual Americans waited until they were married to have sex because they were worried about the possibility of pregnancy. The wide availability of birth control made it possible for heterosexuals to have sex without worrying that it might lead to children. It used to be that whether sexually active heterosexuals had children depended largely on whether they were married. For many decades now, it has largely depended on whether they use contraceptives.

It is true, of course, that many couples today wait until they are married to have children. It is also the case, however, that a majority of heterosexual couples cohabit before they marry. What keeps these couples from procreating during their (sometimes extended periods of) cohabitation is not their unmarried status, but is instead their use of contraceptives. And many couples, after they marry, do not have children immediately, showing once again that the primary factor in determining whether procreation takes place is the use (or nonuse) of contraceptives rather than marriage.

Before the wide availability of contraceptives, marriage played a crucial social role in channeling procreation. As the use of birth control increased throughout the twentieth century and sex outside of marriage became more common and socially tolerated, the link between marriage and procreation began to fray, to the point where marital status came to play a relatively minor regulatory role in how, when, and with whom heterosexuals exercised their procreative capabilities.

Fornication, Adultery, and Sodomy Laws

From the colonial period through the nineteenth century, the criminal law played an important role in regulating nonmarital sex, particularly through its prohibition of fornication and adultery. The applicability of these two sets of laws turned on the marital status of the sexual partners—by imposing criminal liability on unmarried sexual partners and on married individuals who had sex with someone other than their spouses, these laws helped to channel procreative sexual conduct into marriage. Indeed, the existence of fornication and adultery statutes made it impossible for individuals to engage in sexual intercourse outside of marriage without running afoul of the law. Even when not enforced criminally, engaging in fornication or adultery could have negative consequences for the participants, as was reflected not only in social ostracism, but also in the loss of government jobs, housing, and child custody.[89]

A third category of criminal laws, those proscribing sodomy, was aimed at the distinction not between marital and nonmarital but between procreative and nonprocreative sex. Colonial sodomy statutes, as well as the state sodomy laws that followed them, prohibited men from having anal sex with men or women. (The statutes also proscribed sex with animals.) Beginning in the late nineteenth century and continuing through the early twentieth century, sodomy statutes were expanded (either through the enactment of new laws or the judicial interpretation of old ones) to include oral sex. The statutes also came to be interpreted as prohibiting sexual conduct between women.[90]

Although sodomy statutes later in the twentieth century became associated almost exclusively with same-sex sexual conduct, for most of the nation's history they were understood to apply more generally to nonprocreative sex regardless of the genders of the parties. In addition, for much of that history, the statutes, at least in theory, applied to married couples who engaged in anal and oral sex.

The fact that fornication, adultery, and sodomy statutes were enforced with some regularity from the colonial period until the early twentieth century, coupled with the fact that engaging in such conduct could have negative legal and social consequences even in the absence of criminal enforcement, strongly reinforced the traditional view that sexual intercourse should take place only within marriage and that sexual contact should be procreative in nature. Under this regulatory regime, the only way individuals could be sexually intimate without violating the criminal law was to have penile-vaginal sex with their spouses.

The enforcement of fornication, adultery, and sodomy laws waned as the twentieth century progressed. (The one exception to this trend was the enforcement, well past the century's halfway point, of sodomy laws in cases involving same-sex sexual conduct.)[91] The fact that prosecutors and other law enforcement officials came to largely ignore these laws reflected cultural norms that no longer deemed it appropriate to subject adults who engaged in consensual nonmarital or nonprocreative sex to public condemnation and stigmatization.

This view was reflected in the Model Penal Code of 1962, which was issued by the American Law Institute (ALI) after many years of debate and consideration. The code did not include provisions criminalizing fornication, adultery, or sodomy. The ALI took the position that the criminal law should not be used to enforce private morality, while also noting that the statutes on the books had largely lapsed into desuetude.[92] Many states in subsequent years heeded the ALI's recommendation by decriminalizing consensual sexual conduct between consenting adults.

The constitutional viability of the consensual sex laws that remained on the books became vulnerable to challenge once the Supreme Court, during the 1960s and 1970s, recognized the privacy-based rights of sexual partners to use contraceptives and of women to choose abortions.[93] Although those cases did not necessarily stand for the proposition that adults had a constitutional right to engage in the consensual sexual acts of their choice, that is essentially what the Supreme Court held in 2003 when it ruled in *Lawrence v. Texas* that sodomy laws were unconstitutional.[94]

Before *Lawrence*, which addressed the constitutionality of Texas's Homosexual Conduct Law—a sodomy statute that, as its name suggested, applied only to same-sex sexual partners—the marked changes that had taken place over the course of several decades in the way the criminal law regulated consensual sexual intimacy had had little to do with lesbians and gay men or their relationships. That is, fornication, adultery, and sodomy laws fell first into desuetude, and then later into constitutional infirmity, as a result of changing legal and cultural norms related to the advisability of punishing heterosexuals for having either sex (of any kind) outside of marriage or nonprocreative sex within marriage. By the time the Court decided *Lawrence*, the criminal law had ceased playing a meaningful role, either directly or indirectly, in encouraging heterosexuals to procreate within the institution of marriage.

Cohabitation

Almost every state in the nation has had cohabitation laws on the books at some point, with most jurisdictions enacting them in the nineteenth century.[95] Like fornication laws, statutes that criminalized cohabitation were intended to discourage nonmarital sex. However, unlike fornication (and adultery) laws, which, at least in theory, could be violated by engaging in only one sexual act outside of marriage, cohabitation statutes were aimed more specifically at discouraging ongoing nonmarital sexual relationships between individuals who shared a household.

The same forces that contributed to the decriminalization of fornication, adultery, and sodomy led to either the repeal of cohabitation laws or their judicial invalidation. By 1978, only sixteen states still criminalized cohabitation.[96]

The move toward decriminalization was accompanied by the courts' greater willingness to provide some legal protections to cohabitants, particularly following the dissolution of their relationships. In 1976, the California Supreme Court, in the "palimony" case of *Marvin v. Marvin*, held that cohabitants could generally avail themselves of contract or equitable principles to bring support and property allocation claims against their former partners.[97] Following *Marvin*, a growing number of jurisdictions, primarily through judicial decisionmaking rather than statutory enactments, began providing some legal recognition to cohabiting relationships.[98]

The growing toleration of Americans toward cohabitation, when coupled with legal reforms, contributed to large increases in the number of cohabiting couples. In 1970, there were just over five hundred thousand different-sex cohabiting couples in the United States. By 2000, that number had grown tenfold to 5.5 million.[99] By the late

1990s, more than 50 percent of married couples had previously cohabited, up from 10 percent twenty years earlier.[100]

As the popularity of cohabitation as a precursor, or even as an alternative, to marriage grew, the rate at which Americans married dropped. In 1970, there were 10.6 marriages for every one thousand Americans. By 1990, the number was down to 9.8, and a decade later it was 8.3, a drop of 22 percent in thirty years.[101] The growing rates of cohabitation also contributed to increases in the age at which individuals married for the first time. In 1970, the median age at first marriage was 20.8 for women and 23.2 for men. By 2000, the median age had increased to 25.1 for women and 26.8 for men.[102]

The pervasiveness of cohabitation, to put it bluntly, resulted in a lot of sex outside of marriage. But cohabitation's contribution to the delinking of sex from marriage was different from that of the decriminalization of fornication and adultery. As a general matter, neither fornication nor adultery was associated with long-term relationships. This meant that sexual relationships involving fornication or adultery were usually quite different from marital ones, in terms of the parties' conduct and expectations. In contrast, important aspects of marital relationships were reflected in cohabiting ones— cohabiting couples, like married ones, not only lived together, but also generally did so with similar expectations regarding sexual exclusivity, the intermingling of financial assets, and the sharing of household responsibilities. Although the legal rights and benefits that accompany marriage in the United States have always been much greater than those available to cohabiting couples, their day-to-day lives, for several decades now, have not differed in significant ways from those of married couples.

The growing cultural and legal acceptance of cohabitation not only helped to delink sex in long-term relationships from marriage, but also contributed to the weakening of the normative monopoly that marriage once enjoyed over procreation. This delinking was most clearly apparent in the growing number of cohabiting couples who were raising children together.

In 1960, 196,000 children under the age of fifteen were living with their two unmarried parents. A decade later, that number had gone up by only 1,000. By 1980, the number was up to 431,000, an increase of 119 percent. And by 2000, 1,675,000 children under fifteen were living with different-sex cohabiting partners, an astounding 750 percent increase since 1970.[103]

While the number of cohabiting couples who were raising children together was growing at a breathtaking pace, the percentage of households consisting of married couples raising their children was decreasing, falling from 40 percent in 1970 to 24 percent in 2000.[104] In fact, by that year, 41 percent of different-sex cohabiting partners were raising children under the age of eighteen, only slightly lower than the 46 percent of married couples who were doing the same.[105] In addition, about two-fifths of all children spent some time in households headed by cohabiting partners.[106]

It was clear by the turn of the twenty-first century, therefore, that marriage no longer had the monopoly it enjoyed a century earlier in linking long-term heterosexual relationships with the bearing and raising of children. The living together without being married, and the raising of children by couples outside of marriage, had come to be widely practiced and accepted throughout society.

Divorce

For most of American history, individuals were expected not only to get married, but to remain married until death. Until the end of the nineteenth century, the only way married couples could divorce in many states was by petitioning the legislature, an occurrence that was quite rare. Even after all the states (except South Carolina) had, by the turn of the twentieth century, established judicial processes for granting divorces, courts could end marriages only after finding that one of the spouses had wronged the other by, for example, committing adultery or an act of cruelty.

The legal requirement that a good reason or justification exist before a court could dissolve a marriage was consistent with the strong social disapproval of divorce. As the legal historian Lawrence Friedman explains, in the first part of the twentieth century,

> many influential people disapproved of divorce, the Catholic church positively forbade it, the clergy in general were hostile, and divorce carried considerable stigma in society. There was something vaguely immoral about a divorced woman; the very term "divorcée" carried a certain pejorative ring. Perhaps it was the fact that a divorced woman, even a wronged one, was used goods, or that the moral duty of a woman was to stick a bad marriage out and make the best of it. There was certainly the idea that divorce was, if not a cause, then at least an indicator of moral dry rot.[107]

Under the prevailing fault-based regime, divorce proceedings were intended to be adversarial affairs in which one of the spouses contested the marital termination. The reality, however, was that as the twentieth century progressed, most couples who divorced first agreed to end their marriages and then later participated in largely sham divorce "lawsuits." (It was almost always the wives who petitioned courts by accusing husbands of having committed a wrong against the marriage.) By the 1950s, the fault system of divorce masked the underlying reality that most unhappily married couples were essentially able to terminate their marriages at will.

The growing disconnect between what the law was trying to achieve and how courts were actually adjudicating divorce cases led to calls for reform. The change in the law, when it came, was swift and created little controversy.[108] In 1970, California became the first state to adopt a no-fault divorce system. In a matter of only a few years, almost every state in the nation followed suit, effectively allowing spouses to divorce at any time and for any reason. The ability to exit without legal impediments became part of the social understanding of what it meant to be married. Although couples, at the moment of marriage, still expected to be together for life, they also knew from the beginning of the marriage that neither the law nor social stigma would prevent them from divorcing if they so chose.

Experts disagree on whether the adoption of no-fault divorce caused an increase in the divorce rate or whether that rate would have increased at a similar pace even under the old fault regime. Either way, there is no denying that the divorce rate increased significantly: in 1965, there were 2.5 divorces per one thousand Americans; by 1980, the number had more than doubled, reaching an all-time high of 5.2. Although the divorce rate decreased during the 1990s—perhaps reflecting the fact that the marriage rate was declining and more Americans were cohabiting—it was still at 4.1 by the turn of the century, significantly higher than thirty-five years earlier.[109]

The ease with which it became possible for spouses to exit marriage helped to attenuate the distinction between marriage and cohabitation. Although a judicial process was required to end the former but not the latter, that process became relatively simple and quick. The adoption of no-fault divorce also served to further fray the link between marriage and procreation. At the beginning of the twentieth century, marriage had been understood to be a relationship for life, an expectation that reinforced the view that procreation should only take place within marriage. The prevailing understanding had been that most individuals should spend most of their adult years within the institution of marriage. In contrast, by the end of the century, marriage did not have a preset duration (i.e. for life), but depended almost entirely on the preferences of the individuals involved. A large segment of the population were now spending significant portions of their adult lives *outside* of marriage, either before (often in cohabiting relationships), or after, following a divorce.

Single Parenting

The traditional understanding of marriage as a lifelong commitment and of procreation as appropriate only within marriage that prevailed through the early twentieth century meant that single parenting was socially acceptable only in the case of spousal death or abandonment (the latter almost always done by husbands). Single parenting, when it was largely limited to widows/widowers and to deserted wives, was a relatively rare phenomenon. Starting around the last third of the century, however, single-parent households became increasingly common.

In 1970, there were three million single-mother and 393,000 single-father families in the United States. By 2000, the numbers had grown to 10 million single-mother and 2 million single-father families, increases of over 200 and 400 percent, respectively.[110] Also by 2000, 27 percent of children were living with a single parent, up from 9 percent in 1960.[111] Although the majority of those children were living with a divorced mother, a significant minority (41 percent in 2000) were living with a never-married mother.[112] Furthermore, between 1970 and 2000, the percentage of births that were nonmarital increased from 11 to 34 percent.[113]

The large, steady growth in single parenting and nonmarital births followed changes in cultural norms and legal policies that had previously encouraged individuals to have children only within the institution of marriage. For example, as noted, the Supreme Court by the early 1970s had largely prohibited states from imposing legal disabilities on nonmarital children as a way of promoting marital births. At the same time, the strong stigma that had once turned single mothers into social outcasts had largely disappeared in a society that—in part as a result of the political mobilizing by the sexual liberation and women's rights movements—was becoming increasingly tolerant of nonmarital sex and of allowing women to decide whether and when to have children.

These cultural and legal changes further delinked marriage from procreation. Whether to have children, and whether to do so within the institution of marriage, was now less a matter of social compulsion and more of individual choice.

Undoubtedly, the push for gay rights, which began in earnest in the 1970s, benefited from the growing value society was placing on individualism, autonomy, and personal freedom in matters related to marriage, parenting, and relationships. It is crucial to understand, however, that *neither the push for gay rights in general nor the struggle for same-sex marriage in particular was the primary cause of the transformational shifts in cultural norms and legal rules that frayed the connection between marriage and procreation.* Whatever one thinks of the cultural and legal changes that occurred, it is a fact that they were largely induced and implemented by heterosexuals. Indeed, these changes would not have taken place had heterosexuals not decisively embraced greater personal choice and freedom in matters related to intimate and familial relationships. The wide use of birth control, the lack of enforcement of fornication, adultery, and sodomy laws, and the marked increases in the rates of cohabitation, divorce, and single parenting were firmly in place long before the first same-sex couples were permitted to legally marry. The LGBT rights movement's push for same-sex marriage did not weaken the link between marriage and procreation; heterosexuals did that on their own.

The question then arises why, starting in the mid-1990s, those who believed that irresponsible procreation was the cause of many of society's ills focused so intently on same-sex marriages and not on the primary factors that had led to the fraying of the relationship between marriage and procreation. If social conservatives had truly wanted to restore the monopoly marriage had once had over procreation, the way to have done so was not to push back against same-sex marriage, but was instead to attempt to return to the legal and cultural frameworks prevalent at the beginning of the twentieth century. Promoters of so-called responsible procreation drew the line in front of same-sex marriage, when the line, so to speak, was behind them.

What made same-sex marriage a tempting target for social conservatives in the 1990s and early 2000s was that, for the first time in several decades, a hotly contested issue of family law and policy arose that seemed to offer them a chance to defeat the forces of liberalization. It was unlikely, for example, that the public would accept the reimposition of legal hurdles that had once made it more difficult to get a divorce. Indeed, a concerted push by social conservatives in the 1990s to persuade states to adopt covenant marriages, which deny those who enter into them the ability to seek no-fault divorces, fizzled.[114] In addition, although it had been politically possible, as noted, to place stringent new conditions on single-mother welfare recipients, a particularly vulnerable and politically weak group, in the hope of discouraging them from having nonmarital children, no other meaningful plans were in the offing to limit the ability of Americans, most of whom were not on welfare, to procreate outside of marriage. But even if it was no longer possible to persuade a majority of Americans that getting a divorce should be made more difficult, that unmarried cohabitation should be discouraged, and that out-of-wedlock births should be stigmatized, it seemed quite likely that most Americans would reject the idea that marriage laws should be changed in order to permit two men or two women to marry.

Efforts aimed at reducing the rates of divorce and illegitimacy—to say nothing about reinstating legal proscriptions against fornication, adultery, sodomy, and
cohabitation—required changes to the legal status quo that were politically unfeasible
because they would have limited the freedom of heterosexuals to make important decisions about family, marriage, and procreation. In contrast, social conservatives in the
1990s and early 2000s had reasons for optimism about their ability to thwart the push
for same-sex marriage. Not only was the legal status quo on their side, but the issue of
same-sex marriage only impacted lesbians, gay men, and bisexuals, a small, stigmatized, and politically marginalized segment of society. It was therefore strategically and
politically more appealing to promote so-called responsible procreation by targeting
same-sex relationships rather than different-sex ones, in the same way that it had been
strategically and politically more convenient to promote responsible procreation by
attacking the procreative choices of single mothers on welfare rather than those of the
broader population.

The connection between marriage and procreation, then, had significantly weakened before same-sex marriage even became a political and legal issue. The question
remains whether the recognition of same-sex marriage by some states, as marriage
equality opponents claimed would happen, contributed to the further weakening of
heterosexual marriage as a procreative institution. To that question I turn next.

HETEROSEXUAL MARRIAGE AFTER SAME-SEX
MARRIAGE: THE EMPIRICAL EVIDENCE

During the decade that followed the Hawai'i Supreme Court's 1993 ruling questioning the constitutionality of same-sex marriage bans, gay rights opponents repeatedly
raised a slew of hypothetical fears about what the impact on society would be of permitting same-sex couples to marry. For opponents of same-sex marriage, it seemed as
if the sky was the limit when it came to the likely negative social repercussions of gay
marriages. Social conservatives claimed, in effect, that the sky would fall—nothing less
than the very foundations of society and the future well-being of families were at stake.

After Massachusetts in 2004 became the first state to issue marriage licenses to
same-sex couples, it became possible to assess the earlier, and by necessity, hypothetical claims that conservatives had made about the effects of recognizing same-sex
unions on marriages and families. In particular, it became possible to study whether
the recognition of same-sex marriages was associated with fewer heterosexual marriages and more out-of-wedlock births. As it turns out, the empirical evidence does not
support the conservative critics' claims regarding the effects that same-sex marriages
have on heterosexual relationships.

For example, although the marriage rate in the United States, as noted, had been falling for several decades, the drop in the national marriage rate between 2003 and 2011,
as shown in Table 2.1, was *six times* the drop in the Massachusetts marriage rate.[115]

Furthermore, the marriage rate in Massachusetts dropped by 29 percent (from 7.9
to 5.6 per one thousand residents) between 1990 in 2003, *before* the recognition of
same-sex marriages. In contrast, the marriage rate in Massachusetts dropped by only

Table 2.1 Marriage Rates, 2003 and 2011 (per 1,000)

	2003	2011	Change
Massachusetts	5.6	5.5	− 2%
United States	7.7	6.8	− 12%

Source: Centers for Disease Control and Prevention.

2 percent (from 5.6 to 5.5 per one thousand residents) between 2003 and 2011, *following* the recognition of same-sex marriages. The data show that allowing same-sex couples to marry in Massachusetts is not associated with a drop in the state's overall marriage rate. In fact, nearly the opposite is the case: Allowing same-sex couples to marry is associated with a substantial slowing down in the decrease in the state's marriage rate.

The year 2004 was a momentous one for same-sex marriage. At one end of the spectrum, Massachusetts took the lead by becoming the first state to allow lesbian and gay couples to marry. At the other end of the spectrum, thirteen states amended their constitutions to forbid the recognition of gay marriages, by far the largest number of states that did so in any one year. A comparison of the change in the Massachusetts marriage rate with the change in the marriage rate of those states in the years that followed is particularly relevant here, because by adopting the constitutional amendments, they were attempting to do precisely what opponents of gay marriages hoped for, that is, to send a clear message that marriage should remain an exclusively heterosexual institution available only to couples who can (generally speaking) procreate. Nonetheless, as Table 2.2 shows, the marriage rates in most of the states that constitutionalized their

Table 2.2 Marriage Rates, 2003 and 2011 (per 1,000)

State	2003	2011	Change
Montana	7.2	7.8	+ 8%
North Dakota	7.1	6.7	+ 6%
Massachusetts	**5.6**	**5.5**	**− 2%**
Georgia	7.0	6.6	− 6%
Missouri	7.2	6.6	− 8%
Oregon	7.2	6.6	− 8%
Michigan	6.3	5.7	− 10%
Ohio	6.7	5.9	− 12%
Utah	10.2	8.6	− 16%
Kentucky	9.1	7.5	− 18%
Mississippi	6.2	4.9	− 21%
Arkansas	13.4	10.4	− 22%
Louisiana	8.2	6.4	− 22%

State in bold recognized same-sex marriages in 2004. Other states constitutionally prohibited same-sex marriages in the same year.
The Oklahoma marriage rate for 2003 is not available.
Source: Centers for Disease Control and Prevention.

same-sex marriage bans in 2004 dropped at a greater rate (in several cases *significantly greater*) than the Massachusetts marriage rate.

The two states that recognized same-sex marriages after Massachusetts were Connecticut (2008) and Iowa (2009). Following that change in marriage eligibility rules, the marriage rate in Connecticut remained steady (the rate in 2011 was 5.5, the same as in 2007), while the marriage rate in Iowa inched up (from 6.5 in 2008 to 6.7 in 2011). In contrast, the marriage rate in the United States *dropped 7 percent* (from 7.3 to 6.8) between 2007 and 2011.

One would also expect that if, as opponents of marriage equality claim, the recognition of same-sex marriages somehow weakens the institution of marriage, that phenomenon would be reflected in higher divorce rates. However, as shown in Table 2.3, Massachusetts in 2011 had a lower divorce rate (2.7 per one thousand residents) than any of the states (for which data are available) that constitutionally prohibited same-sex marriages in 2004, except for North Dakota, which had the same divorce rate as Massachusetts. It is also worth noting that Connecticut had a lower divorce rate (3.1) in 2011 than any of the states (for which data are available) that constitutionally prohibited same-sex marriages in 2004, except for North Dakota. And Iowa in 2011 had the *lowest divorce rate of any state in the nation* (2.4).

There is also little evidence of an association between the recognition of same-sex marriage and a higher rate of nonmarital births. As Table 2.4 shows, unmarried women in Connecticut, Massachusetts, and Iowa (the three states that first recognized same-sex marriages) in 2011 gave birth to children at lower rates than in most

Table 2.3 Divorce Rates, 2011

State	Per 1,000
Iowa	**2.4**
Massachusetts	**2.7**
North Dakota	2.7
Connecticut	**3.1**
Michigan	3.4
Ohio	3.4
Utah	3.7
Oregon	3.8
Missouri	3.9
Mississippi	4.0
Montana	4.0
Kentucky	4.4
Oklahoma	5.2
Arkansas	5.3

States in bold recognize same-sex marriages. Other states constitutionally prohibited same-sex marriages in 2004.
The Georgia and Louisiana divorce rates for 2011 are not available.
Source: Centers for Disease Control and Prevention.

Table 2.4 Percent Births to Unmarried Women, 2011

State	Percent
Utah	19
North Dakota	33
Iowa	**34**
Massachusetts	**35**
Montana	36
Oregon	36
Connecticut	**38**
Missouri	40
Kentucky	41
United States	41
Oklahoma	42
Michigan	42
Ohio	43
Arkansas	45
Georgia	45
Louisiana	53
Mississippi	54

States in bold recognize same-sex marriages. Other states constitutionally prohibited same-sex marriages in 2004.
Source: Centers for Disease Control and Prevention.

of the states that amended their constitutions in 2004 to ban same-sex marriages. The out-of-wedlock birthrates in these three states in 2011 were also lower than the national average of 41 percent.

If the recognition of same-sex marriages had weakened the institution of marriage and encouraged heterosexuals to procreate outside of marriage, we would expect to see that reflected in the marriage, divorce, and out-of-wedlock birth rates in states that allow same-sex couples to marry. At the same time, if same-sex marriage bans effectively and meaningfully reinforced traditional understandings of marriage, we would expect to see that reflected in the marriage, divorce, and out-of-wedlock birth rates of states that took the highly visible step of amending their constitutions to ban same-sex marriages. As the data presented here show, neither of those propositions is supported by the empirical evidence.[116]

The lack of an association between the legal recognition of same-sex relationships and the marital and childbearing proclivities of heterosexuals has not been limited to the United States. Two books, one by the law professor Bill Eskridge and the lawyer Darren Spedale, the other by the economist M. V. Lee Badgett, have refuted the claim by some opponents of gay marriage that the recognition of same-sex relationships by Scandinavian countries negatively affected the marriages and relationships of heterosexuals in those nations. The two books show that the heterosexual marriage rates in Scandinavia either increased or remained steady following the legal recognition of same-sex relationships there in the late 1980s and early 1990s. (Badgett also includes an analysis of marital rates in two other European countries—Iceland and Holland—that took the lead in legally recognizing lesbian and gay relationships, finding no evidence that such recognition is associated with changes in the marital rates of heterosexuals.) Similarly, the divorce rates among heterosexuals either remained steady or declined following the legal recognition of same-sex relationships by several northern European countries.[117]

The empirical evidence, therefore, simply fails to support the claim that the recognition of same-sex marriages either makes it less likely that heterosexuals will marry or more likely that they will procreate outside of marriage. Although it is true that the heterosexual marriage rate in the United States has been declining for decades, and that, during the same period, the percentage of heterosexual women who give birth outside of marriage has increased significantly, there is no evidence that the legal recognition of same-sex marriages has contributed to those changes.

It would seem that the decision of individuals to marry and to have children depends on the interaction of a large set of social, economic, and personal factors that are beyond the influence of any one legal standard, even one as seemingly important as who is eligible to marry. Furthermore, as the law professors Naomi Cahn and June Carbone have pointed out, the so-called red states, where cultural norms continue to "celebrate the unity of sex, marriage, and procreation," have "higher teen pregnancy rates [and] more shotgun marriages." In contrast, the so-called blue states, where fewer people believe in a traditional understanding of marriage that normatively links it to procreation, have "low divorce rates [and] relatively few teen births."[118] These regional differences suggest that notwithstanding the protestations of marriage equality opponents, there is little connection between maintaining the traditional understanding of marriage on the one hand and the rates of marriage, divorce, and out-of-wedlock births on the other.

The ineffectiveness of family cap welfare policies also illustrates the limitations of targeted policies aimed at influencing the childbearing decisions of individuals. As noted, many in the welfare reform movement who were concerned about the so-called irresponsible procreation of single mothers on welfare, and wanted to discourage non-marital births, pushed for the adoption of family cap provisions that denied increases in cash benefits to unmarried mothers who had additional children while on welfare. The federal government, starting in 1992, began granting waivers under the old AFDC program to states that wanted to implement family caps. The Personal Responsibility and Work Opportunity Reconciliation Act of 1996 eliminated the need for waivers, leaving the decision of whether to adopt the caps entirely to the discretion of the states. Fifteen states implemented family caps prior to the enactment of PRWORA; nine did so afterward.[119] Despite the fact that almost half of the states at some point adopted family caps, the studies have consistently found that they have not influenced the procreative decisions of women on welfare.[120]

It is important to note that the implementation of family caps is a much more targeted policy than the refusal to recognize same-sex marriages. While the prohibition of same-sex marriages denies benefits to one group (lesbians and gay men) ostensibly to encourage so-called responsible procreation by another group (heterosexuals), family welfare caps are intended to promote responsible procreation among the same individuals who are denied the (additional) benefits in question. Despite the fact that family caps are narrowly tailored—because the intent is to influence the procreative decisions of those who are negatively impacted—there is little indication that they have played a role in reducing the number of nonmarital births among mothers on welfare. It is not particularly surprising, therefore, that there is also little evidence that the denying (or granting) of marital benefits to lesbians and gay men influences the marital and procreative decisions of heterosexuals.

At the end of the day, the data suggest that there is no connection between increasing marital rates and decreasing nonmarital births among heterosexuals (the ends) and denying same-sex couples the opportunity to marry (the means). What is true empirically in the aggregate is consistent with the common sense intuition that heterosexual couples do not decide to marry, or to have children only while married, simply because lesbians and gay men are prohibited from marrying the individuals of their choice.

A CRUCIAL MORAL OBJECTION TO THE RESPONSIBLE PROCREATION JUSTIFICATION

Assume, counterfactually, that the empirical evidence showed an association between allowing same-sex couples the opportunity to marry and the rates at which heterosexuals marry and have children within marriage. Even if this were true, defending same-sex marriage bans based on the need to promote responsible procreation among heterosexuals is morally objectionable, because it uses lesbians and gay men (and their children) instrumentally in order to advance the interests of others.

That this is the case is perhaps clearest when one analyzes the accidental procreation version of the responsible procreation claim. As explained earlier, that version emphasizes the fact that different-sex couples frequently conceive children unintentionally, a mistake same-sex couples cannot make. Since same-sex couples are required to plan before becoming parents (by, for example, pursuing adoption or relying on reproductive technologies), they are more likely to be better prepared for parenthood than heterosexuals, who can become parents as a result, in effect, of a one-night stand. It is therefore claimed that different-sex couples need the structure and support provided by marriage in ways that same-sex couples do not.

The accidental procreation justification for same-sex marriage bans crystallizes the moral problem with denying rights to members of group X, who in this instance, according to the claim, act responsibly, in order to help members of group Y, who, again according to the claim, often act irresponsibly. Even if there were empirical support for the proposition that keeping marriage as an exclusively heterosexual institution would make it less likely that heterosexuals would have children accidentally, it is morally problematic to achieve that goal by disadvantaging lesbians and gay men. The latter have not in any way contributed to the rate of procreation (whether accidental or otherwise) among opposite-sex sexual partners. Penalizing same-sex couples in order to create the proper procreative incentives for heterosexuals is simply unfair. Perhaps it is for this reason that we do not in this country have a tradition of denying legal benefits to one group of individuals in order to encourage another group to act more responsibly.

Same-sex couples are not the only ones harmed when they are denied access to the hundreds of legal rights and benefits that accompany marriage; their children are disadvantaged as well. It is nothing less than morally perverse to harm children—by denying them the social and legal support that comes with having parents who are married—in order to encourage others to marry and to not have children outside of marriage. Even if the children of heterosexuals are better off when their parents marry (a claim I return to in chapter 3), and even if heterosexuals are more likely to marry when lesbians and gay men are prohibited from doing so (a claim I have already addressed), these outcomes do not justify denying an entirely separate set of children the social and legal benefits that accompany marriage.

There is little difference between how opponents of marriage equality have used the children of same-sex couples to promote their views on responsible procreation and how, as we saw in chapter 1, earlier defenders of legal disabilities imposed on non-marital children justified that differential treatment as a means to promote procreation within marriage. In both instances, innocent children are harmed in order to protect the interests of other children. It is unjust to disadvantage the children of same-sex couples in order to promote the interests of the children of heterosexual ones, in the same way that it is unjust to promote the interests of marital children by denying benefits to nonmarital ones. (In fact, as I explain in chapter 5, the Supreme Court in striking down DOMA emphasized the harm the statute caused the children of lesbians and gay men.)

Opponents of marriage equality have tried, as best they can, to defend same-sex marriage bans by building on the one characteristic that most clearly distinguishes different-sex couples from same-sex ones, namely that only the former are capable of creating new human beings through sexual intimacy. After failing to establish that procreation, as such, justifies prohibiting same-sex couples from marrying, conservative advocates shifted the emphasis to notions of *responsible* procreation. But the claim that marriage must remain an exclusively heterosexual institution in order to maintain the link between marriage and procreation (1) ignores the transformative cultural and legal changes affecting the understanding and regulation of heterosexual relationships and childbearing that preceded the recognition of same-sex marriage, (2) is unsupported by the empirical evidence following such recognition, and (3) is morally problematic.

Marriage equality opponents have not limited their claims to matters associated with *having* children. They have also defended same-sex marriage bans on grounds related to the *raising* of children. To these grounds I turn next.

3

FAMILY OPTIMALITY

In 1994, shortly before the issue of same-sex marriage exploded onto the national scene, Sara McLanahan, a Princeton sociologist, and Gary Sandefur, a sociologist at the University of Wisconsin, published the results of their decade-long research—based on four national surveys—on the effects of single parenting on children. McLanahan and Sandefur concluded that "growing up with only one biological parent frequently deprives children of important economic, parental, and community resources, and that these deprivations ultimately undermine their chances of future success."[1] Specifically, the two sociologists found that children raised by single parents dropped out of high school and out of the job market, and had children as teenagers, at higher rates than children raised in intact (i.e., never-divorced) married households.

Opponents of same-sex marriage quickly began to rely on the McLanahan and Sandefur findings, as well as on those of other studies of single parent and stepparent families that reached similar conclusions, to contend that households led by married mothers and fathers who are biologically related to their children are the optimal family structure for children. Since same-sex couples by definition lack either a man or a woman and since they cannot both be biologically related to their children, the state can appropriately deny them the opportunity to marry. Such a denial, it is argued, encourages the raising of children in the households that are most likely to promote their welfare.[2]

There are two main problems with the "family optimality" argument that is frequently used to defend same-sex marriage bans. The first is the disconnect between the ends (promoting optimality in child-rearing such that children are raised by their married, different-sex biological parents) and the means (denying same-sex couples the opportunity to marry). Even if we assume, for purposes of argument, that married heterosexual parents who are biologically related to their children provide the "optimal" family structure for children, there is no rational connection between promoting so-called optimality in family structure and denying lesbians and gay men the opportunity to marry or to serve as parents. This is because, as noted, heterosexual couples are not more likely to marry, or to accept the responsibilities of parenthood, simply because lesbians and gay men are prohibited from marrying. Since heterosexuals do not marry, or decide to have children within marriage, on the basis of whether lesbians and gay men are banned from marrying, the bans do not further the purpose of promoting the "optimal" family structure for children.[3]

The second problem with the family optimality argument is that its factual premises regarding child welfare are not supported by the empirical evidence. This second flaw in the optimality claim is the subject of this chapter. I begin with a brief discussion of why the government does not and should not use family optimality as a guiding principle in determining which individuals should be allowed to marry and encouraged to raise children. The rest of the chapter presents a longer exploration of why the social science evidence that opponents of marriage equality rely on to defend same-sex marriage bans does not support their child-rearing optimality claims. In particular, the chapter points out that there is little evidence that marital status (by itself), or biological status, or parental gender is associated with better child outcomes.

WHY OPTIMALITY IS THE WRONG STANDARD

Although opponents of LGBT rights make much of the notion of family optimality, the reality is that, outside of the same-sex marriage context, no one argues that it should play a role in the setting of marriage eligibility rules. The social science evidence clearly shows, for example, that children raised by two high-income parents do better in school than children raised by two low-income parents.[4] Studies also consistently show that children raised by parents with more education do better in school and have fewer behavioral problems than do children of parents with less education.[5]

It could be claimed, therefore, that high-income households in which parents are highly educated constitute the "optimal" setting for the raising of children. Yet no one, of course, contends that marriage be limited to high-income individuals or to those with college degrees. (Similarly, no one argues that only those with high incomes or college degrees be permitted to adopt children.) Such social engineering through marriage eligibility rules would clearly be misguided, because it would be inconsistent with the intuitive point, supported by the social science evidence, that there are many factors that account for child outcomes, including not only parental income and education, but also the quality of parent-child relationships, the level of parental care and involvement, and the child's own abilities and temperament.[6] In addition, the setting of marriage eligibility rules on the basis of parental income and education considerations would ignore the fact that millions of parents with limited income and education provide their children with nurturing and caring homes in which they thrive.

Marriage equality opponents' selective use of the family optimality claim to justify depriving only one group of individuals (lesbians and gay men) of the opportunity to marry the individuals of their choice strongly suggests that the purpose of the claim is to target that group rather than promote the well-being of children. Given that neither social conservatives nor any other groups are raising family optimality claims in any other context as justifications for prohibiting individuals from marrying, policymakers and courts should be highly skeptical of attempts to rely on such claims to deprive same-sex couples of the opportunity to marry. (Although it is true that family optimality claims were raised in the past to defend marital restrictions—such as those based on race and disability—these efforts, as noted, were deeply problematic.)

It is also important to emphasize that judges and child welfare officials do not rely on optimality considerations when making custody, adoption, and foster care placement decisions. Instead, they apply the best interests of the child standard, which—rather than concerning itself with generalized questions of which family households are "optimal"—calls for individualized assessments of whether the particular adults who are willing and able to maintain or assume parental responsibilities are likely to promote the best interests of the specific children in question.[7]

At a high level of generality, there is a certain intuitive appeal to considerations of family optimality in matters related to children, given that "optimal" households, by definition, are better for children than "nonoptimal" ones (however "optimality" is defined). But once we put abstractions aside and consider the actual custody, adoption, and foster care placement decisions that judges and child welfare officials make, it quickly becomes clear that generalized optimality serves as an inadequate guiding principle. Placement decisions do not and should not depend on whether the particular family under consideration belongs to a category of households that is deemed "optimal," but rather on whether the particular adults in question are capable of providing the children with the care and support they need to lead healthy and well-adjusted lives.

The family optimality defense of same-sex marriage bans should be rejected not only because optimality is an inappropriate guiding principle in the setting of marriage eligibility rules and in making child placement decisions, but also because little empirical support for it exists, despite the repeated claims of opponents of marriage equality. To see why this is the case, it is helpful to note that the family optimality argument, as deployed by opponents of same-sex marriage, consists of three different empirical claims: that children do better (1) when raised by married couples; (2) when raised by their biological parents; and (3) when raised by a female parent and a male parent.

DO CHILDREN DO BETTER WHEN RAISED BY MARRIED COUPLES?

The social science literature that opponents of marriage equality most frequently rely on compares children in households headed by married couples to children raised by single parents. These studies show that married couples are able to provide their children with greater financial and emotional support than single parents, which in turn generally leads to these children experiencing fewer behavioral and emotional problems and performing better in school than the children of single parents.[8]

It bears emphasizing, however, that some of these studies, as the sociologist Michael Rosenfeld notes, "have indicated that socioeconomic status explains most or all of the advantage of children raised by married couples."[9] It should also be noted that the fact that children in general may do better when raised by married parents as opposed to by single parents does not mean that most children of single parents evince problems in psychological adjustment or social functioning. As the developmental psychologist

Michael Lamb notes, "numerous large-scale studies show that *the vast majority* of the children and adolescents who spend their childhoods living apart from one of their parents are well adjusted."[10]

Despite these important qualifications, some studies do show that children raised in married households do better on some outcomes than children raised in one-parent households, even after controlling for family income. However, those studies do not show, of course, that it is the *marital status,* as opposed to the *number* of parents, which accounts for the better child outcomes. The studies that might be able to show an association between marital status and better child outcomes are studies that compare children raised by married couples to those raised by unmarried couples.

There are studies showing that children of married parents do better than children of cohabiting couples on some measures, though there is disagreement among social scientists on the extent to which these differences are the result of selection, that is, of the fact that individuals who are more likely to provide higher levels of financial and emotional support for their children are more likely to marry. For example, a recent longitudinal study in the United Kingdom of almost ten thousand children found higher cognitive and socioemotional development among the children of married couples than among the children of cohabiting parents. But when the researchers controlled for factors such as the parents' education levels, income, and home ownership, these factors were found to account for all the differences in cognitive development and most of the disparity in socioemotional development. The researchers concluded that "the gaps in cognitive and socio-emotional development between children born to married and cohabiting parents mainly or entirely reflect the fact that different types of people choose to get married (the selection effect), rather than that marriage has a direct effect on child development."[11]

Aside from questions of selection, it should be obvious that even if the "married versus cohabiting parents" studies were to show a clear association between the marital status of parents and better child outcomes, such a link *would not justify prohibiting individuals from marrying.* Although opponents of marriage equality repeatedly make this mistake, it is odd and illogical to point to empirical evidence that marriage helps to promote the well-being of children *in order to defend a legal restriction on the ability of individuals to marry.* If the empirical evidence on the benefits of marriage for children is as strong as those who object to same-sex marriages claim, then that counsels in favor of adopting more expansive marriage eligibility rules, not more circumscribed ones.

Although it should be clear that the "married versus single parents" and "married versus cohabiting parents" studies do not provide empirical support for the policy decision of limiting marriage to heterosexuals, that point is often not fully understood because marriage equality opponents do not, as I am doing here, break down their family optimality argument into its three distinct empirical claims. Even if the first empirical claim—that children do better when raised by married parents—were true, that does not justify prohibiting same-sex couples from marrying. For that reason, we need to assess the merits of the second claim.

DO CHILDREN DO BETTER WHEN RAISED BY BIOLOGICAL PARENTS?

As noted, opponents of marriage equality, from the earliest days of the policy and legal debates over same-sex marriage, have been drawn to the fact that only different-sex couples can create a new human being though physiological processes. These opponents claim not only that this "fact of nature" makes different-sex couples uniquely suited to participate in the institution of marriage, but also that children do better when raised by their biological parents. Both of these claims are then joined to argue that the state is justified in denying same-sex couples the opportunity to marry.

There is little factual support for the contention that a biological connection between parents and children contributes to better child outcomes. The "married versus single parents" studies, upon which opponents of marriage equality rely on so heavily, may support the claim that children do better when raised by two parents, but they do not support the distinct contention that children do better when raised by their biological parents. The vast majority of the parents (both married and single) who participated in those studies were biologically related to the children. As a result, the "married versus single parents" studies do not establish that the differences in child outcomes are attributable to biology.

Opponents of marriage equality also rely on studies showing that children raised in intact married households generally have better outcomes than those raised in stepparent households. At first glance, it may seem that these studies *do* show that there are benefits to children of being raised by their biological parents, because children in stepparent households by definition share their home with an adult to whom they are not biologically related. There are, however, at least three problems with the attempt to rely on the findings of stepparent household studies to justify the denial of marriage to same-sex couples.

First, several of the studies comparing intact married households with other forms of family structures, such as stepparent households, include adoptive parents within the definition of intact married households.[12] These studies therefore fail to establish that the differences in outcomes between children raised in intact married households and those raised in stepparent homes are attributable to the fact that there is a nonbiological parent in the latter.

Second, children in stepparent households have to cope with the challenges associated with adjusting to new home arrangements. As the sociologist Paul Amato, who has written extensively on family structure issues and whose work is often cited in legal briefs by those who raise family optimality claims in same-sex marriage cases, explains, "stepfamily formation is stressful for many children because it often involves moving (generally to a different neighborhood or town), adapting to new people in the household, and learning new rules and routines."[13] It is not possible to conclude, therefore, that the differences in child outcomes between children raised in intact married households and those raised in stepparent households are attributable to the absence of a biological link between the children in the latter group and one of the two adults in the household rather than to other factors, including family disruption and relocation.

Third, there are good reasons to be skeptical of marriage equality opponents' efforts to analogize between same-sex couple parent households and stepparent heterosexual ones.[14] The ostensible basis for the analogy is that in both types of households, only one of the adults can be biologically related to the children. The "stepparent" label, however, does not fit the large number of lesbian and gay parents who have participated in the decision to have children with their same-sex partners and helped raise them from birth, even though they are not biologically related to them. These individuals are not similarly situated to heterosexual stepparents, the vast majority of whom enter the picture by marrying the biological parents several years after the children were born. Nonbiological lesbian and gay parents are frequently a part of their children's lives from the very beginning, and the children often consider them to be indistinguishable from their biological parents.[15] In contrast, stepparents are usually not parents from birth, and children frequently deem them, especially at the beginning of the relationship, to have a status that falls short of actual parents.[16]

The inapplicability of the analogy between same-sex parent couple households and stepparent heterosexual ones is also evident from the fact that opponents of marriage equality, not surprisingly, do not claim that the absence of biological links between stepparents and stepchildren is a sufficient reason for denying stepparents the ability to marry the children's biological parents. In fact, this is another example of how those who rely on optimality-based claims in matters related to marriage and children limit their use to the question of same-sex marriage. It would be absurd, of course, to suggest that biological parents should be prohibited from marrying individuals who are not biologically related to their children because studies show that children raised in intact households generally do better than those raised in stepparent ones. But it is just as absurd to suggest that same-sex couples should be prohibited from marrying because studies show that children raised in intact (heterosexual) households do better than those raised in (heterosexual) stepparent ones.

The analogy between same-sex parent households and heterosexual stepparent ones is not a persuasive one. A better analogy might be to heterosexual couples who use reproductive technologies to conceive children. Like many same-sex parent couples, heterosexual couples who rely on reproductive technologies to conceive children usually make a joint decision to become parents before conception. Both sets of couples also usually proceed to raise the children from birth (unlike most stepparents, who do not enter the picture until later, usually years after birth). In addition, as with same-sex parent couples, frequently only one of the heterosexual parents who use reproductive technologies to conceive is biologically related to the child.

Several recent studies conducted in the United Kingdom have attempted to determine whether the use of assisted reproduction technologies to conceive children (through surrogacy, donor insemination, or embryo donation), and the corresponding absence of a biological link between children and one or both of their parents, is associated with differences in child outcomes. The studies have compared the social and emotional development of children conceived through assisted reproduction with those conceived through so-called natural means. The studies have consistently found that the former are well adjusted and have not been disadvantaged by the lack of a biological connection between themselves and one or both of their parents.[17]

Finally, those who defend same-sex marriage bans on family optimality grounds, in their efforts to show that children benefit from having biological links to those who serve as their parents, have not usually relied on the contention that biological parents are better parents than adoptive ones. For example, David Blankenhorn, the only witness called on by same-sex marriage opponents to discuss child welfare considerations during the federal trial on the constitutionality of California's Proposition 8, testified that "the studies show that adoptive parents, because of the rigorous screening process that they undertake before becoming adoptive parents, actually on some measures outstrip the biological parents in terms of providing protective care for their children."[18] This statement is supported by several studies, including one that found, using a nationally representative sample, that adoptive parents show greater levels of parental investment—as determined by the "economic, cultural, social, and interactional resources that parents provide for their children"—than do biological parents.[19]

Some studies have found that children of adoptive parents are as psychologically well adjusted, and do as well in school, as the children of biological parents.[20] Other studies have found better outcomes among the children of biological than of adoptive parents.[21] Nonetheless, there is a wide consensus among experts that most adopted children are well adjusted and that providing adults with the opportunity to adopt promotes the welfare of children.[22]

Indeed, the issue of adoption presents us with (yet) another illustration of why optimality is a highly problematic guiding principle in the setting of marital and child welfare policies. The empirical findings by some studies that children on some measures do better when raised by their biological parents than by their adoptive parents—differences that may be explained by the family transitions and dislocations that some adopted children experience—have never been translated into policy suggestions that adoption as a parenting option should be discouraged or curtailed. Furthermore, of course, no sensible person would suggest that such studies justify denying prospective adoptive parents the opportunity to marry. Yet these are precisely the kinds of policy suggestions, based on child-rearing optimality grounds, that marriage equality proponents make when it comes to questions related to marriage and parenting by lesbians and gay men.

At the end of the day, there is little empirical support for the proposition that parent-child biological links are associated with better outcomes in children. Neither the "married versus single parents" studies nor the "intact married versus stepparent households" studies that opponents of marriage equality rely on show that having a biological relationship with their parents helps children. In addition, studies of children conceived through reproductive technologies suggest that biological links with both parents do not play an important role in promoting children's well-being. Finally, the absurdity of relying on the absence of biological ties between adoptive parents and their children to either curtail adoption or to deny prospective adoptive parents the opportunity to marry serves to highlight the misguided ways opponents of marriage equality attempt to deploy biology-based optimality claims to defend same-sex marriage bans.

The fact that same-sex couples cannot both be biologically related to their children does not constitute an appropriate ground upon which to justify denying them the opportunity to marry. This leaves only the third, and last, empirical claim behind the family optimality defense of same-sex marriage bans: that children benefit in crucial and unique ways when they are parented by an adult of each gender.

DO CHILDREN DO BETTER WHEN RAISED BY BOTH A FEMALE AND A MALE PARENT?

The social science studies relied on by those who defend same-sex marriage bans on family optimality grounds also fail to support the additional contention that children benefit in important and distinct ways from having both a female and a male parent.

When it comes to the importance of parental gender, as with the other two claims that make up the family optimality argument for same-sex marriage bans, much of the empirical heavy lifting is ostensibly done by studies that compare children raised by married parents to those raised by single ones. According to opponents of same-sex marriage, those studies show that children do better when raised by both a mother and a father.

It is true, of course, that most single-parent households in the United States are headed by mothers. This does not mean, however, that the presence of a male parent in married, different-sex households, as opposed to the presence of a *second* parent, accounts for the better child outcomes found in children raised by married couples. The "married versus single parents" studies repeatedly cited by defenders of the family optimality argument, in other words, do not support the contention that it is the gender of the parents, as opposed to their number, that accounts for the differences in child outcomes.[23]

The studies that *do* explore the role that parental gender may play in child development and outcomes are the ones that compare lesbian couple households with heterosexual couple ones. These studies (discussed in the next chapter) assess whether the presence of a male parent in the latter family type is associated with children's psychological adjustment and social functioning. Those studies, unlike the "married versus single parents" studies that marriage equality opponents rely on, *compare two-parent households*, thus allowing for the finding of associations between family structure and child development and outcomes that are based on the gender rather than on the number of parents.

Defenders of the family optimality defense of same-sex marriage bans also frequently point to studies suggesting that fathers and mothers parent differently. Some of these studies, many of which date back to the 1970s and 1980s, have found some differences in gender-based parenting styles. For example, some researchers have found that male parents spend more time in physical and rough-and-tumble play with their children, whereas female parents spend more time caretaking and nurturing their children.[24] Marriage equality opponents contend that these kinds of studies prove that there are gender-based differences in parenting and that depriving children of a female or a male parent denies them important developmental benefits.

In assessing the appropriateness of using this literature to defend same-sex marriage bans, it is necessary to keep the following points in mind. First, the "gender differences in parenting" studies generally rely on convenience samples rather than random population samples. As a consequence, the study subjects are not representative of the wider population. This does not mean that the studies are intrinsically flawed or useless. The results of studies based on nonrandom samples can contribute to a better understanding of a subject matter, especially when the findings are consistent with those of other studies. However, the fact that the literature on the different parenting styles of female and male parents generally relies on convenience samples exposes the double standard that opponents of marriage equality bring to bear when they discuss the social science evidence on child development. As I explain in the next chapter, these opponents dismiss the large literature showing no association between parental sexual orientation and the psychological adjustment and social functioning of children as essentially worthless because many of the studies rely on convenience samples. It is deeply ironic that the "gender differences in parenting" literature, which opponents of marriage equality consistently rely on to defend the notion that children do better when raised by a mother and father, relies on the *same* types of convenience samples that they (conveniently) find unreliable in assessing the parenting attributes of lesbians and gay men.[25]

Second, the gender-based differences in parenting styles are not as great as marriage equality opponents claim. Although it seems to be true, for example, that fathers spend a higher percentage of their time with their children in play activities than do mothers, fathers spend most of their time with their children engaged in behaviors other than playing—such as teaching, guiding, and caretaking. In addition, most studies show that, in absolute terms, mothers spend more time playing with their children than fathers do.[26] Indeed, the "gender differences in parenting" studies emphasize *average* differences in the attributes of female and male parents while minimizing within-group variation, that is, the extent to which those attributes fall along a continuum that actually shows considerable overlap in the ways mothers and fathers parent.[27]

The relative unimportance of parental gender is clear from studies showing that female and male parents play a variety of *similar* roles within families, from providers to protectors to teachers to caregivers. Although it is possible to find some average differences in discrete activities (such as the proportion of parental time spent on rough-and-tumble play), examination of a wider set of capabilities and responsibilities finds many more similarities than differences between female and male parents. As Michael Lamb, in reviewing the social science literature studying father-child interactions, notes,

> it is now well established that both men and women have the capacity to be good parents. Both parents are physiologically prepared for and changed by parenthood. New mothers and fathers are equivalently competent (or incompetent) at parenting, with most parenting skills learned "on the job." .... It is clear ... that mothers

and fathers influence children's development in the same non-gendered ways—promoting psychological adjustment when they are caring, loving, engaged, and authoritative.[28]

It is not at all surprising, in a society in which men are still expected to be the primary breadwinners and women the main caretakers of children, that fathers spend less time with their children (and that when they do, they spend a higher percentage of that time playing) and mothers spend more time with them and are therefore usually more involved in caretaking activities. But this does not mean that there is something about male parents that is intrinsically different from female parents (or vice versa). Indeed, the fact that the levels of parental involvement by gender vary across time and cultures significantly undermines the contention that humans are somehow biologically destined to carry out different parental responsibilities depending on their gender.[29]

Nonetheless, opponents of marriage equality frequently defend problematic notions of biological determinism in claiming that female parents parent in ways that are fundamentally different from the ways male parents do (and vice versa). For example, in defending the constitutionality of DOMA before the Supreme Court, the Bipartisan Legal Advisory Group to the U.S. House of Representatives (BLAG) contended that "biological differentiation in the roles of mothers and fathers makes it rational to encourage situations in which children have one of each." After claiming that "men and women are different" and that "so are mothers and fathers," BLAG added that "common sense, and the experience of countless parents, informs us that children relate and often react differently to mothers and fathers."[30]

An amicus brief filed with the Court in the same case, as well as in the lawsuit challenging California's constitutional ban on same-sex marriages, by a group of conservative social scientists also focused on the supposed biological differences between men's and women's parenting. The brief claimed that female parents have a "natural biological responsiveness" to infants that male parents lack. It then contended that mothers need to guide fathers in carrying out "routine caretaking activities" of infants and toddlers. The brief added that "this direction is needed in part because fathers do not share equally in the biological and hormonal interconnectedness that develops between a mother and a child during pregnancy, delivery, and lactation."[31]

The notion that female parents are, in effect, hardwired to nurture children and that male parents can be effective caretakers only when guided by women is unfortunately consistent with stereotyped notions of what women and men are each capable of accomplishing. These assumptions remain in place despite the fact that our society has progressively moved away from gender stereotyping in recognition of the immense harm it has caused both women and men through the generations. In some ways, parenting abilities and influences may be the last frontier in the long effort to discredit notions of biologically determined differences between men and women. In thinking about the purported connection between gender and parenting capabilities, it is crucial to keep in mind the troubling ways such notions of "natural" differences between men and women were used in the past to support gender hierarchy, privilege, and subordination.

Marriage equality opponents also place much weight on studies showing that *paternal* involvement benefits children. (In public policy debates, it is largely assumed that maternal involvement is beneficial.) It is true that studies show that the presence of involved and caring fathers in households led by heterosexual couples is associated with several advantages for children, including fewer behavioral problems and better academic performance.[32] But these studies do not establish that the benefits are the result of the fathers' *gender,* as opposed to the positive effects on children of having a *second* involved parent.

Recent studies of low-income, two-parent heterosexual families who participate in Head Start programs suggest that parental gender makes little difference in child development and outcomes. These studies found, not surprisingly, that children had better cognitive outcomes when both parents were supportive and worse outcomes when neither parent was. Also not surprisingly, the cognitive outcomes of children with one supportive and one unsupportive parent fell somewhere in the middle. But what is crucial here is that the researchers found that for the children in the middle category, *the gender of the supportive parent was inconsequential:* children who had supportive mothers (and unsupportive fathers) did not have different cognitive outcomes than children who had supportive fathers (and unsupportive mothers).[33]

Furthermore, as the sociologist and human development expert Joseph Pleck has pointed out, those who argue that parents contribute to the well-being of their children in unique ways depending on their gender fail to distinguish between parental influences that are independent of the actions of the other parent (statistical independence) and influences that could not be brought about by the other parent (nonsubstitutability). Some studies, for example, show that paternal influences are associated with child outcomes even when controlling for maternal influences.[34] But those studies do not show that "fathers' influence...is distinct from mothers' in the sense of not being substitutable or replaceable by mothers'. That is [they do not show] that for children whose fathers do not provide a particular influence, mothers' providing it will not have the same effect."[35] Indeed, the studies of the aforementioned Head Start families indicate that parental *gender* (in contrast to parental *support*) is not associated with better cognitive outcomes.

There was a time when social scientists thought that fathers might serve a gender role development function, in particular by promoting masculinity in their sons. But studies that sought to compare the degree of masculinity of fathers with that of their children found little correlation between the two. On further investigation, the researchers determined that what mattered was not the masculinity of fathers, but the warmth and intimacy of their relationships with their sons—sons tended to resemble their fathers, and to show improved psychological adjustment and social functioning, when they felt close to them.[36]

Proponents of same-sex marriage bans sometimes claim that children benefit from having a parent of their own gender and that the influence of fathers on sons and of mothers on daughters is particularly important. However, little empirical support exists for the proposition that male children benefit uniquely from having a male parent or that female children benefit uniquely from having a female parent. For example, a study in the *American Sociological Review* that compared households led by single mothers to those led by single fathers did not find that daughters fared better in the former than the latter or that sons did better in the latter than the former.[37] The researchers noted that "what is striking is the extent to which the match between the sex of the parent and the sex of the child is unimportant." They also concluded that "our findings...suggest that given comparable situations, fathers can provide as strong a role model to girls as to boys, just as mothers can be models to boys and girls."[38]

Despite the lack of empirical support, opponents of marriage equality continue to claim that female and male parents each contribute to the well-being of children in unique, essential, and unsubstitutable ways. In doing so, they tap into long-standing, powerful understandings of motherhood and fatherhood as distinct forms of parenting, as well as the fact that, as a general matter, children do better when raised by married heterosexual parents than by single parents. These critics then contend that in order to support same-sex marriage, one has to adhere to the view that whether children have a mother and a father is irrelevant for purposes of promoting their well-being.

There is a crucial difference, however, between claiming, on the one hand, that two female parents, for example, are capable of providing children with the same benefits provided by a female and a male parent and, on the other, that it does not matter to *the children of heterosexuals* whether they have both a supportive mother and father. The studies are clear that the children of heterosexuals benefit from having present and engaged mothers and fathers. However, the same studies, which do not compare households led by heterosexual parents to those led by lesbians and gay men, fail to show that these benefits cannot be provided by present and engaged same-sex parents.

Ultimately, then, it is not possible to assess the merits of the family optimality defense of same-sex marriage bans by focusing only on studies—such as the "married versus single parents" and "gender differences in parenting" studies—that have researched child development and outcomes in the context of heterosexual families. Studies that compare one group of heterosexual parents (e.g., married couples; mothers in heterosexual marriages) with another group of such parents (e.g., single parents; fathers in heterosexual marriages) do not address the two fundamental questions raised by efforts to deny same-sex couples the opportunity to marry on the basis of child welfare considerations: first, whether parental gender plays a unique and unsubstitutable role in child development and outcomes; second, whether parental sexual orientation is associated with child development and outcomes.

The social science studies that seek to answer both of these questions are the ones that have studied the children of lesbians and gay men. As noted, and as I further explore in the next chapter, opponents of marriage equality dismiss those studies' findings because the research is purportedly biased and methodologically flawed. However, as this chapter has shown, the studies the opponents *do* rely on fail to support their claims. While the (1) "married versus single parents" and the (2) "married versus cohabiting parents" studies may justify the expansion of marital rights, they do not justify their restriction. In addition, neither these studies nor the (3) "intact married parents versus stepparents" studies nor the (4) "gender differences in parenting" studies show that either biological parental status or parental gender is associated with better outcomes in children.

The empirical weakness of the family optimality defense of same-sex marriage bans may explain the frequency with which opponents of marriage equality eventually fall back on vague and unempirical notions of "common sense" and "instinct" to defend the idea that it is best for children to be raised by married mothers and fathers who are biologically related to them.[39] It is undoubtedly true that most Americans for most of the nation's history have *assumed* the correctness of that premise, perhaps because most Americans for most of the nation's history have been raised by married couples who were biologically related to them. But it is problematic to deny an entire class of individuals the opportunity to marry those whom they love on the basis of an assumption. Once the assumption is carefully scrutinized, it becomes clear that it lacks empirical support.

4

SEXUAL ORIENTATION AND PARENTING

The legal and policy questions associated with parental sexual orientation first arose in child custody and visitation disputes. Around the time that the first same-sex marriage lawsuits were filed in the early 1970s, a small but growing number of lesbian and gay parents started coming out of the closet. Most of these individuals became parents while married to someone of the opposite gender. After their marriages ended, many were confronted with ex-spouses who attempted to use their recently revealed same-sex sexual orientation to deny or limit their custody and visitation rights. Issues related to child custody and visitation were the first legal matters involving out-of-the-closet LGBT people in the United States that began appearing repeatedly in court dockets. Indeed, family law judges were the first group of jurists in the country to routinely grapple with the legal relevance of sexual orientation.

At first, courts were almost uniformly hostile to the idea that openly lesbian and gay parents should be awarded custody following the dissolution of their different-sex marriages, as well as the notion that they should have unrestricted rights to visit with their children. In fact, several courts in the 1980s concluded that the sexual orientation and same-sex relationships of lesbian and gay parents constituted sufficient grounds to deny or restrict their custody and visitation rights.[1]

By the 1990s, however, most courts had eschewed such reasoning in favor of applying a legal standard known as the "nexus test." That test requires that specific evidence of actual or potential harm to the children be introduced before courts can take into account parents' sexual orientation and relationships in making custody and visitation decisions. Although courts did not always apply the test correctly—some continued to hold the sexual orientation of lesbian and gay parents against them even in the absence of any particularized evidence that it negatively affected their children—the focus was now on the evidentiary question of whether having an openly lesbian or gay parent harmed children.[2]

Around the same time that custody and visitation cases involving lesbian and gay parents were first litigated, social conservatives started raising questions about the impact of parental sexual orientation on children. In 1977, Florida became the first state to prohibit adoption by lesbians, gay men, and bisexuals. At a time when many believed that being attracted to individuals of the same sex was a psychological abnormality—it was not until 1973 that the American Psychiatric Association removed homosexuality from its official manual of mental and emotional disorders—conservative politicians and activists began to claim that having lesbian or gay parents was harmful to children. Critics also suggested that the same-sex sexual orientation of parents might interfere with children's "normal" gender and sexual development. One of the commonly expressed fears was that having lesbian or gay parents might lead boys to be feminine and girls to be masculine. Another concern was that children of lesbians and gay men might be confused about their sexuality, perhaps leading them to experiment sexually and even "to become" lesbian or gay themselves.[3]

In addition, some gay rights critics, taking advantage of the prevailing stereotype of lesbians and gay men (in particular the latter) as oversexualized beings, began raising concerns about the threat of sexual abuse and molestation of children. In fact, a significant part of the antigay activism of the 1970s and early 1980s was built around the notion that society needed to protect its children from lesbians and gay men who might either take sexual advantage of them or try to "recruit" them.

Conservative activists raised these accusations in Florida in 1977 as part of their effort to overturn via the ballot box an ordinance passed by Dade County prohibiting discrimination on the basis of sexual orientation—the first enacted by a southern municipality. The repeal effort was led by Anita Bryant—a singer, former runner-up in the Miss America Pageant in the 1950s, and born-again Baptist—who founded an organization called "Save Our Children." As its name suggested, the group claimed that gay rights laws were not about civil rights but about the gay movement's desire to recruit young people. "The recruitment of our children," Bryant's group explained in an ad that appeared in the *Miami Herald*, "is absolutely necessary for the survival and growth of homosexuality—for since homosexuals cannot reproduce, they *must* recruit, *must* freshen their ranks." Another of the group's newspaper ads went even further by warning that "many parents are confused and don't know the real dangers posed by many homosexuals and perceive them as all being gentle, non-aggressive types. The other side of the homosexual coin is a hair-raising pattern of recruitment and outright seduction and molestation, a growing pattern that predictably will intensify if society approves laws bringing legitimacy to the sexually perverted."[4]

Given the focus, both inside and outside courtrooms, on the question of whether lesbians and gay men constituted a threat to children, it was not surprising that when social scientists began studying lesbian and gay families, they did so with the view of trying to determine whether the children were negatively affected by their parents' same-sex sexual orientation and relationships. The 1980s saw the publication of a handful of studies aimed at answering this question; each ensuing decade has brought larger numbers of studies.

The vast majority of the studies have found no differences between the children of lesbians and gay men and those of heterosexual parents. Some courts have relied on these findings to reject efforts to defend same-sex marriage bans on the basis of child welfare considerations.[5] In contrast, other courts have concluded that the studies fail to undermine "commonsense premise[s]" and "unprovable assumptions" about the benefits to children of being raised by married heterosexual parents.[6] From these courts' perspective, child welfare arguments based on parental sexual orientation are sufficient to uphold the constitutionality of same-sex marriage bans (and of laws prohibiting lesbians and gay men from serving as adoptive and foster care parents).[7]

Despite reaching different results, courts have consistently approached the social science studies in a unitary fashion, that is, they have treated the empirical literature as an undifferentiated whole without distinguishing among different areas of investigation. This unitary approach is problematic, given that the literature on the children of lesbians and gay men has looked into three broad and distinct subject matters. The first area of study has involved the children's psychological adjustment and social functioning. The former has included matters such as behavioral adjustment, emotional well-being, and self-esteem; the latter has included measures such as peer relations and school performance. The second area of study has consisted of the gender role development of children, in particular their gender attitudes and interests. Finally, the third set of studies has examined the children's sexual orientation.

This chapter explores the social science studies in each of these three areas to determine whether their findings are relevant to the question of whether the state can ban same-sex marriages without violating constitutional equality principles.

As an initial matter, it is important to understand that the constitutional analysis is driven by which level of judicial scrutiny is appropriate in cases challenging laws and regulations, such as same-sex marriage bans, that classify individuals according to their sexual orientation. Some courts have concluded that sexual orientation classifications—like sex/gender classifications—merit the application of a heightened judicial scrutiny that places on the government the obligation to show that the policy in question is substantially related to the attainment of an important state interest.[8] This level of judicial scrutiny presumes that the law or regulation in question is unconstitutional and places the burden on the government to show otherwise.

In contrast, other courts have concluded that sexual orientation classifications are only entitled to "rational basis" review.[9] The Supreme Court, in other contexts, has explained that under this highly deferential form of judicial review, laws and regulations "must be upheld against equal protection challenge if there is any reasonably conceivable state of facts that could provide a rational basis for the classification."[10] In addition, the rational basis test "is not a license for courts to judge the wisdom, fairness, or logic of legislative choices" and "do[es] not demand of legislatures scientifically certain criteria of legislation."[11]

The Supreme Court, in the two same-sex marriage cases that it heard in 2013, one involving California's ban on same-sex marriages and the other DOMA, declined the opportunity to decide which level of judicial review should be applied to sexual orientation classifications under the federal constitution. Given our nation's long and unfortunate history of invidious discrimination against lesbians, gay men, and bisexuals, coupled with the fact that sexual orientation does not affect the ability of individuals to participate in or contribute to society, I believe that courts should apply heightened scrutiny when sexual orientation classifications are challenged constitutionally. In this chapter, however, I assume for purposes of argument that rational basis is the appropriate standard to apply to those classifications. If the government, as I will argue, is precluded under the rational basis test from relying on claims of harm to children arising from their parents' same-sex sexual orientation to justify same-sex marriage bans, then it will also be precluded from doing so under more rigorous forms of judicial scrutiny.

The rational basis test, despite its clear deference toward the government's legislative and policy choices, imposes at least two limitations on the state's authority to regulate. The first is a requirement that there be a "reasonably conceivable state of facts" that supports the differential treatment in question. This requirement demands that laws be defended on grounds that have not been shown to be erroneous. As the Supreme Court has explained, "even the standard of rationality ... must find some footing in the realities of the subject addressed by the legislation."[12]

The rational basis standard imposes a second limitation on state action: the government, when it makes rights and benefits available to some but not others, must do so in the pursuit of a *legitimate* state interest.[13] The absence of such an interest requires courts to find the law in question constitutionally invalid.[14] (Some courts and commentators have argued that the Supreme Court has applied a form of heightened rational basis review in cases involving historically disadvantaged or unpopular groups like lesbians and gay men.[15] Even if this claim is correct, I do not here deploy a heightened form of rational basis review; instead, my analysis tracks the traditional, and highly deferential, understanding of that review.)

With this basic understanding of the relevant constitutional principles, we can proceed to explore what the social science literature on the children of lesbians and gay men means for marriage equality litigation, keeping in mind the three broad and distinct subject areas of study already noted (psychological adjustment and social functioning; gender role development; and sexual orientation). The empirical evidence showing the lack of an association between parental sexual orientation and the psychological adjustment and social functioning of children is so uniform and conclusive that there is no conceivable factual basis for suggesting otherwise. It is therefore constitutionally impermissible to rely on the psychological adjustment and social functioning of the children of lesbians and gay men to defend same-sex marriage bans.

The social science literature is slightly less consistent on questions related to the gender role development and sexual orientation of children, with a minority of studies suggesting possible associations with parental sexual orientation. Although *the empirical evidence does not permit us to conclude that there is an association between the sexual orientation of lesbian and gay parents and either the gender attitudes/interests or the sexual orientation of their children*, that evidence contains sufficient suggestions of possible differences in these two areas to meet the easy-to-satisfy factual component of the rational basis test. The empirical literature, in other words, suggests that we cannot rule out a "reasonably conceivable state of facts" showing differences between the children of lesbians and gay men and children of heterosexuals in matters related to gender role development and sexual orientation.

The mere existence of possible differences, however, is not enough to satisfy the rational basis test's second—and more normative—requirement: that the differences in question have a rational relationship to a *legitimate* state interest. Constitutional principles prohibit the government from instituting policies on the basis of possible differences in gender role development and sexual orientation between the children of lesbian and gay parents and children of heterosexual parents. The state does not have a legitimate interest in encouraging individuals to behave in certain ways, or to pursue certain preferences, on the basis of their gender. The government also does not have a legitimate interest in attempting to influence the sexual orientation of individuals or in discouraging individuals (including adolescents) from engaging in same-sex as opposed to different-sex sexual conduct.

This means that the empirical findings of studies that have investigated whether there is an association between parental sexual orientation and the gender role development and sexual orientation of children are, in effect, *constitutionally irrelevant*.

It is important to note, before proceeding with an exploration of the social science literature on the children of lesbians and gay men, that although I focus my discussion on the relevance of that literature to the constitutionality of same-sex marriage bans, the same analysis applies to regulations restricting the ability of lesbians and gay men to serve as adoptive and foster care parents. These parenting restrictions, like same-sex marriage bans, cannot be constitutionally defended on child welfare grounds, even when applying the rational basis test.

CHILDREN'S PSYCHOLOGICAL ADJUSTMENT AND SOCIAL FUNCTIONING

The studies that have looked at the psychological adjustment and social functioning of children have found no differences in outcomes between the children of lesbian and gay parents and children of heterosexual ones. In fact, as I explain in this section, the studies' findings on these questions are so uniform and consistent that they render efforts to defend same-sex marriage bans on the basis of concerns about children's psychological adjustment and social functioning irrational (and therefore unconstitutional) because they lack a defensible factual foundation.

In this section I also respond to critics who contend that the social science studies on the children of lesbian and gay parents are unreliable because they are methodologically flawed. In addition, I explain why a recent study by the sociologist Mark Regnerus, which purports to show an association between having a lesbian or gay parent and negative child outcomes, should not be given any weight by policymakers or courts.[16]

The Early Studies: Children of Dissolved Heterosexual Marriages

Almost all of the children who were raised by out-of-the-closet LGBT individuals in the 1970s and 1980s were raised by lesbian mothers following the dissolution of their different-sex marriages with the children's fathers. Not surprisingly, these were the families that social scientists first studied in seeking to determine the existence of possible associations between parental sexual orientation and child outcomes. Given the nature of the child population in question, it made sense for the control groups in the early studies to consist of children raised by divorced heterosexual mothers. In this way, the studies controlled for the effects of familial dissolution on child outcomes.

Although some of the early studies looked at questions of gender role development and sexual orientation, their main focus was on the children's psychological development, behavioral adjustment, and peer relations. The studies gathered data by interviewing parents and children (the interviewers usually did not know the sexual orientation of the parents) and having them fill out questionnaires. The researchers in these early studies did not find significant differences in the rates of emotional problems, degree of self-esteem, or strength of peer relations between the children of lesbian mothers and children of heterosexual mothers.[17]

Given the unavailability of randomly selected samples of lesbian mothers, early researchers identified lesbian-headed households through convenience sampling, by means that included word of mouth, placing advertisements in lesbian/gay publications, and contacting lesbian and gay organizations and community groups. When the issue of same-sex marriage first began to be debated several years later, opponents of marriage equality repeatedly urged courts and policymakers to disregard the findings of the early studies, as well as other convenience sample studies conducted later, because they were not based on random population samples. These critics vigorously complained that the nature of the samples precluded the reaching of definitive conclusions about how children were doing in families headed by lesbians mothers who did not participate in the studies. Some judges relied on this criticism to raise doubts about the studies' validity, doubts that in their view were sufficient to justify upholding the constitutionality of same-sex marriage bans (and of parenting restrictions on lesbians and gay men).[18]

There is an entirely valid reason for the limited availability of random samples of lesbian and gay parents: these parents, along with their children, are vulnerable to discrimination and stigmatization. It might be possible, in a society in which there are no legal or other consequences to being identified as lesbian or gay, to easily collect data on children of randomly selected lesbian and gay parents. But since the United States is not such a society, social scientists must do the best they can with the limitations they confront.

Social scientists routinely use convenience samples to identify study subjects, especially when there is limited or no availability of random samples. As the law professor Michael Wald has noted, the use of convenience samples is "common in virtually all research related to controversial family law policies, such as the desirability of transracial adoptions, fathers as parents, the desirability of joint custody, the conditions under which a custodial parent should be allowed to relocate to a home distant from a noncustodial parent, or the impact of grandparent visitation."[19] Indeed, it bears reemphasizing here that much of the literature on the parenting styles of mothers and fathers that those who rely on family optimality claims to defend same-sex marriage bans frequently cite is based on the *same* types of convenience samples that the same opponents (conveniently) find unreliable in assessing the attributes of lesbian and gay parents.

It is incorrect to dismiss the findings of the early studies of children of lesbian mothers because they were based on convenience samples. The results of studies based on nonrandom samples can contribute to a better understanding of the subject matter, especially when the findings are consistent with those of other studies. The results of the early studies were entirely consistent with those of later studies, some of which were based on random population samples.

The Study of Children of Planned Lesbian Families

Beginning around the mid-1980s, a growing number of lesbian women started coming out of the closet *before* having children. Many of these women conceived children through donor insemination and then proceeded to raise their children, either by themselves or with female partners, without fathers from birth. As the number of these so-called planned lesbian families grew, social scientists turned their attention to them.

Researchers became particularly interested in conducting studies comparing children in two-mother households with children raised by their mothers and fathers. These studies allowed for an exploration of whether the presence of male parents in the latter households was associated with differences in the children's psychological adjustment and social functioning. These are the studies that compare two-parent households—*not* the "married versus single parents" studies that opponents of marriage equality rely on to defend same-sex marriage bans on family optimality grounds. It is these studies that investigate the possibility of associations between family structure and child outcomes that are based on the parents' *gender* rather than *number*.

Starting in the mid-1990s, studies began appearing in peer review journals comparing the psychological adjustment and social functioning of children of planned lesbian families with those of heterosexual parents. These studies included comparisons of children of two-parent lesbian households with those of two-parent heterosexual ones. (Some of the studies also compared lesbian-parent households with single-mother heterosexual ones.) *None* of the studies found that the children of lesbian mothers had greater emotional, behavioral, self-esteem, school performance, or peer relations problems or difficulties than the children of heterosexual parents.[20]

Several of these studies sought to address the sampling concerns raised by critics. One of the concerns about convenience samples in this area is the selection problem, that is, the possibility that lesbian parents who volunteer for the studies might have children who are doing better than those who do not. However, the growth in the number of lesbians who were becoming parents through donor insemination allowed researchers to rely on more systematic sampling methods. One group of Dutch researchers, for example, focused on a consecutive sample of all thirty lesbian mother families that used the services of a fertility clinic at a Dutch hospital to conceive children between 1986 and 1991.[21] Similarly, another team of researchers studied lesbian mothers who used a California sperm bank to conceive children prior to 1990.[22] This type of sampling, which targeted for study all of the lesbian mothers who used the services of a particular clinic or sperm bank during a particular period of time, made it less likely that the findings would be skewed by selection bias.

Researchers also sought to address the possibility of volunteer bias by gathering information not only from the parents, but also from third parties such as the children's teachers and caregivers.[23] Finally, researchers who conducted an important longitudinal study of lesbian mothers and their children sought to address the potential for volunteer bias by identifying study subjects *before* they had children.[24]

More Recent Studies: Random Sampling

The first study of children of lesbian mothers based on a sample gathered from a large population segment was conducted in the United Kingdom in the 1990s. Susan Golombok and a team of British researchers used data from the Avon Longitudinal Study of Parents and Children (ALSPAC) to identify lesbian mothers.[25] This study consisted of almost fourteen thousand mothers and their children who were expecting babies between April 1, 1991, and December 31, 1992, in an area of southwest England. Golombok and her team studied the children in thirty-nine lesbian-mother families and compared them to two control groups (also drawn from the ALSPAC), one consisting of seventy-four two-parent heterosexual families and the other of sixty families headed by single heterosexual mothers. The researchers, after interviewing the parents and the children's teachers, found "that children reared by lesbian mothers appear to be functioning well and do not experience negative psychological consequences arising from the nature of their family environment."[26]

Since then, several studies have been published in peer review journals using representative samples of lesbians and gay men. For example, Jennifer Wainwright and a team of researchers used a large national sample of American adolescents called the National Longitudinal Study of Adolescent Health (Add Health).[27] Through the Add Health dataset, Wainwright and her team identified forty-four adolescents raised in households headed by two women. The researchers then matched each of them with another adolescent from the Add Health database raised by opposite-sex parents using criteria such as sex, age, ethnic background, family income, and parent's educational attainment.

The researchers did not find any differences in psychological adjustment, as reflected in depressive symptoms, anxiety, and self-esteem, between the two groups of adolescents. They also found no differences in school functioning as measured by the students' grade point averages. They did find, however, that family type was associated with the degree to which adolescents felt connected to their schools, with adolescents raised by same-sex parents showing a higher degree of school connectedness (that is, they felt safer and more comfortable at school) than adolescents raised by different-sex couples.

Using the same data, Wainwright and Charlotte Patterson published two additional articles. In the first, they reported finding no differences in the rates of delinquency, victimization, and substance use among adolescent children of lesbian mothers compared to children of heterosexual parents.[28] In the second article, they shared findings that showed no association between parental sexual orientation and the quality of adolescents' peer relations.[29] A British study based on data collected from a large group of adolescents also found no differences in victimization by peers or in rates of depression and anxiety between children of lesbian-mother couples and those of different-sex couples.[30]

Two other studies have used representative population samples to assess the academic performance of children of lesbians and gay men. In one of the studies, the Stanford sociologist Michael Rosenfeld used data from the 2000 census to identify over two thousand children raised by lesbian couples and over fourteen hundred children raised by gay male couples.[31] Rosenfeld compared these children's rates of "grade retention"—the extent to which they had to repeat grades—with the grade retention rates of children of married heterosexual couples. After accounting for socioeconomic status (married heterosexual households had higher incomes than lesbian and gay ones), Rosenfeld found no differences in the rates of grade retention.

Another study of academic performance based on a random sample was published by Daniel Potter using data collected from over twenty thousand children as part of the Early Childhood Longitudinal Study–Kindergarten Cohort (ELCS–K).[32] Out of all the children in the ELCS–K, 158 were identified as living in households led by same-sex couples, both female and male.

Potter initially found that the math scores of children of same-sex couples were lower than those of children raised by married heterosexuals. But when he accounted for the number of family transitions (i.e., the number of changes in a child's family structure), there were no differences in the math assessment scores of children of different-sex couples compared to those of same-sex ones. This meant that the lower scores found among children raised by same-sex couples were associated with the number of changes in the children's family structures and not with parental sexual orientation.

The findings of studies that have relied on large numbers of randomly selected subjects are entirely consistent with those that have used small and nonrandom samples. Indeed, the crucial point is that, *regardless of the sampling procedures used*, the empirical evidence, uniformly and consistently, shows no association between parental sexual orientation and children's psychological adjustment and social functioning.

The Age of the Children

In addition to raising questions about the sampling methods used in the studies of children of lesbian and gay parents, critics have also claimed that because studies have been largely limited to young children, insufficient empirical information exists to determine the role that parental sexual orientation may play in the long-term well-being of children. Some judges have relied on this criticism to raise doubts about the validity of the studies, doubts that in their view are sufficient to justify upholding the constitutionality of same-sex marriage bans (and of parenting restrictions on lesbians and gay men).[33]

It should not strike anyone as particularly surprising that the children in the early studies on lesbian and gay parenting were relatively young. When researchers, for example, turned their attention to planned lesbian families shortly after those families were first formed, the children were still quite young. As the years progressed, the children in these families grew older, making it possible to study adolescents and young adults. One study from 1995, for example, focused on young adult children of lesbian mothers.[34] In

1999, a study was published on children aged eleven to eighteen, followed three years later by another on children between seven and seventeen.[35] In 2004, and then again in 2006 and 2008, researchers published studies of teenage children of lesbian mothers identified through Add Health.[36] In 2008 and 2009, two additional studies of adolescents were published, one of British youth and the other of American teenagers adopted by lesbian or gay male parents when they were young.[37] Since 2010, researchers have published several studies of older children, including one of seventeen-year-olds whose lesbian mothers were part of the National Longitudinal Lesbian Family Study (NLLFS) and another of young adults who were part of a British longitudinal study.[38] It is simply incorrect to suggest, therefore, that the social science evidence on the children of lesbian and gay parents has focused almost exclusively on young children.

A related contention some courts have raised in critiquing the social science literature is that parenting by lesbians and gay men is a new phenomenon and that, as a result, not enough time has elapsed to adequately study its impact on children. For example, the U.S. Court of Appeals for the Eleventh Circuit has claimed that "scientific attempts to study homosexual parenting in general are still in their nascent stages."[39] The New York Court of Appeals has concluded that "there has not been enough time to study the long-term results of…child-rearing" by lesbians and gay men.[40] During the 2013 oral arguments before the Supreme Court in the California Proposition 8 case, Justice Samuel Alito made a similar point when he noted that cell phones and the Internet have been around longer than same-sex marriages and that therefore not enough time has gone by to allow adequate study of their effects.

The judges who have raised these concerns have not provided us with the amount of time—perhaps fifty years? perhaps a century?—that would have to pass before they would consider it appropriate to trust the studies' findings. It is a fact, however, that parenting by openly lesbian and gay individuals has been occurring for at least four decades. It is also a fact that social scientists began studying such parenting in the 1980s, with every ensuing decade bringing additional studies. Some of those studies have been longitudinal, that is, they have followed the same children over the course of several years.[41] And it has been possible to study the children of lesbians and gay men into adolescence and adulthood. It is simply not persuasive to claim, therefore, that the "recent" advent of lesbian and gay parenting *by itself* provides a sufficient reason— *regardless* of what the empirical studies actually show—to justify prohibiting same-sex couples from marrying.

Studies of Adoptive Parents and Gay Fathers

Until a few years ago, almost all of the studies examining the psychological adjustment and social functioning of children raised by sexual-minority parents focused on the biological children of lesbian mothers. More recently, however, researchers have begun conducting a growing number of studies that look at adopted families headed by both lesbians and gay men.

Two of those studies were led by Stephen Erich. In the first, he and a team of researchers assessed sixty-eight young adopted children raised in twenty-four lesbian and twenty-three gay male households. After collecting data through parental questionnaires, the researchers found that "the overwhelming majority of the adopted children of these gay and/or lesbian parents are not exhibiting any significant behavioral problems."[42] In the second study, Erich and another team compared 176 adolescents raised by 127 heterosexual adoptive parents to 34 adolescents raised by 27 lesbian or gay male parents. In assessing the questionnaires the adolescents completed, the researchers found no differences in their attachments to parents or to peers. The researchers also found no differences in "adolescent life satisfaction [and] adolescent social desirability score[s]."[43]

Rachel Farr and a team of researchers also published a study comparing children adopted by fifty-six same-sex couples (both male and female) to those adopted by fifty different-sex parents. This study, which included interviews of parents, children, teachers, and outside caregivers, found that child behavioral problems were associated with the degree of stress felt by the parents, but not with parental sexual orientation.[44] A follow-up analysis of the data found that positive child behavior was associated with supportive coparenting and that child conduct problems were associated with strained and competitive coparenting. Parental sexual orientation, however, was not associated with child outcomes.[45]

Another study of adopted children, led by Justin Lavner, focused on high-risk children in Los Angeles County who transitioned from the foster care system to adoptive homes. (The children's high-risk background was reflected in the fact that, for example, 89 percent were born with symptoms associated with exposure to illegal drugs during gestation.) Sixty of the participating families were headed by heterosexuals, fifteen by gay men, and seven by lesbians. Most of the adoptive parents (68 percent) were either married or living with a domestic partner. Lavner and his team of researchers assessed the children's cognitive development and levels of behavioral problems at two months, one year, and two years after placement, through parental questionnaires and interviews and tests of the children. They found no significant differences in cognitive development or behavioral problems, despite the fact "that the children adopted by gay and lesbian parents had significantly higher levels of background risk and were more likely to be of a different ethnicity than their adoptive parents compared with children in heterosexual households."[46]

In another study, Abbie Goldberg and JuliAnna Smith compared adjustment outcomes—as reported by the parents—among toddlers raised by forty female same-sex, thirty-five male same-sex, and forty-five different-sex adoptive parents. The researchers found that the children's psychological adjustment problems were associated with lack of parental preparation for adoption, parental depressive symptoms, and parental relationship conflict. The study, however, did not find any association between parental sexual orientation and the children's psychological adjustment.[47]

The adoption studies are significant because their findings are consistent with those of the more numerous studies of biological children of lesbian mothers. The former studies suggest that the biological link between lesbian mothers and their children does not explain the latter studies' findings of no association between parental sexual orientation and children's psychological adjustment and social functioning. Regardless of whether parents are related to their children via biology or adoption, no association

has been found between parental sexual orientation and psychological or social outcomes among children.

It is also significant that the adopted child studies have included children of gay
fathers. These studies join a handful of others—including Rosenfeld and Potter's school
performance studies based on representative samples—that have looked at children of
gay fathers. The fact that the small but growing number of studies on such children
are consistent with the larger number of studies that have found no differences in the
psychological adjustment and social functioning of children of lesbian mothers, compared to those of heterosexual parents, also suggests that neither sexual orientation nor
gender is associated with children's psychological and social outcomes. Regardless of
whether the parents are men or women, or biological or adoptive, the studies show no
association between parental sexual orientation and children's psychological adjustment and social functioning. A possible exception is a study published in 2012 by the
University of Texas sociologist Mark Regnerus.

The Regnerus Study

The participants in Regnerus's study were recruited randomly by a research firm that
identified them through telephone and mail surveys. Participants answered questionnaires via the Internet. According to Regnerus, of the three thousand young adults
(between the ages of eighteen and thirty-nine) who participated in his study, 175 had
lesbian mothers and 73 had gay fathers.

After comparing the answers given by adult children raised by individuals identified in the study as lesbian or gay to those raised from birth by married heterosexuals,
Regnerus found several differences. The adult children of lesbian mothers, for example, reported higher levels of unemployment, depression, cigarette smoking, mari-
juana use, and criminal arrests and a lower level of educational attainment than did
the adult children of married heterosexual parents. Although there were fewer differences between the latter and the young adult children of gay fathers, Regnerus found
that those with gay fathers reported, for example, higher levels of depression, cigarette
smoking, and criminal arrests.[48]

Not surprisingly, critics of parenting by lesbians and gay men were quick to rely
on the Regnerus study to question the broad consensus in the social science literature
that parental sexual orientation is not associated with the well-being of children. The
Regnerus study, however, *does not show an association between parental sexual orientation and child outcomes because it relies on an unreasonably broad characterization of
who is a "lesbian mother" or a "gay father."* The study attempted to identify lesbian and
gay parents by asking adult children whether their parents had a same-sex relationship between the time they were born until they turned eighteen (or whenever they
left home). Rather than inquiring whether the respondents considered their parents
to be lesbian or gay, or whether the parents self-identified as such, Regnerus simply
asked the children whether their parents had ever been in a same-sex relationship. If
a respondent's answer to that question was yes, then Regnerus identified the parent in
question as either a lesbian mother or a gay father.

Although it is possible to reasonably disagree about how best to define and deter-mine individuals' sexual orientation, it is unreasonable to posit that participation in *one* same-sex relationship (as reported by a nonparticipant in that relationship) over the course of eighteen years (or more), *regardless of the relationship's duration or level of commitment*, is enough to characterize the individual in question as lesbian or gay. Indeed, the study's unreasonably broad criteria for determining who is a "lesbian mother" or a "gay father" meant that the vast majority of the parents identified as such did not live with a partner of the same sex for any extended period of time while rais-ing the respondent children.[49]

Less than a quarter (23 percent) of the respondents in Regnerus's study who reported that their mothers had participated in a same-sex relationship had lived with both their mother and her female partner for at least three years. In addition, *close to half* (43 percent) of the respondents who reported that their mothers had participated in a same-sex relationship either *had never lived* with their mothers and a female partner *or had done so for a period of less than four months* before reaching the age of eighteen.[50]

Furthermore, *almost two-thirds* (58 percent) of the respondents who reported that their fathers had had a same-sex relationship had not lived with their fathers *at all* during the course of that relationship. In addition, *only one or two* (2 percent) of the seventy-three respondents who claimed that their fathers had participated in a same-sex relationship had lived with their father and a male partner for at least three years. And less than a quarter (23 percent) of the respondents reported living with their father and a male partner for more than four months.[51]

The first fatal flaw in Regnerus's study, then, is the nonsensical way it identified lesbian mothers and gay fathers. The second flaw is that it failed to control for the effects of family disruption on children. As one commentator has explained, because the sample of children of "lesbian mothers" in Regnerus's study was "comprised of young adults who experienced multiple family forms and transitions, it is impossible to isolate the effects of living with a lesbian mother from experiencing divorce, remar-riage, or living with a single parent."[52]

It is widely recognized that children raised in intact two-parent households from a young age do better than children who experience family instability.[53] The Regnerus study does nothing more than reflect the well-understood point that family insta-bility is associated with negative outcomes in children. It is not at all surprising, for example, that the children of "lesbian mothers" (as defined in the Regnerus study) had worse outcomes than the children raised in intact heterosexual households, given that (1) nearly half of the children of women identified as "lesbian mothers" reported that their biological parents had once been married, but no longer were; (2) 58 per-cent of these children reported that their mothers had left the household during their childhood; and (3) about 14 percent of them reported spending time in the foster care system.

The question raised by the efforts to restrict the marital and parental rights of les-bians and gay men is not whether familial instability is associated with negative child outcomes (it clearly is). The question is instead whether parental sexual orientation is associated with those outcomes. The Regnerus study fails to address that crucial issue, because most of the adult children of "lesbian mothers" or "gay fathers" who participated in the research—unlike the children raised by heterosexual parents who served as comparators—were raised in households that experienced significant familial disruptions. Regnerus, in effect, stacked the deck by comparing children raised in stable and intact heterosexual households with children raised by "lesbian mothers" and "gay fathers" who experienced family disruption and instability. The design of this study was as flawed as would be a study that set out to investigate possible associations between parental sexual orientation and child outcomes by comparing children raised by *married* same-sex couples since birth to children raised by divorced and remarried heterosexuals. Critics of parenting by lesbians and gay men would quickly—and appropriately—dismiss the relevance of such a study because it would conflate parental sexual orientation with familial dislocation and transitions.

Policymakers and courts should therefore reject efforts by conservative advocates to rely on the Regnerus study to undermine the broad consensus among social scientists that parental sexual orientation is not associated with the well-being of children. Aside from the deeply flawed Regnerus study, social scientists have found little evidence that parental sexual orientation is associated with negative child outcomes related to psychological adjustment and social functioning. Indeed, the evidence showing that parental sexual orientation is not associated with the psychological adjustment and social functioning of children has been remarkably consistent through the decades. Studies going back thirty years have found no differences between the children of lesbian and gay parents and children of heterosexuals in a broad array of measures, including emotional adjustment, behavioral problems, cognitive functioning, anxiety or depression, self-esteem, delinquency and substance abuse, attachment to parents, victimization, social competence, peer relations, and school performance. The remarkable degree of consistency in the empirical findings has led several professional organizations, including the American Psychological Association and the American Academy of Pediatrics, to issue reports concluding that the social science evidence does not support the contention that children are harmed by their parents' same-sex sexual orientation.[54]

Therefore, the claim that same-sex marriage bans are justified by differences in the psychological adjustment and social functioning of the children of lesbians and gay men compared to those of children of heterosexuals has no empirical basis of fact. The absence of a factual foundation means that efforts to justify the differential treatment of lesbians and gay men in matters related to marriage and parenting on the basis of the psychological adjustment and social functioning of their children does not pass constitutional muster, even under the highly deferential rational basis test.

THE GENDER ROLE DEVELOPMENT OF CHILDREN

The researchers who have studied the children of lesbians and gay men have not limited themselves to investigating their psychological adjustment and social functioning. They have also looked at other matters, including whether parental sexual orientation is associated with children's gender role development. These studies have sought to determine the extent to which the children of lesbians and gay men have preferences and engage in activities that conform to what has traditionally been expected of children based on their gender.

It is important as an initial matter to distinguish gender *identity* development from gender *role* development. A handful of studies have looked at the extent to which the sons and daughters of lesbian mothers are comfortable with their respective male and female identities. The researchers have failed to find disparities between these children's biological sex and the sex with which they identify.[55] A significantly larger number of studies have looked into the issue addressed here, that is, whether the gender attitudes and interests of the children of lesbian and gay parents differ from those of heterosexual parents. This second issue has been of most interest to researchers because, as one developmental psychology article notes, "it is well established within the psychological literature that [while] gender identity [is] relatively fixed, [gender] attitudes are more open to parental influence and change."[56] At the same time, however, social scientists generally agree that parents are only one source of gender influence and that peers, teachers, and the media also play important roles.[57]

In this section, I summarize the social science studies that have looked into the gender role development of children raised in lesbian and gay households. I then assess that empirical evidence from the perspective of the rational basis test and conclude that there is a "conceivable state of facts" under which there may be an association between parental sexual orientation and the gender attitudes and interests of children. In particular, a minority of studies suggest that the daughters of lesbian mothers have gender preferences and engage in activities that are less consistent with traditional gender expectations when compared to the daughters of heterosexual parents.

I also argue, however, that the goal of encouraging children to form attitudes and pursue interests that are consistent with what has traditionally been expected of them depending on their gender does not constitute a legitimate state interest. As a result, the state cannot constitutionally justify same-sex marriage bans on the basis of a factually conceivable association between parental sexual orientation and the gender attitudes and interests of children.

Before proceeding, it is important to emphasize that I am not suggesting that the social science evidence shows an association between parental sexual orientation and the gender role development of children. More studies will have to be conducted before such an association can be claimed to exist. My point is simply that the suggestion of possible differences in gender role development between the children of lesbian and gay parents and children of heterosexual parents reported in some of the studies is sufficient to meet the easy-to-satisfy factual component of the rational basis test, which only requires a *conceivable* basis of fact to support the governmental policy in question.

I recognize that my claim regarding indications of possible differences in gender role development may make some supporters of LGBT rights uncomfortable, given that their opponents have shown a marked willingness through the decades to pounce on any suggestion of differences between the children of lesbian and gay parents and children of straight parents to justify the unequal treatment of sexual minorities in matters related to marriage and parenting. Although I understand this concern, it seems to me that it is better to acknowledge the possibility of difference and then to proceed to the more important question: whether those differences, even if they can be shown conclusively to exist, should matter in the setting of policy. Constitutional principles prohibit the government from setting policy on the basis of differences in the gender role development of the children of lesbians and gay men compared to children of heterosexuals. Thus, the possibility of difference in this area cannot be used to justify the differential treatment of sexual minorities.

The Studies

Researchers who have looked at the gender interests and attitudes of the children of lesbians and gay men have investigated whether these children differ from the children of heterosexuals in matters such as play, dress, and career preferences. Three studies published in the early 1980s found no differences in these preferences between the children of lesbian mothers and children of heterosexual parents.[58] A fourth study, published in 1986, replicated those findings as to the boys of lesbian mothers. However, that study also found that the daughters of lesbian mothers were "less traditionally feminine" in their dress choices and in their preferred school and play activities. In addition, the girls raised by lesbian mothers expressed greater interest in careers traditionally dominated by men (such as law, medicine, and engineering) than did the daughters of straight mothers.[59]

Largely on the basis of the findings of the 1986 study, the sociologists Judith Stacey and Timothy Biblarz published an article in the *American Sociological Review* in 2001 that received an immense amount of attention, in part because it contended that researchers were not being sufficiently open to the possibility that parental sexual orientation might influence the gender attitudes and interests of children.[60] (The article also suggested that the same-sex sexual orientation of lesbian mothers might influence the sexual orientation of their children, in particular their daughters.) In fact, a handful of studies published since 1986 suggest that there may be gender-related differences between the children of lesbians and gay men and children of heterosexual parents.

One of those studies, led by Abbie Goldberg and published in 2012, looked at the gender preferences of children raised in adoptive heterosexual families, comparing them to those of children adopted by lesbians and by gay men. The researchers, with the assistance of adoption agencies across the country, identified 126 adoptive families (48 headed by heterosexual couples, 44 by lesbian couples, and 34 by gay male couples) with similar incomes, education levels, and racial profiles.

Goldberg and her team of researchers found that the differences in gender-based play preferences between the boys and girls of heterosexual couples were greater than the differences between the boys and girls in the other two sets of families. In other words, when the researchers compared the children's play preferences "*between genders* (boy versus girl) by family type," they found that the children of heterosexual parents showed a greater divide in their play preferences based on their gender than did children of lesbian and gay parents. The researchers also found that the play preferences of the boys of lesbian mothers were less traditionally masculine compared to those of the boys of gay fathers and of heterosexual parents. (There was, however, no difference in the play-related femininity rating of the girls of gay fathers when compared to that of girls in the other two sets of families.)[61]

A few years earlier, Dutch researchers published a study that, while finding no differences in "gender typicality, gender contentedness [or gender-related] pressure from peers" between the children of lesbian-couple mothers and children of heterosexual two-parent families, did find that the children of lesbian mothers were less likely to think that their gender was superior to the other and reported less parental pressure to conform to gender stereotypes.[62]

Most studies, however, have found no association between parental sexual orientation and the gender role development of children. In fact, since Stacey and Biblarz published their widely discussed article in 2001, five different studies that have looked at the extent to which the children of lesbian mothers evince attitudes and behaviors that are typically male or female, have found no differences associated with parental sexual orientation.[63]

A clear majority of the studies dating back to the early 1980s, therefore, have concluded that having lesbian or gay parents is not associated with gender-related differences in children. Nonetheless, the first issue under the rational basis test is not whether there is conclusive evidence of difference; instead, the issue is whether there is *any* conceivable basis of fact to support the claim of possible differences between the children of lesbians and gay men and children of heterosexual parents. Although there have been only a handful of studies suggesting such an association—in contrast to the greater number suggesting the opposite—it seems to me that their findings constitute sufficient evidence of possible differences to meet the easy-to-satisfy factual component of the rational basis test.

The fact, however, that some of the empirical literature suggests possible differences between the children of lesbian and gay parents and children of heterosexual parents on some measures does not end the constitutional inquiry. The rational basis test also requires that the differences in question be rationally related to the attainment of a legitimate state interest.

Opponents of marriage equality, therefore, cannot simply argue that the possible differences in the gender role development of the children of lesbians and gay men are enough to justify same-sex marriage bans. Instead, under the rational basis test, they must also contend that the differences in question have some connection to the promotion of a legitimate state interest. In order to do so, marriage equality opponents would have to claim that the government has the authority to set policies with the view of encouraging children to behave in gender-typical ways. However, this would leave the government in the constitutionally untenable position of contending that the promotion of specific gender attitudes and interests is a legitimate state interest.

Promotion of Gender Interests and Attitudes as a State Interest

The Supreme Court has left little doubt that it is constitutionally impermissible for the government to set policy with the objective of encouraging individuals to pursue particular priorities and preferences depending on their gender. The first time the Court so held was in its 1975 ruling in *Weinberger v. Wiesenfeld*. In that case, the plaintiff's wife died while giving birth to the couple's son. The deceased, who had worked for years as a teacher, had been the family's principal source of income. After his wife's death, the plaintiff applied for a "mother's insurance benefit" under the Social Security Act. According to the relevant statutory provision, a widow with children was entitled to a survivor benefit based on the earnings of her deceased husband. The provision did not afford the same benefit to surviving widowers, leading social security officials to reject the plaintiff's benefit application. He then sued the government arguing that the provision was unconstitutional because it denied him (and all other similarly situated men) equal protection under the Fifth Amendment.

The government contended that the statutory provision did not violate the Constitution because it was a benign measure "reasonably designed to compensate women beneficiaries as a group for the economic difficulties which still confront women who seek to support themselves and their families." But after reviewing the measure's legislative history, the Court determined that its purpose was instead to encourage widows to stay at home caring for their minor children rather than join the workforce. As the Court put it, Congress enacted the provision "because it believed that [women with minor children] should not be required to work."[64]

The Court made clear that the stereotypical view that women should stay at home caring for children while men should work outside the home was an impermissible basis for a law. The Court explained that even if "a man is working while there is a wife at home, [that] does not mean that he would, or should be required to, continue to work if his wife dies." The justices added that "it is no less important for a child to be cared for by its sole surviving parent when that parent is male rather than female."[65]

Since *Wiesenfeld*, the Court has repeatedly held that the government cannot adopt policies with the goal of encouraging different preferences and choices among individuals depending on whether they are men or women. Less than a month after *Wiesenfeld*, the Court, in *Stanton v. Stanton*, addressed the constitutionality of a Utah statute that required parents to support their sons until they reached the age of twenty-one, but only support their daughters until they turned eighteen. The state supreme court had upheld the provision on the basis of the reasonableness of "old notions" such as (1) that men are expected to support their family through work and therefore need more education than women, which in turn means that male offspring need to be supported longer by their parents; (2) that "girls tend generally to mature physically, emotionally and mentally before boys"; and (3) that women "generally tend to marry earlier."[66]

The U.S. Supreme Court rejected the state court's reasoning, explaining that "no longer is the female destined solely for the home and the rearing of the family, and only the male for the marketplace and the world of ideas." The Court added that "to distinguish between [men and women] on educational grounds is to be self-serving: if the female is not to be supported so long as the male, she hardly can be expected to attend school as long as he does, and bringing her education to an end earlier coincides with the role-typing society has long imposed."[67]

The same reasoning is evident in a 1978 ruling in which the Court struck down an Alabama statute rendering husbands, but not wives, liable for child support following a divorce. The government claimed that its statute "effectively announc[ed] the State's preference for an allocation of family responsibilities under which the wife plays a dependent role" and that it was "seeking... the reinforcement of that model among the State's citizens." But the justices held that "this purpose cannot sustain the statute, and that, therefore, if it is to survive constitutional attack,... it must be validated on some other basis."[68]

A few years later, the Court dealt with a Mississippi law that prohibited men from enrolling in a state-supported nursing school. The Court, in striking down the statute, explained that the

> policy of excluding males from admission to the School of Nursing tends to per-
> petuate the stereotyped view of nursing as an exclusively woman's job. By assur-
> ing that Mississippi allots more openings in its state-supported nursing schools to
> women than it does to men, [the school's] admissions policy lends credibility to
> the old view that women, not men, should become nurses, and makes the assump-
> tion that nursing is a field for women a self-fulfilling prophecy.[69]

A more recent elaboration of the same principles can be found in *United States v. Virginia*. At issue in that case was the Virginia Military Institute's policy of admitting only male students. The state argued that women were incapable of benefiting from the Institute's "adversative" method of instruction, which was characterized by "physical rigor, mental stress, absolute equality of treatment, absence of privacy, minute regula-tion of behavior, and indoctrination in desirable values." The government claimed that there were important "psychological and sociological differences" between men and women that made the application of the adversative educational method to women less beneficial and effective. But the Court had little patience with such essentialized understandings of gender differences, noting that "state actors controlling gates to opportunity... may not exclude qualified individuals based on fixed notions concern-ing the roles and abilities of males and females."[70]

It is clear, therefore, that it is constitutionally impermissible for the government to craft policies based on its views regarding which interests and preferences individuals should pursue depending on their gender. Thus, even if it could be shown conclusively that the sexual orientation of parents was associated with differences in their children's gender role development, those who defend same-sex marriage bans could not rely on that factual basis to justify their constitutionality.

It may be objected that the gender discrimination cases of the U.S. Supreme Court that I have explored here involved the application of heightened scrutiny—because the statutes and policies in question contained explicit gender classifications—and are therefore not relevant to the issue that I am addressing in this chapter: the interplay between the empirical literature on lesbian and gay parenting and the application of the highly deferential rational basis test. Although the Court's review of the relation-ship between the government's means and its ends in the gender cases has undoubtedly been more searching than it would have been had it applied the rational basis test, that fact does not undermine my point that the government's promotion of gender-based attitudes and interests among individuals can never constitute a legitimate state interest as is required by the rational basis standard. Indeed, the Court has expressed most of its concerns about state-promoted gender stereotyping when it has analyzed the appropriateness of the government's objectives, not when it has assessed the link between those objectives and the means chosen by the state to achieve them.[71]

The Court has never suggested that the promotion of what the government considers proper gender-based preferences and behaviors would be a legitimate interest under the rational basis test. In fact, the opposite is the case. While discussing the state's stereotypical views regarding the different interests and choices of men and women in *Stanton*, the Court noted that it "perceive[d] nothing rational in the distinction drawn by" the statute in requiring parents to support their sons for more years than their daughters. The Court made clear that the statute was unconstitutional "under any test—compelling state interest, or rational basis, or something in between."[72]

Opponents of marriage equality, therefore, cannot simply argue that the possible differences between the gender attitudes and interests of the children of lesbians and gay men and those of the children of heterosexual parents, as suggested by a handful of social science studies, are sufficient to justify same-sex marriage bans. Instead, they must contend that the differences in question have some connection to the promotion of a legitimate state interest. In order to do so, opponents would have to claim that the government has the authority to set policies with the view of encouraging children to behave in gender-typical ways. This position is constitutionally untenable because the promotion of specific gender-based preferences and priorities among individuals can never constitute a proper governmental objective.

THE SEXUAL ORIENTATION OF CHILDREN

Of the three broad areas investigated by social scientists who have studied the children of lesbians and gay men (psychological adjustment and social functioning, gender role development, and sexual orientation), that of sexual orientation is likely fraught with the greatest uncertainty. One reason for this uncertainty is the absence of a consensus among experts on how to determine an individual's sexual orientation. It has been suggested, for example, that whether someone is lesbian or gay depends on the presence of one or more of several factors, including same-sex sexual attraction, same-sex sexual behavior, and self-identification as lesbian or gay.[73] It has also been suggested, however, that while these measures "capture related dimensions of sexual orientation[,] ... none of the[m] ... completely addresses the concept."[74]

In addition, little consensus exists among experts on the reasons why different individuals develop different sexual orientations. One possible determinant of sexual orientation may be genetics. Some studies of siblings have found that identical twins are more likely to have the same sexual orientation than fraternal ones.[75] There are also some studies suggesting that hormonal factors in a mother's womb may play a role in the determination of sexual orientation. Some studies, for example, have found an association between higher levels of the hormone androgen in mothers and a greater degree of same-sex sexual attraction among their offspring.[76]

It has also been suggested that environmental factors may play a role in the determination of sexual orientation. For a good part of the twentieth century, for example, many experts adhered to a Freudian psychoanalytic theory of sexuality that traced homosexuality to difficult relationships with parents. Such a view is rarely defended these days, in part because there is little empirical support for it.

There is little certainty, then, about the factors that account for different sexual orientations in different individuals. As the American Psychological Association notes, "although much research has examined the possible genetic, hormonal, developmental, social, and cultural influences on sexual orientation, no findings have emerged that permit scientists to conclude that sexual orientation is determined by any particular factor or factors. Many think that nature and nurture both play complex roles."[77]

Despite the difficulties that inhere both in defining sexual orientation and in accounting for why different individuals develop different sexualities, social scientists have attempted to determine whether there is an association between the sexual orientation of lesbian and gay parents and that of their children. A majority of these studies have not found such an association. Some studies, however, suggest that the daughters of lesbian mothers might be more likely to participate in same-sex sexual relationships than the daughters of heterosexual parents. However, as I explain at the end of this chapter, even if it could be shown conclusively that the sexual orientation of parents is associated with their children's sexual orientation, the government could not constitutionally rely on that factual basis to defend same-sex marriage bans.

The two caveats noted at the beginning of the previous section also apply here. First, I want to make it clear that I am not suggesting that the social science evidence shows an association between parents' and children's sexual orientation. More studies will have to be conducted before such an association can be claimed to exist. My point is simply that the suggestion of difference between the children of lesbian and gay parents and children of heterosexual ones in matters related to sexuality reported in some of the studies is enough to meet the easy-to-satisfy factual component of the rational basis test, which only requires that there be a *conceivable* basis of fact to support the governmental policy in question.

Second, I fully recognize that my claim regarding the existence of possible differences in sexual orientation may make some supporters of LGBT rights uncomfortable, given that their opponents have consistently shown a marked willingness to pounce on any suggestion of differences between the children of lesbian and gay parents and children of straight parents to justify the unequal treatment of sexual minorities in matters related to marriage and parenting. Once again, it seems to me that the better course is to acknowledge the possibility of difference and then proceed to the more important question: whether such differences, even if they can be shown conclusively to exist, should matter in the setting of policy. It seems clear that, as with the question of gender role development, constitutional principles prohibit the government from setting policy on the basis of possible differences in the sexual orientation of the children of lesbians and gay men. Thus, the possibility of difference in this area cannot be used to justify the differential treatment of sexual minorities.

The Studies

The first published study that compared the sexual orientation of children of lesbian parents with a control group composed of children of heterosexual parents appeared in 1995.[78] This investigation, conducted by Susan Golombok and a team of British researchers, focused on children of lesbian women born into heterosexual relationships. (To distinguish this study from another study led by Golombok discussed later, I will refer to it as the "Golombok Study 1.") The study compared twenty-five young adult children of lesbian mothers with twenty-one young adults raised by single heterosexual mothers. When interviewing the adult children about sexual orientation issues, the investigators distinguished between sexual attraction, self-identification as lesbian or gay, and sexual behavior. They found no difference between the two groups in the extent of sexual attraction to someone of the same gender. There was also no difference between the two groups of young adults in their rates of self-identification as lesbian or gay. In addition, the researchers found that the sons in both groups did not show differences in their interest in participating in same-sex relationships.

However, the results on the latter measurement—interest in participating in same-sex relationships—were different for daughters. A statistically significant greater number of the daughters of lesbian mothers had had at least one sexual relationship with someone of the same sex. In addition, a statistically significant greater number of the daughters of lesbian mothers thought they might in the future experience same-sex attraction or enter into a lesbian relationship.[79]

In 2010, the Dutch researchers Henny Bos and Theo Sandfort, in comparing sixty-three children between the ages of eight and twelve raised by lesbian mothers with sixty-eight children of the same age range raised by heterosexual parents, "measure[d] children's expectations of future heterosexual romantic involvement." The researchers found that "children in lesbian families were less certain that in the future they would experience heterosexual attraction and engage in heterosexual relationships."[80]

In the same year that Bos and Sandfort published their study, Susan Golombok and Shirlene Badger reported on a follow-up study ("Golombok Study 2") to one conducted in the 1990s that had compared children raised in three different kinds of families: planned lesbian families, families headed by single heterosexual mothers, and families headed by different-sex couples. After the children in the Golombok Study 2 became young adults, researchers inquired about their sexual orientation. Of the seventy young men and women in the study, none identified as gay or lesbian, and only one (a daughter raised by lesbian parents) identified as bisexual. This study, therefore, showed no significant difference between the sexual orientation (as measured by self-identification) of children of lesbian mothers and that of children of heterosexual parents.[81]

Another study investigating a possible association between the sexual orientation of parents and that of their children was published in 2011. This report is part of the ongoing study known as the National Longitudinal Lesbian Family Study (NLLFS), which began in 1986. The 2011 article reported on the sexual orientation and behavior of seventy-eight seventeen-year-olds raised by lesbian mothers from birth.[82]

Interestingly, *20 percent* of the daughters of lesbian mothers in the study identified themselves as bisexual, which is quite high compared to population-wide studies of rates of bisexuality. At the same time, however, none of the daughters of lesbians identified themselves "as predominantly-to-exclusively lesbian." As for the lesbian mothers' sons, "2.7% self-identified in the bisexual spectrum, and 5.4% as predominantly or exclusively homosexual."[83] These findings are generally consistent with the rates of self-identification found among the general population in recent national surveys.[84]

The NLLFS researchers did not compare the rate of sexual orientation *self-identification* of the lesbian mothers' children with a national probability sample. They did, however, compare the reported rates of same-sex sexual *behavior* with data from the 2002 National Survey of Family Growth (NSFG), which was conducted by the U.S. Department of Health and Human Services (HHS). The NLLFS researchers found that the lesbian mothers' "adolescent girls were significantly more likely to have had sexual contact with other girls...than NSFG adolescent girls."[85] At the same time, the researchers found that the adolescent boys of lesbian mothers in the study were not more likely to have engaged in same-sex sexual behavior than the boys in the NSFG.

After the publication of the NLLFS report, HHS released new NSFG data collected between 2006 and 2008, a period closer to the time when the NLLFS researchers collected their data on the seventeen-year-old children of lesbian mothers. When the NLLFS researchers compared their data with that of the more recent NSFG study, they found no difference in the rates of same-sex sexual conduct between the adolescent sons *or daughters* of lesbian mothers in the NLLFS and the adolescents in the NSFG.[86]

Much of the social science literature, then, fails to show an association between the sexual orientation of lesbian mothers and that of their children. There is little evidence, for example, that a larger percentage of children of lesbians identify as either lesbian or gay than do the children of heterosexuals. Neither the Golombok Study 1 nor the Golombok Study 2 found such an association. In addition, the rate of lesbian or gay self-identification among the children of lesbian mothers found in the NLLFS study is comparable with the rates of self-identification found among the general population in recent national surveys.

Furthermore, the Golombok Study 1 and the NLLFS study did not find that the sons of lesbian mothers showed a greater interest in same-sex sexual relationships than did the sons of heterosexual parents. In addition, the NLLFS study that used the more recent NSFG data did not find differences in the rates of same-sex sexual behavior among girls.

As noted, however, two other studies (the Golombok Study 1 and the NLLFS study that used the older NSFG data) did find that the daughters of lesbian mothers engaged in same-sex sexual conduct more frequently than the daughters of heterosexual parents. In addition, the Bos and Sandfort study found lower rates of expected heterosexual attraction among the children of lesbian mothers. (It bears emphasizing, however, that that study focused on preadolescents, who were significantly younger than the young adults and seventeen-year-olds who were the subjects of the Golombok Study 1 and the NLLFS study, respectively. It is reasonable to believe that, data gathered from children who are adolescents or older are more reliable in assessing sexual orientation than data gathered from preadolescents.)

The studies that have found that the daughters of lesbian mothers have engaged in more same-sex sexual conduct than the daughters of straight parents do not explore why the difference exists. Although some critics of LGBT rights have claimed that having lesbian or gay parents makes it more likely that the children will themselves be lesbian or gay, there is nothing in the studies that supports this causation theory. Indeed, the studies may reflect nothing more than that the daughters of lesbian mothers may feel more comfortable acknowledging that they have experienced same-sex sexual attraction than the daughters of heterosexual parents.

The first question under the rational basis test, however, is not whether the empirical evidence shows a causal connection, or even a clear association, between the sexual orientation of lesbian parents and that of their children. Instead, the issue is whether the empirical evidence might lead a reasonable observer to conclude that the question of a possible association between the two has a conceivable empirical basis. This is a close call, given that most studies have found no such association. Nonetheless, it seems to me that the data provide a sufficient indication of a possible association to meet the easy-to-satisfy factual component of the rational basis test.

However, the existence of conceivable empirical support for the claim that there may be differences in the sexual orientation of the children of lesbian and gay parents when compared to children of heterosexual parents does not end the constitutional inquiry. The rational basis test also requires that the possible differences in question be rationally related to the attainment of a legitimate state interest.

Opponents of marriage equality, therefore, cannot simply argue that the possible differences in the sexual orientation of the children of lesbians and gay men are enough to justify same-sex marriage bans. Instead, under the rational basis test, they must also contend that the possible differences have some connection to the promotion of a legitimate state interest. In order to do so, marriage equality opponents would have to claim that it is better for individuals to develop a different-sex sexual orientation than a same-sex one, or at least that it is better for sexually active individuals (in particular, perhaps, adolescents) to engage in different-sex sexual acts than in same-sex sexual ones. However, the government does not have a legitimate interest in discouraging individuals from either "developing" a same-sex sexual orientation or engaging in same-sex sexual conduct.

Discouraging Same-Sex Sexual Orientation or Conduct as a State Interest

The first time the Supreme Court addressed the question of whether the state has a legitimate interest in discouraging same-sex sexual conduct was in 1986 when it assessed the constitutionality of Georgia's sodomy law in *Bowers v. Hardwick*. The *Hardwick* Court, after rejecting the argument that sodomy laws, as applied to same-sex sexual conduct, violated the constitutional right to privacy, upheld those statutes by holding that majoritarian moral disapproval of homosexuality constituted a legitimate ground upon which to prohibit same-sex sexual conduct under the due process clause of the federal constitution.[87]

Ten years later, however, the Court followed a vastly different approach in the equal protection case of *Romer v. Evans*. Colorado voters in 1994 approved a state constitutional amendment that would have deprived lesbians, gay men, and bisexuals (but no others) of antidiscrimination protection under state and local law. The *Romer* Court, in striking down the amendment under the federal constitution, made clear that the enactment of laws aimed at expressing disapproval of a disfavored group does not constitute a legitimate state interest under the rational basis test. As the Court explained, the rational basis inquiry is intended to "ensure that classifications are not drawn for the purpose of disadvantaging the group burdened by the law."[88] This means that a law enacted in order to discourage individuals from identifying as lesbian, gay, or bisexual cannot pass constitutional muster. As the constitutional scholar Cass Sunstein notes, "the underlying judgment in *Romer* must be that, at least for purposes of the Equal Protection Clause, it is no longer legitimate to discriminate against homosexuals as a class simply because the state wants to discourage homosexuality.... The state must justify discrimination on some other, public-regarding ground."[89]

Efforts to justify restrictions on the marital (and parental) rights of lesbians and gay men because of the possibility that their children will identify as lesbian or gay is nothing more than an expression of dislike and disapproval of sexual minorities. As the law professor Clifford Rosky explains, "it is difficult to think of a clearer example of animosity toward a class than the simple fear that the class will gain new members— other than the hope that the class will lose existing members, which is closely related."[90]

The Colorado constitutional amendment at issue in *Romer* was a "status-based enactment" that sought to discourage individuals from identifying as lesbian, gay, or bisexual by withholding from them the protections afforded by antidiscrimination laws. Defenders of same-sex marriage bans may argue that even if the state does not have a legitimate interest in discouraging same-sex sexual *orientation*, it does have such an interest in discouraging same-sex sexual *conduct*. The problem with this argument, of course, is that it runs head-on into *Lawrence v. Texas*, the case in which the Court overruled *Bowers* by striking down sodomy laws as unconstitutional under the due process clause.[91]

One of the crucial principles that emerges from *Lawrence* is that a law that is intended to discourage same-sex sexual behavior is no more legitimate than one aimed at the status of being lesbian, gay, or bisexual. Indeed, the Court later cited *Lawrence* in asserting that "our decisions have declined to distinguish between status and conduct" in the context of sexual orientation.[92]

In *Lawrence*, the government argued that it had a legitimate interest in having its laws reflect moral disapproval of same-sex sexual conduct. The Court, however, rejected the view that moral disapproval of particular conduct by itself constitutes a legitimate state interest. In doing so, the Court emphasized that gay people, like straight ones, have autonomy-based interests in making decisions related to their sexuality. The freedom to make those choices without state interference, the Court made clear, is a central component of human dignity. The liberty interests of individuals in matters related to sexuality, therefore, limit the government's authority to discourage same-sex sexual conduct.

It is true, of course, that *Lawrence* involved the state's exercise of its most coercive power: the authority to criminalize conduct. In seeking to discourage same-sex sexual conduct through marriage bans, the government would not be threatening to incarcerate anyone. Nonetheless, there is something deeply troubling, even Orwellian, about the government setting policy with the goal of attempting to influence the sexual orientation of individuals, as well as the choices they make when deciding how (and with whom) to be sexually intimate. Such a goal is clearly inconsistent with the considerations of human autonomy and dignity that served as the normative foundations of the Court's ruling in *Lawrence*.

That disapproval of same-sex relationships is not a legitimate basis for government action is also clear from the Court's ruling striking down DOMA in *United States v. Windsor*. As I explore in more detail in the next chapter, the Court in *Windsor* emphasized that when states legally recognize same-sex relationships as marital, they confer dignity on same-sex couples and their relationships. One of the primary reasons why DOMA failed to pass constitutional muster was that Congress, in enacting the statute, sought to strip lesbians and gay men of that dignity by expressing disapproval of their intimate relationships. As the Court explained, "the avowed purpose and practical effect of the law here in question are to impose a disadvantage, a separate status, and so a stigma upon all who enter into same-sex marriages made lawful by the unquestioned authority of the States." The Court added that "the history of DOMA's enactment and its own text demonstrate that interference with the equal dignity of same-sex marriages, a dignity conferred by the States in the exercise of their sovereign power, was more than an incidental effect of the federal statute. It was its essence."[93]

It is clear, then, that the combination of *Romer, Lawrence*, and *Windsor* prevents the government from defending the differential treatment of lesbians and gay men on the basis of a purported interest in discouraging same-sex relationships or conduct. The sexual orientation of individuals, and how they choose to manifest their sexuality, is a matter of individual autonomy and dignity, not of state concern. For that reason, the government cannot ban same-sex marriages (or impose restrictions on parenting by lesbians and gay men) on the ground that parental sexual orientation may be associated with the sexual orientation of children.

Discouraging Same-Sex Sexual Conduct among Adolescents as a State Interest

Opponents of marriage equality may argue that even if the government does not have the constitutional authority to try to influence the sexual orientation or conduct of adults, it does have a legitimate interest in seeking to influence the sexual conduct of minors. Specifically, opponents may rely on the possibility of a higher rate of non-heterosexuality among the children of lesbian and gay parents to justify imposing same-sex marriage bans by contending that the state has a legitimate interest in discouraging same-sex sexual behavior among adolescents.

It may be true that the government has a legitimate interest in generally discouraging sexual conduct by minors.[94] That is not, however, the interest that is at issue here. Instead, the question is whether the state has a legitimate interest in discouraging adolescents from engaging in *same-sex* sexual conduct in particular. Unfortunately for supporters of same-sex marriage bans, the effort to discourage same-sex sexual conduct by minors to a greater extent than different-sex sexual conduct by the same age group has not survived equal protection analysis under the rational basis test.

In 1999, the Kansas legislature approved a measure, commonly known as the "Romeo and Juliet" law, which authorized judges to impose a significantly shorter prison sentence on a teenage criminal defendant who had sex with a minor than would be imposed if the defendant had been an adult. But in order to qualify for the shorter sentence, the defendant had to be of a different sex than the minor. This made teenage defendants who had sex with minors of the same sex ineligible for the significant reduction in jail time available to teenagers who had sex with minors of a different sex.

The state of Kansas, in defending its Romeo and Juliet law from an equal protection challenge, asserted that it had a particular legitimate interest in discouraging same-sex sexual conduct among minors. As the government explained in its brief to the Kansas Supreme Court, "the statute observes the delicate nature of child sexual orientation and appreciates the fact that children will gravitate toward the traditional sexual relationships throughout their teen years." The brief added that "a rational basis exists for the Legislature…to limit the Romeo and Juliet provisions to heterosexual teens as the law furthers the legitimate purpose of recognizing and, in part, promoting traditional sexual relationships between teenagers."[95]

The Kansas Supreme Court, however, rejected the proposition that the government has a distinct legitimate interest in discouraging same-sex sexual conduct among minors. Although the court acknowledged that "the state has broad powers to protect minors," it ruled that that authority did not allow the government to discourage same-sex sexual conduct among teenagers in the absence of evidence that "homosexual sexual activity is more harmful to minors than adults." The court made clear that even when it comes to minors, and even under the rational basis test, the government must justify the differential treatment of individuals by doing more than simply stating that society has an interest in having children develop as heterosexuals, as opposed to as lesbians, gay men, or bisexuals.[96]

At the end of the day, it is constitutionally untenable for opponents of LGBT rights to argue that laws which treat lesbians and gay men differently than heterosexuals in matters related to marriage and parenting can be justified by a governmental preference that individuals, whether they be adults or minors, do not identify as lesbian or gay and that they not engage in same-sex sexual acts. This means that even if the question of whether there is an association between the sexual orientation of lesbian and gay parents and that of their children is subject to reasonable dispute within the meaning of the rational basis test, the government is precluded from relying on the possibility of such an association to justify same-sex marriage bans (as well as parenting restrictions affecting lesbians and gay men).

An assessment of the relevance of the social science evidence on the children of lesbians and gay men as it relates to the constitutionality of same-sex marriage bans requires that a distinction be made between studies that have investigated children's psychological adjustment and social functioning and those that have investigated their gender role development and sexual orientation. For obvious reasons, there is wide agreement on the normative questions surrounding the former studies. Everyone agrees that it is better for children to be well adjusted psychologically and to have higher social functioning. There is no room for reasonable disagreement on this point. As a result, the constitutional relevance of the studies, in justifying the differential treatment of lesbians and gay men, depends entirely on the nature of the empirical findings. The fact that the studies consistently and uniformly show that parental sexual orientation is not associated with the psychological adjustment and social functioning of children means that same-sex marriage bans cannot be defended on the basis of needing to promote the well-being of children in these matters.

In contrast, the implications of the studies addressing gender role development and sexual orientation are different because their empirical findings are, in effect, *constitutionally irrelevant*. The crucial question in matters related to gender role development and sexual orientation is not whether empirical differences in these matters exist between the children of lesbian and gay parents and children of heterosexual parents, but is instead whether the government can properly legislate or regulate on the basis of those differences. The key question, in other words, is normative rather than empirical. And the Constitution, it turns out, takes sides in the normative debate over whether the government should be in the business either of promoting particular gender-based conduct and interests or of encouraging heterosexuality. Neither of these goals is a legitimate state interest. As a result, whatever differences may exist between the children of lesbians and gay men and children of heterosexuals in matters related to gender role development and sexual orientation are irrelevant to the question of whether the government can prohibit same-sex couples from marrying.

Opponents of LGBT rights seem to believe that *any* evidence of difference between the children of lesbians and gay men and children of heterosexuals is enough to justify the differential treatment of lesbian and gay individuals in matters related to marriage and parenting. Some courts have adopted this reasoning by treating the social science evidence as an undifferentiated whole, relying on any possible findings of difference to uphold same-sex marriage bans (as well as parenting restrictions affecting lesbians and gay men) under the rational basis test. However, constitutional principles require courts to make distinctions among the different categories of findings in the social science literature on the children of lesbians and gay men. It turns out that, as a constitutional matter, not all differences in this area are equal.

5

SAME-SEX MARRIAGE BEFORE
THE SUPREME COURT

In 2008, the California Supreme Court struck down the state's statutory ban on same-sex marriages, concluding that it was inconsistent with the due process and equality protections afforded by the state constitution.[1] A few months later, marriage equality opponents gathered enough signatures to place a referendum provision, named Proposition 8, before California voters, asking them to amend the constitution to prohibit the recognition of same-sex marriages.

Since the late 1970s, conservative activists have routinely turned to the ballot box to try to block or overturn LGBT rights measures. The conservatives' early use of the referendum process focused primarily on efforts to void the enactment of laws protecting individuals from discrimination on the basis of sexual orientation. Between 1977 and 1992, opponents of gay rights succeeded in placing twenty-two such measures on ballots across the country; voters approved eleven of them.[2]

The Supreme Court in 1996 essentially stopped the use of ballot referenda as a way of denying lesbians, gay men, and bisexuals antidiscrimination protection when it struck down a voter-approved amendment to the Colorado constitution that had sought to prohibit the adoption of any law, regulation, or policy protecting sexual minorities from discrimination.[3] But only two years later, conservative activists, responding to judicial rulings favorable to marriage equality, succeeded in persuading voters in Alaska and Hawai'i to amend their constitutions to ban same-sex marriages.[4]

By the time the question of same-sex marriage came to a vote in California in 2008, voters in twenty-nine states had approved amendments to their constitutions banning same-sex marriages.[5] (Some of those amendments not only prohibited the recognition of same-sex marriages, but also barred civil unions and domestic partnerships.) In fact, marriage equality opponents had previously won all but one of the anti–gay marriage ballot box measures.[6]

After a hard-fought campaign, Proposition 8 was approved by 52 percent of California's voters. Four years later, the U.S. Supreme Court accepted an appeal in a case challenging the measure's validity under the federal constitution. This chapter explores the role that procreation and child welfare considerations played in the political campaign in favor of Proposition 8, as well as in the constitutional litigation that followed the provision's approval by voters. The chapter also looks at how the same considerations impacted a second same-sex marriage case that reached the Supreme Court, this one involving the constitutionality of DOMA.

In the end, the Supreme Court only decided the substantive issues in the DOMA lawsuit. (The Court upheld the striking down of Proposition 8 on procedural grounds without assessing its constitutionality.) But in ruling that DOMA was unconstitutional, the Court dealt a major blow to the child welfare justifications for same-sex marriage bans by concluding that children are harmed not by the recognition of same-sex marriages, but by the government's failure—in this case the federal government—to recognize the relationships of same-sex couples as marital. Child welfare considerations, in other words, played an important role in the Court's reasoning, but in ways that significantly undermined rather than supported the constitutionality of same-sex marriage bans.

PROPOSITION 8 OUTSIDE THE COURTROOM: IT'S ABOUT YOUNG CHILDREN

A few months after voters approved Proposition 8, the two political consultants who orchestrated the campaign in its favor published an article in which they discussed the challenges proponents faced in persuading a majority of voters in California, a liberal and tolerant state, to amend the state constitution in order to ban same-sex marriages.[7] Focus groups and voter survey research predicted that Californians would reject Proposition 8 if proponents relied on negative portrayals of gay people and their relationships. However, the research suggested that voters might approve the measure if proponents focused on the impact the recognition of same-sex marriages would have on the religious liberty rights of those who opposed such marriages and on the education of children in the schools.

On the latter point, the campaign produced a series of highly successful television ads in which parents and teachers claimed that if Proposition 8 was defeated, young children would be taught about same-sex marriage in the schools. One ad showed a mother preparing food in her kitchen as she is approached by her young daughter, who breathlessly tells her that in school that day she had "learned how a prince married a prince, and I ... can marry a princess!" After the girl excitedly handed her horrified mother a children's book about two princes who married each other, a law professor appeared on screen telling viewers that while they might think something like this could never happen, it had already occurred in Massachusetts. The professor explained that after same-sex marriages were permitted in that state, "schools began teaching second graders that boys can marry boys" and the "courts ruled parents had no right to object." The television ad ended with a voiceover narrator intoning that "teaching children about gay marriage will happen here unless we pass Proposition 8."[8] A report published after the election concluded that this ad was particularly effective in persuading parents of children under the age of eighteen to vote in favor of the constitutional marriage ban.[9]

The measure's supporters raised a similar specter of children being "exposed" to same-sex relationships in the official ballot pamphlet provided by the California

Secretary of State to voters. (The pamphlet contains statements by opponents and sup-porters of ballot initiatives.) In that pamphlet, proponents warned that "if the gay mar-riage ruling is not overturned, TEACHERS COULD BE REQUIRED to teach young children there is *no difference* between gay marriage and traditional marriage." The vot-ers' guide added that "we should not accept a court decision that may result in public schools teaching our kids that gay marriage is okay."[10]

As noted, the Save Our Children campaign in Florida in the late 1970s, aimed at overturning Dade County's ordinance prohibiting discrimination on the basis of sex-ual orientation, had claimed that gay people were interested in either molesting or recruiting children. Similarly, in the early 1990s, supporters of Colorado's constitu-tional amendment that would have denied antidiscrimination protection to lesbians, gay men, and bisexuals had it not been struck down by the Supreme Court, portrayed gay people as sexual predators. In fact, Colorado for Family Values, the main organiza-tion behind the measure, distributed over eight hundred thousand copies of a pam-phlet that warned voters not to "let gay militant double-talk hide their true intentions. Sexual molestation of children is a large part of many homosexuals' lifestyle—part of the very lifestyle 'gay-rights' activists want government to give special class, ethnic sta-tus! Say no to sexual perversion with children—vote Yes on Amendment 2!"[11]

By 2008, however, such brazen stereotyping of lesbians and gay men was too overt to be politically effective, especially in a tolerant state like California. For this reason, the child-focused component of the Proposition 8 campaign was less explicit. While suggesting that parents should be concerned about their children's exposure to gay people and their relationships, the campaign did so in less overt ways than earlier political rhetoric deployed against gay rights.

One less overt approach the Proposition 8 campaign took was to insinuate that the recognition of same-sex marriage would encourage schools to expose children to sexual matters at a very young age. For example, a mother who appeared in one of the television ads complained to viewers that she did not want same-sex marriage taught in the schools and added anxiously that her child was only in the second grade.[12] The campaign also hinted that if children learned about same-sex marriage in the schools, it might lead them to become gay. This was suggested by the little girl in the afore-mentioned ad who excitedly told her concerned mother that she, too, could marry a princess. As the federal judge who heard the Proposition 8 trial later concluded, the campaign's advertisements did not explicitly articulate why children needed "to be protected from same-sex marriage.... Nevertheless, the advertisements insinuated that learning about same-sex marriage could make a child gay or lesbian and that parents should dread having a gay or lesbian child."[13]

The political campaign on behalf of Proposition 8 was extremely effective in framing the debate as involving not the rights to equality of same-sex couples, but the impact the recognition of same-sex marriages would have on the rest of society, in particular on young and vulnerable children. However, when the federal constitutional lawsuit was filed against Proposition 8 and the focus shifted from the political campaign to the courts, the measure's proponents did not introduce any evidence regarding how young children would be affected by learning that same-sex couples could marry. It seems that while suggesting that young children would be harmed by being exposed to gay people and their relationships had worked well on the campaign trail, proponents knew that such insinuations would not survive legal scrutiny.

PROPOSITION 8 INSIDE THE COURTROOM: IT'S ABOUT THE "DEINSTUTIONALIZATION OF MARRIAGE"

Eight months after voters approved Proposition 8, two same-sex couples filed a federal lawsuit challenging its constitutionality. After California officials refused to defend it, the measure's official proponents successfully petitioned the court to allow them to intervene in the lawsuit. In 2010, the proponents and the lesbian and gay plaintiffs faced off at a trial held before the federal district court judge Vaughn Walker in San Francisco.

The trial provided Proposition 8 proponents with the opportunity to introduce evidence that the recognition of same-sex marriage threatened the well-being of society and children. In their pretrial filings, proponents "promised to demonstrate that redefining marriage to encompass same-sex relationships would effect some twenty-three specific harmful consequences."[14] Once the trial began, however, proponents did not come close to proving what they had said they would. In fact, they called on only two witnesses to testify, only one of whom, David Blankenhorn, the president of the Institute for American Values, addressed the effects of same-sex marriage on society and children.

During his direct testimony, Blankenhorn opined that children do best when raised by married mothers and fathers who are biologically related to them.[15] But during cross-examination, Blankenhorn acknowledged that he did not know of studies showing that biological parents are better at raising children than adoptive parents or that children raised from birth by same-sex couples have worse outcomes than children raised from birth by two biological parents.[16]

Although Blankenhorn raised the family optimality claim during his testimony, the principal harm resulting from the recognition of same-sex marriage he identified was that it contributed to the "deinstutionalization" of marriage. He told the court that the reason marriage existed everywhere was that it was the only institution "that performed the task of bringing together the three dimensions of parenthood: the biological, the social—that is the caring for the child—and the legal." Blankenhorn claimed that this historical and universal understanding of marriage, one that was intrinsically linked to its essential purpose of channeling reproduction, was threatened by the more contemporary view that marriage was not about procreation and children, but was instead about recognizing the committed relationships of consenting adults. This newer and ascendant understanding of marriage served to deinstitutionalize marriage, that is, to weaken it by making its rules and purposes less comprehensible and authoritative. Blankenhorn claimed that the result of this process of deinstitutionalization was that marriage "loses esteem in the society. It loses respect. It loses its sense of being held in high regard. And the institution becomes less and less able to carry out its contributions to the society." Although he recognized that heterosexuals had contributed to the deinstitutionalization of marriage, he warned that "scholars are telling us that the process of deinstitutionalization would be furthered and accelerated significantly by adopting same-sex marriage."[17]

Blankenhorn's testimony was only the latest illustration of how social conservatives, in opposing same-sex marriage, have repeatedly defended a rigid and static understanding of marriage. For many social conservatives, marriage is essentially a prepolitical institution: one that, in effect, precedes both society and the state.[18] From this perspective, government does not create marriage, but takes it, in effect, as it finds it. As a result, the state's role in marriage is limited to protecting and maintaining the institution's basic features rather than trying to reform it according to changing values and priorities. Any alteration to the fundamental components and purposes of marriage, the argument goes, is illegitimate and dangerous.

Although marriage traditionalists like to invoke history to support their claims, their understanding of marriage is, in fact, deeply ahistorical. The plaintiffs in the Proposition 8 case made this point through the trial testimony of the Harvard historian Nancy Cott. Cott, the author of *Public Vows: A History of Marriage and the Nation*, largely acknowledged to be among the most important books on the history of marriage in the United States, testified that while channeling procreation has been *one* of the purposes of marriage, it has by no means been the *only* one. Cott explained that from the state's perspective, marriage has served other equally important functions, including the need to "create stable and enduring unions between couples,...so that they would support one another, whether or not they had children." Cott added that "the institution of marriage has always been at least as much about supporting adults as it has been about supporting minors."[19]

Rather than describing marriage as a fixed and static institution, Cott provided the court with a historical synopsis of the ways marriage in the United States has changed through time. One of the most important of these changes, which took hold in the second half of the twentieth century, was the development of a privacy-based component to marriage. This new understanding of marriage sought to promote liberty and autonomy by protecting married individuals and their intimacy choices from intrusive state regulation. But even before the twentieth century, marriage had been associated with questions of freedom and civil rights, most clearly shown by the role it played in helping to establish the citizenship rights of former slaves who, before emancipation, had been legally barred from marrying.

Cott also described the way differing understandings of marriage helped to dictate different roles for spouses. During the first few decades of the nation's history, marital relations were governed by the common law doctrine of coverture, under which women's legal and economic identities were subsumed into those of their husbands. Coverture principles were understood to be part of a broad bargain in which wives "agreed" to serve and obey their husbands in return for husbands' promises to support their wives and children. This legally enforceable understanding of spousal roles was based on a sexual division of labor, in which men were considered naturally capable of being good providers and women destined to care for the home and children.

Social and economic changes, including industrialization and urbanization, helped to make the traditional sexual division of spousal labor less rigid and uniform, particularly as growing numbers of women joined the workforce in the twentieth century. These structural changes, coupled with legal reforms, such as the enactment of the Civil Rights Act of 1964 barring employment discrimination on the basis of sex and the subsequent Supreme Court rulings prohibiting the government from assigning spousal roles by gender, meant that during the last third of the twentieth century, the state ceased dictating intrafamily roles. The question of how spouses should divide their labor and responsibilities, once entirely determined by legal rules and social norms, now became much more a matter of married couples' choices and arrangements.

Cott explained to the court that the purposes and meanings of marriage in the United States, far from being static and unchanging as the opponents of marriage equality claimed, had varied over time. As a result, society's interests in marriage, and what the institution means to spouses, are very different in the early twenty-first century from what they were at the beginning of the previous century, which were, in turn, quite different from a century earlier.

Cott is not the only marriage scholar who has provided us with a more complex, nuanced, and ultimately more accurate understanding of the institution of marriage over time than the simplistic, rigid, and ahistorical version that opponents of same-sex marriage propound. The historian Stephanie Coontz, for example, explains in her book *Marriage, A History: How Love Conquered Marriage* that for centuries marriage was not primarily about serving the needs of spouses or their children, but about establishing social networks beyond the immediate family. The political and economic importance of marriage meant that, for most of recorded history, it was parents, religious figures, and community leaders, not prospective spouses, who decided who married whom. Not until the eighteenth and nineteenth centuries did a new understanding of marriage emerge in Western societies, such that individuals were permitted to choose whom to marry based on considerations of love and affection. This new model of marriage, however, came with a highly patriarchal understanding of the nuclear unit that allowed husbands to rule their families as they saw fit. Not until the second half of the twentieth century did women succeed in attaining some parity and equal treatment within marriage under U.S. law, which helped reform marriage from a rigidly hierarchical institution into one that is more fair and equal.[20]

David Blankenhorn, during his testimony in the Proposition 8 trial, emphasized that same-sex marriage significantly contributed to the "deinstitutionalization of marriage." That phrase, as Blankenhorn acknowledged, was coined by the prominent family sociologist Andrew Cherlin in a 2004 article published under that title.[21] However, Cherlin—unlike Blankenhorn and other proponents of same-sex marriage bans—did not in his article defend a "true" understanding of marriage that was static and unchanging. Instead, he explained the way the meaning of marriage in the United States changed throughout the twentieth century. Specifically, Cherlin noted the way social and economic forces during the century's early decades transformed marriage "from an institution to a companionship." Years later, as "the roles of wives and husbands became more flexible and open to negotiation," another crucial shift took place, "from the companionate marriage to what we might call the individualized marriage." Under this understanding of marriage, which prevails today, it is seen to be as much about individual self-expression and satisfaction as about "building a family and playing the roles of spouse and parent."[22]

At the end of the day, then, in order to accept the type of fixed, unchanging understanding of marriage that Blankenhorn articulated during the Proposition 8 trial, one has to ignore the social, political, economic, and legal changes that have transformed both the purposes of marriage and the expectations of its participants over the centuries. This is not to deny, of course, that marriage and procreation have been linked in important ways. However, it is to deny the idea that channeling procreation has always been, and should always remain, the primary function of marriage.

The federal judge hearing the Proposition 8 trial was not persuaded by either Blankenhorn's family optimality claim or his argument that same-sex marriage would lead to the further deinstitutionalization of marriage. Judge Walker also concluded, after reviewing the evidence introduced by the lesbian and gay plaintiffs, that parental gender and sexual orientation were not associated with either good parenting or child adjustment. He explained that "children raised by gay or lesbian parents are as likely as children raised by heterosexual parents to be healthy, successful and well-adjusted. The research supporting this conclusion is accepted beyond serious debate in the field of developmental psychology."[23]

As noted, empirical questions related to procreation and child welfare have been at the center of policy and legal debates over same-sex marriage. The Proposition 8 trial presented opponents of marriage equality with a seemingly valuable opportunity to introduce evidence supporting their long-standing claims that same-sex marriage harms society and children. And yet, the best these opponents could muster was to offer Blankenhorn's questionable and unpersuasive testimony. (More than two years after the Proposition 8 trial, Blankenhorn wrote an op-ed in the *New York Times* announcing that he would no longer oppose the right of same-sex couples to marry.)[24] The failure of the defenders of same-sex marriage bans to introduce evidence of harm to society and to children during the Proposition 8 trial speaks volumes about the dearth of empirical support for their claims. These claims are long on so-called tradition, apparent intuition, and purported common sense; they are (extremely) short on provable facts.

After the U.S. Court of Appeals for the Ninth Circuit affirmed Judge Walker's ruling striking down Proposition 8 as unconstitutional, the measure's proponents persuaded the Supreme Court to hear the case.[25] In arguing that the state constitutional amendment promoted important state interests and that it did not, therefore, violate the equal protection provision of the federal constitution, the proponents in their brief to the Supreme Court relied almost exclusively on procreative and child-rearing considerations. The brief noted, for example, that same-sex couples and different-sex couples are not similarly situated because of the "natural capacity" of the latter to create children, an "indisputable biological" fact that justifies their preferential treatment when it comes to marriage. Marriage, the brief claimed, quoting the anthropologist Claude Levi-Strauss, is "a social institution with a biological foundation."[26] The brief also cited Blackstone, Locke, and Montesquieu in support of the proposition that the primary purpose of marriage is to promote responsible procreation so that children will be cared for by those who bring them into this world. It is this primary purpose of marriage, the brief added, that explains the institution's universality. Finally, the brief raised the family optimality claim, asserting that children do best when raised by their biological parents.

The petitioners' brief in the Proposition 8 case illustrates the way opponents of marriage equality, twenty years after the issue of same-sex marriage first exploded onto the national scene, were still defending the constitutionality of the marital bans largely on procreative and child welfare grounds. Indeed, it seemed in early 2013 that the question of whether lesbians and gay men had a constitutional right to marry the individuals of their choice might come down to whether a majority of the Supreme Court justices agreed with the responsible procreation and child optimality claims made by supporters of Proposition 8.

THE DEFENSE OF MARRIAGE ACT LITIGATION

At the same time the Supreme Court agreed to hear the Proposition 8 case, it also accepted an appeal in a lawsuit challenging DOMA. As noted, procreative and child welfare considerations, along with concerns about the morality of same-sex relationships and fears that a ruling by "activist" judges in Hawai'i might result in same-sex marriages being recognized nationwide, had led Congress to enact DOMA, by large margins, in 1996. Although there had been some earlier challenges to DOMA's constitutionality, the legal pressure on the statute intensified around the time that Barack Obama became president in 2009.[27] At first, the Obama administration defended the statute in the courts. In doing so, however, the Department of Justice explicitly disavowed the claim that DOMA was justified on the basis of procreative or child welfare considerations. Instead, government lawyers limited themselves to the contention that Congress had acted within its constitutional authority in enacting DOMA because it had sought to preserve the status quo, that is, to maintain the definition of marriage, as it related to gender, that had until then prevailed.[28]

However, in 2011, after lesbian and gay plaintiffs filed two federal lawsuits challenging DOMA's constitutionality in the Second Circuit (which covers Connecticut, New York, and Vermont), President Obama determined that the government should no longer defend the statute in the courts. The administration took the position that sexual orientation classifications deserved heightened judicial scrutiny under the equal protection clause of the federal constitution, an issue the U.S. Court of Appeals for the Second Circuit had never addressed before. The administration argued that DOMA failed to pass constitutional muster under heightened scrutiny and therefore should be struck down.[29]

Although the executive branch continued to enforce DOMA, its refusal to defend it in the courts infuriated many congressional Republicans. The GOP leadership of the House of Representatives hired lawyers to defend DOMA on behalf of the Bipartisan Legal Advisory Group of the United States House of Representatives (BLAG). (This entity was "bipartisan" in name only, since House Democratic leaders did not agree that Congress should defend DOMA's constitutionality.)

The DOMA lawsuit that reached the Supreme Court was filed by Edith Windsor, an eighty-three-year-old resident of New York City who in 2007 had married Thea Spyer, her female partner of many decades. (Although the marriage took place in Canada, its validity was recognized by the state of New York.) When Thea died in 2009, she left her entire estate to Edith. Federal tax law permits a decedent's estate to pass to her surviving spouse tax free. But since DOMA prohibited the federal government from recognizing the lesbian couple's marriage for any purpose, the Internal Revenue Service required Edith to pay $363,053 in estate taxes.

The biggest challenge for BLAG in *United States v. Windsor* was how to articulate the federal government's interest in refusing to recognize the marriage of an eighty-three-year-old woman who was married under the law of her state. In this regard, BLAG did not fare well in the lower courts. The trial court granted Windsor's motion for summary judgment after concluding that the statute did not pass constitutional muster even under the highly deferential rational basis test.[30] Even more problematically for BLAG, and for opponents of LGBT rights generally, the U.S. Court of Appeals for the Second Circuit, in ruling on behalf of Windsor, became the first federal appellate court to hold that a law like DOMA, which classifies individuals on the basis of sexual orientation, must survive the application of heightened judicial scrutiny, a standard that places a high burden on the government to show that the law substantially advances an important governmental interest.[31]

Not surprisingly, BLAG contended in its brief to the Supreme Court that the rational basis test was the appropriate standard to apply and that several rational bases justified DOMA's enactment, including the federal government's interest in applying uniform rules to determine who is eligible for federal benefits based on marital status. Of course, before DOMA, there had been a uniform rule: if couples were married under the law of their state, they were married for federal purposes. But this uniformity was not enough, according to BLAG, because the recognition by some states of same-sex marriages meant that whether same-sex couples were eligible for federal marital benefits might depend solely on which states they lived in. According to BLAG, it was legitimate for Congress to demand a gender-based marital eligibility rule for federal benefits that applied across the country.

The group's brief to the Supreme Court also contended that the federal government, like the states, could constitutionally treat same-sex couples differently from heterosexual couples in order to address "the undeniable and distinct tendency of opposite-sex relationships to produce unplanned and unintended pregnancies."[32] Relying heavily on the accidental procreation argument explored in chapter 2, BLAG claimed that heterosexual couples need the structure and stability of marriage more than same-sex couples because only heterosexuals can become parents unintentionally.

In addition, BLAG placed much emphasis on biological considerations, arguing that "common sense and human experience" justified giving preferential treatment to biological parents and their children. "Biological parents," BLAG's brief explained, "have a genetic stake in the success of their children that no one else does." Furthermore, BLAG claimed that there was a "biological differentiation in the roles of mothers and fathers" that justified excluding same-sex couples from marriage. According to BLAG, the statute's constitutionality could be premised on the fact that "men and women are different" and "so are mothers and fathers." At the end of the day, BLAG argued, it was reasonable to believe "that children relate and often react differently to mothers and fathers" and that it was "thus rational for governments to offer special encouragement for family structures in which these differing parental roles can complement each other."[33]

Given that the preceding chapters have assessed the merits of these claims, it is not necessary to do so here. Note, however, that the defense of same-sex marriage bans on procreative and child welfare grounds seemed to ring particularly hollow in a case involving the question of whether an eighty-three-year-old lesbian widow was entitled to a tax benefit afforded heterosexual widows. It took nothing less than a creative imagination to contend that denying Windsor an estate tax exemption benefited society in any meaningful, or even discernible, way. Or, to view it from the other side of the coin, it required a creative imagination to contend that granting Windsor the tax exemption available to other married couples harmed society in any meaningful, or even discernible, way. Despite BLAG's best efforts in its brief, questions related to procreation and child-rearing seemed far removed from the issue of whether the federal government could justify denying an octogenarian lesbian a tax benefit it would have provided her had she been married to a man.

THE ORAL ARGUMENTS

For two consecutive days in March 2013, the oral arguments before the Supreme Court in the Proposition 8 and DOMA cases captured much of the nation's attention. Those who wanted to hear the arguments in person started lining up outside the court building several days earlier. Court officials released the arguments' audiotapes and transcripts only a few hours after the sessions ended, something they do only in cases the public follows closely. Commentators across the political spectrum agreed that the two cases were among the most important civil rights cases heard by the Court in recent decades.

First before the Court was *Hollingsworth v. Perry*, the Proposition 8 case. Early on in the argument, Justice Sonia Sotomayor asked Charles Cooper, a former assistant attorney general during the Reagan administration and the lead lawyer defending Proposition 8, whether any rational reason existed, outside of the marriage context, for using sexual orientation as a basis for denying government benefits. Cooper responded by saying that he could not provide an answer to that question, but even if the government could not constitutionally discriminate against lesbians and gay men in other areas, marriage was different. This was because same-sex couples were not similarly situated to different-sex couples vis-à-vis that institution, given that they could not procreate.

Cooper added that same-sex marriage constituted a "profound redefinition of a bedrock social institution" and that the California voters who approved Proposition 8 could have been reasonably concerned about the uncertainty arising from that redefinition's long-term consequences. However, when two of the justices asked Cooper what those consequences might be, he seemed reluctant to provide specific examples, instead claiming that uncertainty was by itself a sufficiently valid reason to proceed cautiously before changing the definition of marriage.

Cooper's hesitation on this point left the conservative justice Antonin Scalia dissatisfied. Scalia chided Cooper for not mentioning "concrete things" about the possible impact of same-sex marriage. Specifically, Scalia claimed that "there's considerable disagreement…among sociologists as to what [are] the consequences of raising a child…in a single-sex family, whether that is harmful to the child or not. Some states…do not permit adoption by same-sex couples for that reason."

Although Cooper proceeded to agree with Scalia's point, there is, in fact, as explained in chapter 4, no "considerable disagreement" among developmental psychologists and sociologists on the question of whether being raised by same-sex couples harms children. The truth is just the opposite: there is an overwhelming consensus among experts that there is no association between parental sexual orientation and harm to children. Justice Scalia's contention was nothing more than an attempt to introduce factual uncertainty where one did not exist.

A few minutes later, Justice Anthony Kennedy, whom most commentators expected would cast the deciding vote in the case, noted that about forty thousand children in California were being raised by same-sex couples and that these children were vulnerable to an "immediate legal injury" when the state refused to allow their parents to marry. Kennedy asked Cooper whether it was not correct that "the voices of those children [are] important in this case."

Cooper responded by claiming, first, that "no data" showed that the children of same-sex couples were harmed if their parents were not permitted to marry (especially if they were allowed to register as domestic partners), and second, that under the rational basis test, a law can "be sustained even if it operates to the disadvantage of a group, if it…otherwise advances rationally a legitimate state interest."

There are at least three problems with Cooper's response. First, there is considerable tension, to say the least, between contending, on the one hand, that children benefit from marriage and that marriage promotes the well-being of children in innumerable ways and then suggesting, on the other hand, that whether same-sex couples are permitted to marry has no impact on their children. Second, the trial court, after hearing all the evidence presented by both sides, had concluded that the children of same-sex couples benefit in meaningful ways when their parents are permitted to marry.[34] Indeed, even David Blankenhorn, the only witness Proposition 8 supporters had called on to testify about child welfare considerations, had acknowledged that "adopting same-sex marriage would be likely to improve the well-being of gay and lesbian households and their children."[35]

Finally, and most problematically of all, Cooper's response is indicative of the willingness of marriage equality opponents to use the children of lesbians and gay men instrumentally, that is, as means to promote (what the opponents believe is) the social good. Cooper essentially told the Court that even if the forty thousand children of same-sex couples in California were harmed or disadvantaged because the state prohibited their parents from marrying, that was a constitutionally permissible price to pay in order to promote the state's interest in procreative and family optimality. Although such a cavalier attitude toward the well-being of children would be troubling in any context, it is particularly so coming from a lawyer representing a movement which claims that its normative polestar is the promotion of child welfare.

The day after hearing arguments in the Proposition 8 lawsuit, the Supreme Court heard *Windsor*, the DOMA case. As in *Perry*, part of the argument addressed a procedural question. In *Perry*, the procedural question had been whether the Proposition 8 proponents, who were private parties representing their interests and not those of California, had standing to appeal the case. In *Windsor*, the procedural question was whether the Court had jurisdiction even though the two principal parties—the plaintiff (Windsor) and the defendant (the United States)—agreed with the lower court's ruling invalidating DOMA. (Although BLAG had been allowed to intervene, it was not a main party in the case.)

After the lawyers addressed the procedural issue in *Windsor*, most of the remainder of the argument involved the question of whether the federal government had a constitutionally permissible justification for refusing to recognize legally valid (under state law) same-sex marriages, given two important and long-standing traditions: first, that it was the states and not the federal government that regulated marriage, and second, that couples were married for federal purposes as long as they were married under the law of their state.

In addressing this issue, Paul Clement, a former solicitor general under President George W. Bush and the lawyer representing BLAG, claimed that the federal government had a valid interest in establishing uniform benefit eligibility rules on the basis of marital status. In addition, Clement told the Court, as he wrote in his brief, that if states had a legitimate interest in promoting marriage as a procreative institution, then the federal government did as well.

Despite Clement's latter point, matters related to procreation and child welfare did not seem to concern the justices during the oral argument in *Windsor*. Instead, they peppered the lawyers with questions about the procedural issue in the case and about the federal–state divide in authority when it comes to regulating marriage. After a second day of spirited exchanges between the justices and the lawyers on both sides, the cases, and the future of same-sex marriage, lay in the Supreme Court's hands.

THE SUPREME COURT'S RULINGS ON SAME-SEX MARRIAGE

The Court, in the end, refused to address the merits of the case in *Perry*. Instead, a majority of the justices concluded that the Proposition 8 proponents did not have standing because they were not subject to personal and tangible harm if they lost the case. Although the measure's supporters wanted the courts to uphold its constitutionality, of course, their keen interest in the outcome did not provide them with the requisite direct stake in the lawsuit necessary to provide them with legal standing to appeal.

The Supreme Court therefore vacated the ruling by the U.S. Court of Appeals for the Ninth Circuit, leaving in place only the trial court's conclusion that Proposition 8 violated the plaintiffs' due process and equal protection rights.[36] Although this outcome was a major victory for marriage equality supporters because it allowed same-sex couples in California to marry, the Court left for another day the question of whether lesbians and gay men have a constitutional right to marry the individuals of their choice.

The Court did address the underlying constitutional issues in *Windsor*. In an opinion written by Justice Kennedy, the Court emphasized that it is the states that have traditionally defined and regulated marriage, with federal involvement playing a decidedly secondary role. The states' interests in defining and regulating marriage arise "from the understanding that marriage is more than a routine classification for purposes of certain statutory benefits." Citing his opinion in *Lawrence v. Texas*, Justice Kennedy explained that "private, consensual sexual intimacy between two adult persons of the same sex may not be punished by the State, and it can form but one element in a personal bond that is more enduring."[37]

The Court explained that some states, like New York, where Windsor and her spouse had lived, chose to provide same-sex couples with the rights and dignity that came with marriage. In stark contrast, Congress, which as a general matter had always permitted states to decide who was married for purposes of awarding federal rights and benefits, had enacted a statute that specifically deprived same-sex couples of the status and dignity afforded by state marriage laws.

After reviewing DOMA's text and legislative history, the Court concluded that the "essence" of the statute was to treat state-recognized same-sex marriages as "second-class marriages for purposes of federal law." The statute was unconstitutional because its "avowed purpose and practical effect... are to impose a disadvantage, a separate status, and so a stigma upon all who enter into same-sex marriages made lawful by the unquestioned authority of the States."[38] The goal behind DOMA was to impose inequality and to express congressional disapproval of same-sex relationships. As such, the statute violated the due process and equal protection rights of lesbians and gay men.

As noted, BLAG in its brief relied in part on the responsible procreation and family optimality claims in defending DOMA's constitutionality. Although the Court did not directly address the merits of these claims, there are two reasons to believe that it implicitly rejected them. First, the fact that the Court found DOMA unconstitutional strongly suggests that it believed that neither the responsible procreation nor the family optimality claim presented a constitutionally valid justification for the statute. Second, the Court explicitly concluded that DOMA *harmed* children. In particular, the Court explained that when the federal government treats state-sanctioned same-sex unions as second-tier marriages, it "humiliates tens of thousands of children now being raised by same-sex couples." This stigmatization harms children because it makes it "more difficult for [them] to understand the integrity and closeness of their own family and its concord with other families in their community and in their daily lives." The Court found it unacceptable that "DOMA instructed all federal officials, and indeed all persons with whom same-sex couples interact, including their own children, that their marriage is less worthy than the marriages of others."[39]

In addition to emphasizing the stigma and humiliation that DOMA imposed on children, the Court noted that the law financially harmed the children of married same-sex couples by denying their parents a wide range of federal rights and benefits. The statute, for example, made it more expensive for families to pay for health care because it required taxation of health benefits provided by employers to their workers' same-sex spouses. The law also denied Social Security benefits to surviving same-sex spouses to care for the couples' children, benefits the government made available to surviving heterosexual spouses.

The welfare of children, then, played a crucial role in the Court's constitutional assessment of DOMA, but in ways that were the opposite of what opponents of marriage equality advocated. The Court did not conclude, as the opponents had urged it to do, that the recognition of same-sex marriages was harmful to children. Instead, the Court concluded that it was the federal government's *refusal to recognize* state-sanctioned same-sex marriages that harmed children, a harm that helped render the statute unconstitutional. At the end of the day, child welfare considerations played an important role in the Court's reasoning, but in ways that significantly undermined rather than supported the statute's constitutionality.

The Court's concern about the dignitary and financial harms to children caused by DOMA means that a majority of the justices, as a matter of logic, did not believe that having lesbian or gay parents was harmful to children. If the Court believed that children are harmed by the recognition of same-sex marriages, it would have been illogical for it to emphasize the harms that flow from a statutory *refusal* to recognize such marriages.

It is clear, therefore, that the Court's ruling in *Windsor* dealt a major blow to the procreative and child welfare justifications for same-sex marriage bans. Opponents of marriage equality, however, will undoubtedly urge a narrow interpretation of *Windsor* that will permit them to continue to raise these justifications. That narrow interpretation will be based on two main points. First, that the Court did not explicitly assess the merits of the two justifications and therefore it is incorrect to conclude that it rejected them. Second, that the Court stated, at the end of its opinion, that its holding and reasoning were limited to the federal government's refusal to recognize same-sex marriages already sanctioned by the states, thus making it clear that it was not addressing the underlying (and larger) question of whether states can ban same-sex marriages without offending the federal constitution.

There is good reason to be skeptical of this limited reading of *Windsor*. After all, the same dignitary and other injuries to same-sex couples and their children that required the invalidation of DOMA would seem to compel the invalidation of state bans on same-sex marriage. Whether the refusal to recognize the relationships in question is the result of decisions made at the federal or state level does not in any way diminish the harms to couples and to children that flow from that refusal. Nonetheless, until the Supreme Court explicitly makes that point, opponents of marriage equality can be expected to continue to defend same-sex marriage bans on the basis of procreative and child welfare considerations.

If the past is any indication, future courts, in assessing the merits of those claims, will look to the social science literature for guidance on the question of how the recognition

of same-sex marriages affects families and children. (As already explained, that literature does not support the empirical claims made by opponents of marriage equality.)
I end this chapter with an exploration of an alternative perspective that counsels in
favor of determining the constitutionality of same-sex marriage bans *without* turning
to the social science literature for guidance.

FUTURE RULINGS ON SAME-SEX MARRIAGE:
NO ROLE FOR THE SOCIAL SCIENCES?

A few days before the oral arguments in *Perry* and *Windsor, Pediatrics,* the presti-
gious journal of the American Academy of Pediatrics, published a statement titled
"Promoting the Well-Being of Children Whose Parents Are Gay or Lesbian," written
by the Academy's Committee on Psychosocial Aspects of Child and Family Health.
The committee, after reviewing the social science literature on the children of lesbian
and gay parents, concluded that "scientific evidence affirms that children have similar
developmental and emotional needs and receive similar parenting whether they are
raised by parents of the same or different genders." The statement then announced that
the Academy, in order "to promote optimal health and well-being of all children," supported marital rights for parents regardless of their sexual orientation.[40]

The journal also published online a letter from Douglas Mogul, an assistant professor of pediatrics at Johns Hopkins Hospital, praising the Academy for supporting
same-sex marriage, but expressing deep reservations about the Academy's decision to
base its support on the social science evidence. The letter explained that

> no other demographic is concurrently facing a comparable test of suitability;
> although scientific evidence may exist that certain demographics provide vary-
> ing degrees of ability to develop strong families, I am not aware of any systematic
> attempt to question, undermine, or allow these other groups in this pursuit. As
> such, linking your recommendation to data suggests that data is necessary to rule
> for, or against, gay families. This demand is holding gay families to a different stan-
> dard and is therefore a prejudice in and of itself.[41]

In taking issue with the Academy's approach, Mogul emphasized that it only
encouraged the criticism that more data was needed. He added that "more information
is not necessary to reach the conclusion that equality for gay, lesbian, and gender-queer
families should be supported in every sphere. If people want to prove that any demo-
graphic is harmful to children and that equality should be ignored, the onus is on those
individuals—not the other way around. Otherwise, our founding documents demand
that all people are treated equally."[42]

Mogul is not the only one who has questioned the use of social science evidence to
determine whether same-sex couples have a constitutional right to marry. Interestingly,
a similar point was made in an amicus brief filed in *Perry* on behalf of the Institute for
Marriage and Public Policy and two conservative academics that urged the justices to
reject efforts by same-sex marriage advocates to use social science evidence to justify

striking down Proposition 8. The brief contended that the case should be decided on the basis of the law rather than on advocacy grounded in the social science literature. More specifically, the brief complained that the social sciences were ill equipped to conduct the types of "objective observations and controlled experiments that are standard in the physical sciences" and that, in any event, the social sciences had long been infected by political and ideological biases, especially in controversial matters of social policy.[43]

The brief also argued that the existing research on the impact of same-sex marriage was "radically inconclusive" and that many more years would have to go by, and many more studies conducted, before the effects of such a recent phenomenon as same-sex marriage could be ascertained. Given the dearth of data, the recognition of same-sex marriage was as likely to have harmful effects on society and children as benign ones. The brief concluded that "this case can and should be resolved on the basis of existing law, which should not be altered in response to advocacy posing as science."[44]

Although they do so in radically different ways, both Mogul's letter and the amicus brief encourage the questioning of the assumption, under which both sides of the same-sex marriage debate have been operating for a long time, that social science evidence should play a role in the constitutional review of gay marriage bans. Interestingly, the idea that the constitutional assessment of marital policies should be conducted independently of the social science evidence has support in the Supreme Court's case law. As I noted in chapter 1, the Commonwealth of Virginia, in defending its antimiscegenation law in *Loving v. Virginia*, relied heavily on the writings of a sociologist to claim that the children of interracial couples suffered psychological and social harm as a result of their parents' relationships. Virginia also took the position that the marriage ban was constitutional as long as there were reasonable disagreements among experts about the social consequences that accompanied the recognition of interracial marriages.[45]

However, the Supreme Court in *Loving* rejected the state's position by refusing to link its constitutional analysis to the empirical evidence regarding the possible effects of allowing interracial couples to marry. From the Court's perspective, antimiscegenation laws represented invidious forms of discrimination and thus were unconstitutional, regardless of what experts had to say about the social consequences of interracial marriages.[46]

As I also explained in chapter 1, those who defended laws that imposed legal disabilities on nonmarital children also turned to scientific evidence to support their claims. Specifically, those who argued in favor of the differential treatment of so-called illegitimate children contended that married households constituted the ideal family structure for the raising of children and that having children outside of marriage harmed them socially and psychologically. According to this view, the differential treatment of nonmarital children was constitutionally justified because it channeled procreation into the optimal family structure: households headed by married couples.

However, in assessing the constitutionality of the legal disabilities imposed on nonmarital children, the Supreme Court paid little attention to these types of empirical claims. As the Court saw it, the differential treatment of nonmarital children constituted a form of invidious discrimination and thus the empirical claims of harm used to justify them were constitutionally irrelevant. What experts had to say about the benefits to children of being raised by married couples turned out to be inconsequential as the Court, starting in the late 1960s, repeatedly struck down laws denying benefits to nonmarital children.[47]

It is not entirely clear why the social science evidence has come to play such a crucial role in assessing the constitutionality of same-sex marriage bans, given that it was largely irrelevant in cases involving interracial bans and the differential treatment of nonmarital children. One reason might be that by the time the issue of same-sex marriage began to be litigated with some frequency in the late 1990s and early 2000s, there were extensive empirical literatures on (1) how the children of married couples fared when compared to the children of cohabiting couples, stepparents, divorced parents, and single parents, and (2) whether differences existed between the children of heterosexuals and those of lesbians and gay men. Opponents of marriage equality turned to the former literature to support their claim that recognizing same-sex marriages would harm children; marriage equality proponents turned to the latter literature to argue that there was no evidence that eliminating gender as a marriage eligibility criterion would cause such harm.

There were simply no equivalent social science literatures available when the Supreme Court decided *Loving*. Indeed, at that time there were few empirical studies showing the presence or absence of social difficulties or psychological problems experienced by the children of interracial spouses. Similarly, when the Court turned its attention, shortly after *Loving*, to the question of the law's differential treatment of nonmarital children, there were almost no studies comparing the outcomes of children raised in different types of family structures. Social scientists did not begin to conduct those studies in earnest until a couple of decades later, that is, until after the increase in the number of single parent, stepparent, and cohabiting parent households began to raise significant policy concerns in some quarters.

However, the ready availability of empirical evidence on questions related to family structure in general, and parenting by lesbians and gay men in particular, does not by itself render such evidence essential (or even relevant) to determining the constitutionality of same-sex marriage bans. The fact that the Supreme Court was able to assess the constitutionality of interracial marriage bans and of the differential treatment of nonmarital children without having conclusive empirical evidence about the consequences of lifting the two sets of legal restrictions suggests that future courts should be able to do the same in assessing the constitutionality of same-sex marriage bans.

Indeed, it behooves courts to keep in mind the important point that Mogul made in his letter to *Pediatrics*. No other group of individuals is required to establish empirically that the state's decision to permit them to marry would not have any negative social consequences. Imposing this unique burden on lesbians and gay men before they are permitted to marry the individuals of their choice is, in and of itself, a sign of prejudice.

Despite the Supreme Court's precedents in the areas of antimiscegenation and illegitimacy, it is probably not realistic to expect future courts to decide the constitutionality of same-sex marriage bans without any references to the social science literature on family structure and child welfare. If nothing else, the fact that opponents of marriage equality continue to defend same-sex marriage bans on the basis of the supposed harm to society and children that accompanies the lifting of those bans means that judges will likely continue to pay attention to what social scientists have to say on these issues. At the same time, however, courts should be careful not to require marriage equality proponents to produce conclusive social science evidence regarding the absence of harm before lesbians and gay men are afforded the constitutional right to marry the individuals of their choice. Such a requirement is problematic not only because, as already explained, it is unique, but also because it represents a burden that, in all likelihood, cannot be met. It is exceedingly difficult, after all, for the social sciences to conclusively prove a negative, that is, to establish beyond all reasonable doubt that any given change in policy will not have some negative repercussions. For this reason, the argument that more data need to be collected will always be available to those who oppose the elimination of gender as a marriage eligibility criterion.

This was the position taken by the amicus brief filed by the Institute for Marriage and Public Policy in *Perry*. As noted, the brief urged the Supreme Court to entirely disregard the social science evidence on lesbian and gay families because there were insufficient data to establish conclusively that same-sex marriage would not have harmful social effects. But we need to remember that if the Court had followed that approach in *Loving* and in the illegitimacy cases—that is, if the Court had demanded that social scientists provide conclusive evidence that the striking down of interracial marriage bans and of laws privileging marital children over nonmarital ones would not have any negative social effects—the two sets of laws might still be with us today. If courts were to refuse to strike down the differential treatment of minority groups until equality advocates could show conclusively that no possible social harm will result from a change in the status quo, it would significantly impair the ability of the Constitution to provide equal protection under the law to all.

Conclusion

LESSONS FOR THE FUTURE

This book has focused on the role that procreative and child welfare considerations have played in policy and legal debates involving same-sex marriage. Although those debates have often been heated and have not always been illuminating, they have helped the nation focus on several crucial questions of family policy and law, including what is the purpose of marriage and what constitutes good parenting.

A growing percentage of Americans live in states that recognize same-sex marriages. Given that young Americans overwhelmingly support the idea that same-sex couples should be provided with the opportunity to marry, it seems inevitable that lesbians and gay men in the United States, regardless of where they reside, will eventually be permitted to marry individuals of their choice. But even after the question of gay marriage is settled, other policy decisions will have to be made regarding how the state should structure, support, and regulate familial relationships. This conclusion explores five important lessons to be learned from the role that procreative and child welfare considerations have played in policy and legal debates involving same-sex marriage.

LESSON 1: AVOID EXCLUSIONARY POLICIES LINKED TO PROCREATIVE AND CHILD WELFARE CONSIDERATIONS

As noted in chapter 1, American law has had an unfortunate history of imposing deeply misguided class-based marital disqualifications and benefits limitations on certain classes of adults and children in order to promote particular understandings of procreative and child-rearing optimality. This history shows that marital class-based exclusionary policies justified on the basis of the purported social harm caused by disfavored forms of procreation and child-rearing have almost always turned out to be empirically groundless or normatively problematic (or both).

The troubling nature of these class-based policies was not always immediately apparent. As with same-sex marriage bans until recently, most Americans in decades past assumed that banning interracial marriages, prohibiting disabled individuals from marrying, and denying benefits to nonmarital children were necessary and appropriate means to promote socially useful objectives in matters related to procreation and child welfare. However, as with same-sex marriage prohibitions, most Americans eventually came to understand that these class-based policies sought to achieve social objectives in deeply problematic ways.

It goes without saying that the government has a compelling interest in promoting the well-being of children. But class-based marital disqualifications and benefits limitations are blunt social policy tools. A slew of alternative and more particularized policy options exist that can promote the well-being of children: everything from tax incentives for those who care for children to child-care subsidies for working parents. In contrast, history shows that disqualifying entire classes of individuals from marriage with the objective of promoting child welfare has been more about invidious discrimination than about protecting children.

It may be objected that legislatures, regardless of how the question of same-sex marriage is eventually resolved, are unlikely to implement any new class-based marital restrictions. That is probably true. At the same time, however, the debate over same-sex marriage led some states to create alternatives to marriages, such as civil unions and domestic partnerships, but to *exclude different-sex couples* from their ambit, apparently reflecting the view that society and children are better off if those couples marry than if they, for example, domestically partner.

I believe that these efforts to exclude different-sex couples from civil unions and domestic partnership regimes were misguided. Indeed, it is time to dispense altogether with the idea that, in order to promote procreative goals and child welfare objectives, relationship-recognition regimes, whether marital or not, should be limited to certain classes of individuals. Again, the nation's track record in imposing and defending these types of class-based limitations does not make one optimistic about the advisability of retaining those that remain, much less of adopting new ones.

One of the many benefits that will accompany the eventual settling of the highly divisive issue of same-sex marriage is that the country will be able to move beyond the relatively narrow question of whether lesbian and gay couples should be allowed to marry and instead focus on how society and the state can support and promote the healthy development of all children. Our children will benefit immensely if we as a nation spend as much time, energy, and resources in the next twenty years discussing how best to promote child welfare through particularized and nonexclusionary policies as we have spent during the last twenty years debating the question of whether same-sex couples should be allowed to marry.

LESSON 2: AVOID FAMILY POLICIES BASED ON THE "FACTS OF NATURE"

Opponents of marriage equality have tried to extrapolate a justification for denying lesbians and gay men the opportunity to marry the individuals of their choice from the "natural" fact that only men and women can procreate. But as philosophers of many different stripes have known for a long time, it is problematic to try to determine what "ought to be" primarily on the basis of "what is." As I showed in chapter 2, the fact that only a man and a woman can, as a physiological matter, create a new human being through sexual contact provides a weak and unpersuasive justification for the normative (and policy) position that same-sex couples should be denied the opportunity to marry.

Opponents of marriage equality have also relied on two biology-based arguments to claim that same-sex marriage bans are necessary in order to provide children with an optimal family environment. First, these opponents have insisted that children do better when raised by their biological parents, a contention that, as I showed in chapter 3, is not supported by the social science evidence. Second, in making the optimality argument, these opponents have relied on notions of biological determinism to claim that men and women parent in intrinsically different ways. As noted these opponents are confusing gender-based social norms and expectations with biological differences between men and women. In addition, the notion that men and women are somehow biologically hardwired to parent in different ways is significantly undermined by the many studies showing that the parenting styles, attributes, and influences of female and male parents are much more similar than different.

It is understandable that most Americans would assume, back in the days when almost all children were raised by their biological mothers and fathers (that is, approximately before the last third of the twentieth century), that there was something essential and valuable about having children raised by their two biological parents. The multiplicity of family forms that has ensued since then, however, has led many Americans to reevaluate that assumption. And it turns out that, for the reasons I explained in chapters 3 and 4, neither parent-child biological links nor the presence and involvement of a parent of each gender is associated with healthier child development and better child outcomes.

It therefore behooves the country going forward to not base policies aimed at promoting child welfare on the existence of biological connections between some parents and their children or on the supposed intrinsic differences between female and male parents. In many ways, our society has already moved in this direction by, among other policies, promoting adoption, recognizing that the husbands of women inseminated with the sperm of other men are the legal fathers of the resulting children, and by rendering gender legally irrelevant in determining the obligations of marriage and in establishing rights to custody and visitation.[1] However, as the protracted debates over same-sex marriage show, biology-inspired claims, including claims related to essentialized notions of what men and women are capable of achieving on the basis of their sex/gender, unfortunately remain very much part of family policy debates. The welfare of children will be better promoted if policymakers leave behind these idealized and essentialized notions of what constitutes "optimal" families and instead focus on the social structures and support that all parents need in order to promote their children's well-being.

LESSON 3: THERE ARE NO QUICK FIXES IN PROMOTING RESPONSIBLE PROCREATION

Although this book has been highly critical of the way opponents of marriage equality have relied on responsible procreation claims to defend same-sex marriage bans, I have not taken issue with the point that it is important to encourage those who bring children into this world to take responsibility for them. There is nothing objectionable about wanting to promote that goal. What is problematic is the effort to do so by denying lesbians and gay men the opportunity to marry the individuals of their choice.

Social conservatives who have focused intently on defending heterosexual privilege in marriage have believed simplistically that maintaining the prohibition against same-sex marriages encourages heterosexuals to be more responsible about their procreative decisions. As I showed in chapter 2, however, there is no reason to believe that that is the case.

Those who believe that the well-being of society depends on the extent to which heterosexuals can be persuaded to have children only within marriage face many significant challenges, none of which implicate LGBT individuals or their relationships. One of those challenges is the seemingly unavoidable fact that individuals decide to marry and to have children based on the confluence of a large set of social, economic, and personal factors that are not easily influenced by individual social policies. Even narrowly tailored reforms that have sought to create the appropriate incentives in order to promote "responsible procreation"—such as family cap provisions meant to discourage women on welfare from having additional children—have proven ineffective in encouraging heterosexuals to have children only within marriage.

A second challenge that social conservatives face in promoting their understanding of responsible procreation is represented by well-established cultural and constitutional norms that deem the decisions of whether to marry and to have children as best left to individuals and couples to make without governmental interference. The state could, for example, promote childbearing within marriage by imposing severe penalties on adults who have out-of-wedlock births. Such a solution, however, is entirely inconsistent with prevailing social and legal understandings of the importance of autonomous decisions in matters related to intimate and familial relationships.

Opponents of marriage equality, by focusing so intensely on same-sex marriage bans, have been able to skirt the much more difficult issue of how to promote their conception of responsible procreation without directly questioning the prevailing view that the decisions *of heterosexuals* about when and whom to marry, and whether to have children inside or outside of marriage, are matters of individual choice rather than governmental policy. It is one thing to try to persuade heterosexuals that society is better off when same-sex couples are denied the opportunity to marry. It is quite another to try to persuade heterosexuals that society would be better off if their getting a divorce were made more difficult, if their cohabiting outside of marriage were discouraged, or if their giving birth outside of marriage were penalized or stigmatized. Until recently, it seemed that social conservatives might succeed in restricting marriage to heterosexuals. It has been clear for a long time, however, that conservatives are unlikely to persuade a majority of heterosexuals to limit or restrict their personal autonomy in matters related to families, marriage, and children.

A third challenge faced by those who believe that society's well-being depends on the extent to which heterosexuals can be persuaded to have children only within marriage has more to do with economic forces than with notions of personal freedoms. Social conservatives have paid little attention to how economic factors, such as the globalization of the labor market, income inequality, and job insecurity, contribute to the increased rates at which heterosexuals, in particular those with limited economic means, have children out of wedlock.

The rates of nonmarital births are significantly higher among less affluent women than among middle- and upper-class women. In addition, studies show that most unmarried mothers of limited economic means are interested in marrying, but are likely to do so only when they feel economically secure and their prospective spouses have the financial ability to contribute to household expenses and child support.[2] The apparent link between economic insecurity, out-of-wedlock births, and delayed marriages illustrates the scope of the challenges faced by those who believe that having children within marriage is the only way to procreate responsibly. It has been much easier for social conservatives to defend the heterosexual privilege in marriage than to address market forces that give rise to the kind of income inequality and economic insecurity that seem to contribute to the growing rates of nonmarital births.

In short, those who believe, as opponents of marriage equality do, that responsible procreation is best promoted by privileging marital unions at the expense of all other possible ways of having and raising children face huge, perhaps insurmountable, challenges. An alternative policy vision—one that in my view is not only more appealing normatively, but also more likely to be effective—aimed at encouraging those who have children to take responsibility for them is to provide parents in need with the kind of social and financial support that will permit them to care for their children regardless of whether they are married, cohabiting, single, straight, or biologically related to their children.

Although a full defense of such a vision would go beyond the scope of this book, it is important to note that this vision rejects the efforts of conservatives (both social and libertarian) to privatize care rather than rely on public support for relationships of dependency, such as those between parents and their children. The movements for welfare reform and against same-sex marriage have both contended that the solution to many of the nation's social ills is to have government abstain from policies that promote nontraditional family forms. To the extent that there is a role for government at all, these movements assert, it is to advance only one particular family structure, that headed by married heterosexuals who are biologically related to their children.

The large social science literature showing that lesbians and gay men are raising healthy and well-adjusted children provides only one example of how it is possible for parents who fall outside the traditional mold to promote their children's well-being. More adults will take responsibility for more children if our society commits itself to valuing and supporting multiple familial arrangements through recognition and subsidies instead of trying to adhere to an outmoded policy paradigm that privileges one family form at the expense of all others.

LESSON 4: PROMOTING CHILD WELFARE REQUIRES A FOCUS ON WELL-BEING RATHER THAN DIFFERENCES

It is almost always taken for granted that parental households headed by married, heterosexual parents who are biologically related to their children should serve as the normative (or gold) standard to which all other forms of parental arrangements are compared. As a result, when assessing lesbian and gay parents, many policymakers and judges—to say nothing of conservative commentators and activists—have assumed that any differences in the development of the children of lesbians and gay men, compared to the development of the biological children of married heterosexual parents, constitutes grounds for denying same-sex couples the opportunity to marry.

As I showed in chapter 4, the social science evidence has consistently failed to find associations between parental sexual orientation and children's psychological adjustment and social functioning. When it comes to adjustment and functioning, in other words, there is no evidence of difference. However, some intriguing suggestions in a minority of studies indicate a possible association between parental sexual orientation and the gender role development and sexual orientation of children.

Supporters of LGBT rights have tended to either ignore or minimize possible differences between the children of lesbian and gay parents and children of heterosexuals. This tendency is understandable, given that opponents of LGBT rights have always been eager to pounce on any possible differences in order to defend the differential treatment of current and prospective lesbian and gay parents, including by restricting their ability to marry. It is also understandable because, as a matter of political strategy and legal doctrine, it is easier to make equality claims, and to seek antidiscrimination protection, by emphasizing similarities rather than differences.

At the same time, however, using the existence (or absence) of differences in child development and outcomes as a normative guidepost in the setting of child welfare policies risks reinforcing social privileges and hierarchies that work to the detriment of children raised in households that do not fit the traditional mold. The relevant question is not whether there is evidence that these children are different from children of married heterosexual parents who are biologically related to them, but whether the differences that may exist are problematic because they threaten the well-being of children.

An exclusive focus on well-being would not make policy determinations any easier; in fact, in many instances, it is more difficult to determine whether child well-being is threatened than whether differences exist. This is because the latter question is primarily empirical, one that social scientists can attempt to answer as they search for measurable differences among children raised in different types of family structures. In contrast, the question of whether empirical differences translate into actual or potential threats to well-being demands a more normative approach because it requires assessments of what is good and bad for children.

The critical question in matters related to diversity in familial arrangements is not whether there are measurable differences among children raised by different types of families, but whether the differences are harmful. This question requires a broader— and in many ways more complicated—conversation about which characteristics, attributes, and preferences of children are likely to negatively affect their well-being.

Future research may show that a greater percentage of children of lesbians and gay men than of children of married heterosexual parents have less traditional views on questions of gender and sexuality. Future research may also show that the children of single, adoptive, or divorced parents have different attitudes and interests than children raised by their biological and never-divorced married parents. Social scientists will undoubtedly continue to collect data on these questions. But it will be up to legislators, policymakers, and the voting public to interpret and give meaning to the data by deciding whether the differences that do exist require policy changes or reforms. The mere existence of difference will not be enough to guide those decisions. Instead, determinations will have to be made regarding whether the differences in question threaten the well-being of children and, if so, which policies will work best in eliminating or mitigating these threats.

LESSON 5: GENDER IN PARENTING SHOULD MATTER LESS, NOT MORE

During the oral argument before the Supreme Court in the California same-sex marriage case, one of the justices asked the attorney defending Proposition 8 whether same-sex marriage bans constitute a form of gender classification. The lawyer responded by saying that they do, but only in the sense that "fatherhood" and "motherhood" are also gendered. In doing so, the attorney seems to have been trying to reassure the Court that the gendered component of marriage is both natural and benign.

I have already addressed in this conclusion the problems with suggesting that there are biological and intrinsic differences between female and male parents. But it seems appropriate to end a book that has explored the intersection of procreation, children, and marriage by making an even more fundamental point: family law and policy should emphasize the attributes, capacities, and resources that make for successful *parenting* rather than successful mothering or fathering *as linked to parental gender*. As I explained in chapter 3, the social science literature shows that it is generally better for children to have two involved and caring parents rather than one. Although many of these studies have sought to assess paternal influences on children, the studies do not establish that it is the *gender* of the second parent, as opposed to the *presence and involvement* of that parent, which matters.

These studies, when combined with the studies discussed in chapter 4 that compared children of same-sex couples with children of heterosexual couples (thus controlling for the number of parents but not their gender) and found no reasons to be concerned about the psychological adjustment and social functioning of the children of lesbians and gay men, show that gender in parenting matters much less than either tradition or intuition might suggest.

Defenders of same-sex marriage bans portray themselves as protecting motherhood and fatherhood against gay marriage proponents who seek, in effect, to degender parenthood. It is essential, however, to be clear on what degendering parenthood entails. To argue in favor of same-sex marriage is not to deny that children benefit from parental contributions that have traditionally been associated with motherhood (such as caring, nurturing, and providing emotional support), as well as those that have traditionally defined fatherhood (such as protecting, sheltering, and providing economic support). Instead, what the push for same-sex marriage questions is the presumption that female parents are intrinsically better at providing their children with the former and male parents are intrinsically better at providing them with the latter.

If we can get ourselves to think about "mother" and father" as verbs rather than as nouns—if we focus, in other words, on what it means *to* mother or *to* father a child rather than on the gender of the parent in question—we can continue to value parental qualities and attributes that are clearly beneficial to children without having to defend the empirically unsupported proposition that dual-gender parenting is a prerequisite for successful parenting. Children do best not when they have a female parent and a male parent, but when their parents, *regardless of their gender, sexual orientation, or number*, are able to provide them with the love and support that they need to thrive. What should matter in the setting of child welfare policies is not parental gender, but how parents parent.

Social conservatives are correct that one of the consequences of degendering marriage is that it will degender parenthood. What they ignore is that the process of degendering parenthood began long ago, starting in the second half of the nineteenth century with the elimination of the doctrine of coverture, under which women's social and legal identities were subsumed into those of their husbands following marriage, and proceeding all the way through what has become the mainstream contemporary view that, as the Supreme Court has put it, "no longer is the female destined solely for the home and the rearing of the family, and only the male for the marketplace and the world of ideas."[3]

Social conservatives are also wrong in claiming that the degendering of parenthood is harmful to society and to children. The proposition that children need mothers and fathers is correct if it means that children need caring, involved, and supportive parents. However, as the tens of thousands of same-sex couples who are raising children in this country show every day, the proposition is incorrect if it means that children need a female and a male parent in order to maximize their chances of leading happy, fulfilling, and productive lives.

In the end, the degendering of parenthood is a cause for celebration rather than hand-wringing. It opens new possibilities for human development and accomplishments that are not tied to tired and problematic understandings of what human beings are capable of achieving for themselves, and providing for others, on the basis of their gender. The future of the American family—defined broadly to include its diverse compositions and manifestations—is brighter today than it was a generation ago largely because gender in parenting matters less rather than more.

The push for same-sex marriage has by no means been the only contributor to this positive and exciting change. It is likely, however, that the eventual nationwide recognition of such marriages will dispense, once and for all, with the legal and policy relevance of gender in parenting. Such an outcome will be good for our country in general and for our children in particular.

NOTES

Introduction

1. Ken Bronson, *A Quest for Full Equality* (2004), available at the website of Quatrefoil Library, www.quatrefoillibrary.org/materials/QuestforFull_Equality.pdf, accessed January 2014. For additional information about Jack Baker, Michael McConnell, and their gay rights activism, see Kay Tobin and Randy Wicker, *The Gay Crusaders* (New York: Arno Press, 1975), pp. 135–155.

2. McConnell v. Anderson, 451 F.2d 193 (8th Cir. 1971). The court explained that McConnell did not have "the right to pursue an activist role in implementing his unconventional ideas concerning the societal status to be accorded homosexuals and, thereby, to foist tacit approval of this socially repugnant concept upon his employer"; p. 196.

3. Letter from Gerald R. Nelson, Clerk of District Court, Hennepin County, Minnesota, to Richard John Baker, May 22, 1970 (included in Appellants' Brief and Appendix, Baker v. Nelson, Minnesota Supreme Court, No. 40039 (1971), Appendix, p. 1).

4. David L. Chambers, "Couples: Marriage, Civil Union, and Domestic Partnership," in *Creating Change: Sexuality, Public Policy, and Civil Rights*, John D'Emilio, William B. Turner, and Urvashi Vaid, eds. (New York: St. Martin's Press, 2000), pp. 281, 283.

5. Appellants' Brief and Appendix, *supra* note 3, pp. 7–9. The brief, written by Baker under the supervision of R. Michael Wetherbee, a Minneapolis attorney, sought to educate the court about sexual orientation and gay people by including an impressively comprehensive summary of the social, cultural, psychological, and anthropological literature available on the topics in the early 1970s; pp. 11–44. The brief then contended that denying same-sex couples the opportunity to marry violated the eighth and ninth amendments to the federal Constitution, as well as the rights to liberty and equality under the Fourteenth Amendment; pp. 45–82. The constitutional equality argument was largely grounded in the view that the government's denial of that opportunity was an impermissible form of gender discrimination; pp. 74–77.

6. Respondent's Brief, Baker v. Nelson, Minnesota Supreme Court, No. 40039 (1971), p. 2.

7. Baker v. Nelson, 191 N.W.2d 185 (Minn. 1971). For background information on Paul Barwick, John Singer, and their same-sex marriage case, see Chambers, *supra* note 4, pp. 284–286. Like Michael McConnell, Singer's gay rights activism cost him a job (in his case, with the Equal Employment Opportunity Commission). And, like McConnell, Singer lost a federal lawsuit challenging his firing. Singer v. U.S. Civil Service Commission, 530 F.2d 247, 256 (9th Cir. 1976) (holding that the government properly fired the gay plaintiff because of his "open and public flaunting or advocacy of homosexual conduct").

8. Brief of Appellants, Singer v. Hara, Washington Court of Appeals, No. 1879-I (1972), pp. 5–7. Most of this brief was copied, word for word, from the brief filed in the Minnesota same-sex marriage case.

9. Brief of Respondent, Singer v. Hara, Washington Court of Appeals, 1879-I (1972), p. 16.

10. Brief of Respondent, Singer v. Hara, Washington Court of Appeals, 1879-I (1972), pp. 3–4. The Kentucky Court of Appeals made a similar point in another early same-sex marriage case when it reasoned that "it appears to us that appellants are prevented from marrying, not by the statutes of Kentucky...but rather by their own incapability of entering into a marriage as that term is defined." Jones v. Hallahan, 501 S.W.2d 588, 589 (Ky. Ct. App. 1973).

11. Carlos A. Ball, *The Right to Be Parents: LGBT Families and the Transformation of Parenthood* (New York: New York University Press, 2012), chs. 1 & 2; Daniel Winunwe Rivers, *Radical Relations: Lesbian Mothers, Gay Fathers, and Their Children in the United States since World War II* (Chapel Hill: University of North Carolina Press, 2013), ch. 3.

12. Ball, *supra* note 11, ch. 3.

13. Ball, *supra* note 11, ch. 5.

14. Baehr v. Lewin, 852 P.2d 44 (Haw. 1993). On the background and impact of *Baehr*, see Carlos A. Ball, *From the Closet to the Courtroom: Five LGBT Rights Cases That Have Changed Our Nation* (Boston: Beacon Press, 2010), ch. 4.

15. Debate on the Defense of Marriage Act, U.S. House of Representatives, July 12, 1996, H7482. After leaving Congress, Barr had a change of heart and called for DOMA's repeal. *See, e.g.*, Bob Barr, *The True Marriage Divide*, SCOTUS Blog, August 18, 2011, www.scotusblog.com/2011/08/the-true-marriage-divide/, accessed January 2014.

16. Defense of Marriage Act, Hearing before the Subcommittee on the Constitution of the Committee on the Judiciary, U.S. House of Representatives, 104th Congress, May 15, 1996, pp. 1–2.

17. Debate on the Defense of Marriage Act, *supra* note 15, p. H7488.

18. Report 104–664, Defense of Marriage Act, Committee on the Judiciary, U.S. House of Representatives, July 9, 1996, p. 14.

19. Some of the most explicit references to Christianity during DOMA's enactment were made by Senator Robert Byrd (D-WV), who read scripture from his personal Bible on the floor of the Senate during a forty-five-minute speech decrying same-sex marriage, gay people, and their relationships. Debate on the Defense of Marriage Act, U.S. Senate, September 10, 1996, S10108–S10111. *See also* Report 104–664, *supra* note 18, p. 16 (arguing that DOMA appropriately reflected Congress's "moral disapproval of homosexuality, and a moral conviction that heterosexuality better comports with traditional (especially Judeo–Christian) morality.").

20. Transcript of Proceedings, Baehr v. Miike, Hawai'i Circuit Court, Civ. No. 91-1394-05, September 10, 1996, pp. 4–13.

21. Baehr v. Miike, 1996 WL 694235 (Hawai'i Circ. Ct. 1996).

22. Lynn D. Wardle, "The Potential Impact of Homosexual Parenting on Children," 1997 *University of Illinois* 833, 854. For a response to Wardle's article, see Carlos A. Ball and Janice Pea, "Warring with Wardle: Morality, Social Science and Gay and Lesbian Parents," 1998 *University of Illinois Law Review* 253.

23. Brief of Appellants, Conaway v. Deane, Maryland Court of Appeals, No. 44, September 5, 2006, p. 8.

24. Brief of Intervenors, Andersen v. Kings County, Washington Supreme Court, No. 75934-1, October 18, 2004, p. 36.

25. United States v. Windsor, 133 S.Ct. 2675 (2013).

Chapter 1

1. A. Leon Higginbotham, Jr., and Barbara K. Kopytoff, "Racial Purity and Interracial Sex in the Law of Colonial and Antebellum Virginia," 77 *Georgetown Law Journal* 1967, 1990–1992 (1989).

2. "Negro Womens Children to Serve According to the Condition of the Mother," in *The Statutes at Large; Being a Collection of All the Laws of Virginia* (vol. 2) (William Waller Hening ed., 1823), p. 170. Other colonies soon followed Virginia's lead by linking the free or slave status of children to that of their mothers. Julie Novkov, *Racial Union: Law, Intimacy and the White State in Alabama, 1865–1954* (Ann Arbor: University of Michigan Press, 2008), p. 10.

3. Charles F. Robinson II, *Dangerous Liaisons: Sex and Love in the Segregated South* (Fayetteville: University of Arkansas Press, 2003), p. 3; Joel Williamson, *New People: Miscegenation and Mulattoes in the United States* (New York: Free Press, 1980), p. 8.

4. Robinson, *supra* note 3, p. 8.

5. Loving v. Virginia, 388 U.S. 1 (1967).

6. "An Act for Suppressing Outlying Slaves," in *The Statutes at Large* (vol. 3), *supra* note 2, pp. 86–87. In 1705, the Virginia Assembly changed the punishment for entering into an interracial marriage from lifetime banishment to six months in prison for the white party. Peter Wallenstein, *Tell the Court I Love My Wife: Race, Marriage, and Law—An American History* (New York: Palgrave Macmillan, 2002), p. 18. Edmund Morgan suggested that this new penalty was a "more effective deterrent to racial intermarriage among ordinary people" and did not, after the period of incarceration was completed, deprive the colony of laborers. Edmund S. Morgan, *American Slavery, American Freedom: The Ordeal of Colonial Virginia* (New York: Norton, 1975), p. 335.

7. Kathleen M. Brown, *Good Wives, Nasty Wenches, and Anxious Patriarchs: Gender, Race, and Power in Colonial Virginia* (Chapel Hill: University of North Carolina Press, 1996), p. 199.

8. Morgan, *supra* note 6, p. 336; Robinson, *supra* note 3, p. 6.

9. *The Statutes at Large* (vol. 3), *supra* note 2, p. 87.

10. Peter W. Bardaglio, "'Shamefull Matches': The Regulation of Interracial Sex and Marriage in the South before 1900," in *Sex, Love, Race: Crossing Boundaries in North American History*, Martha Hodes, ed. (New York: New York University Press, 1999), p. 114.

11. Karen Woods Weierman, "'For the Better Government of Servants and Slaves': The Law of Slavery and Miscegenation," 24 *Legal Studies Forum* 133, 141 (2000).

12. Wallenstein, *supra* note 6, p. 40.

13. On the enactment and enforcement of southern antimiscegenation laws in the period leading up to the Civil War, see Robinson, *supra* note 3, pp. 8–20. A few states repealed their antimiscegenation laws prior to the Civil War (e.g., Massachusetts (1840) and Iowa (1851)), while a handful did so in the years following it (e.g., Washington (1867) and Ohio (1887)). Harvey M. Applebaum, "Miscegenation Statutes: A Constitutional and Social Problem," 53 *Georgetown Law Journal* 49, 50 n. 10 (1964).

14. *See, e.g.*, Dodson v. State, 31 S.W. 977 (Ark. 1895) ("it is not true that marriage is only a civil contract. It is more than that. It is a social and domestic relation, subject to the exercise of the highest governmental power of the sovereign states—the police power."); State v. Gibson, 36 Ind. 389 (1871) ("In this State marriage is treated as a civil contract, but it is more than a mere civil contract. It is a public institution established by God himself,

is recognized in all Christian and civilized nations, and is essential to the peace, happiness, and well-being of society. In fact, society could not exist without the institution of marriage, for upon it all the social and domestic relations are based."); State v. Hairston, 63 N.C. 451 (1869) (noting that marriage "is more than a civil contract, it is a *relation, an institution,* affecting not merely the parties, like business contracts, but offspring particularly, and society generally."). Another important question raised by the postbellum challenges to antimiscegenation statutes was the extent of the federal government's authority to adopt laws affecting marriage, an institution that had up until then been a matter of exclusive state control. The postbellum miscegenation rulings consistently denied the authority of the federal government to interfere with state sovereignty in matters related to marriage and the family. *See, e.g.,* State v. Gibson, 36 Ind. 389 (1871) ("The right, in the states, to regulate and control, to guard, protect, and preserve this God-given, civilizing, and Christianizing institution [of marriage] is of inestimable importance, and cannot be surrendered, nor can the states suffer or permit any interference therewith. If the federal government can determine who may marry in a state, there is no limit to its power."); Lonas v. State, 50 Tenn. 287 (1871) ("We are of opinion that the late amendments to the Constitution of the United States, and the laws enacted for their enforcement, do not interfere with the rights of the States, as enjoyed since the foundation of the government, to interdict improper marriages").

15. *See, e.g.,* Ellis v. State, 42 Ala. 525 (1868); Green v. State, 58 Ala. 190 (1877). The Alabama Supreme Court in Burns v. State, 48 Ala. 195 (1872), was the only state supreme court to strike down an antimiscegenation law in the nineteenth century, viewing marriage as a contract and holding that the Fourteenth Amendment and the Civil Rights Act of 1866 precluded the enforcement of interracial marital bans. Five years later, as the harsh racism of Jim Crow began to replace the egalitarian promise of Reconstruction, the Alabama court overruled *Burns,* claiming that "natural law" forbade interracial marriages and "that amalgamation which leads to a corruption of races, is as clearly divine as that which imparted to them different natures." *Green, supra.* And five years after that, the Alabama court upheld a statute that imposed a more severe penalty for interracial adultery and fornication, concluding that "the evil tendency of the crime…is greater when…committed between persons of the two races…. Its result may be the amalgamation of the two races, producing a mongrel population and a degraded civilization, the prevention of which is dictated by a sound public policy affecting the highest interests of society and government." Pace v. State, 69 Ala. 231, 233 (1881). The U.S. Supreme Court affirmed on the ground that the statute treated blacks and whites alike. Pace v. Alabama, 106 U.S. 583 (1883).

16. Bowlin v. Commonwealth, 65 Ky. 5 (1867).

17. Scott v. Georgia, 39 Ga. 321 (1869) (emphasis added).

18. Lonas v. State, 50 Tenn. 287 (1871).

19. State v. Jackson, 80 Mo. 175, 179 (1883). Some of those who called for the strict separation of the races in the nineteenth century believed that whites and blacks were members of different species, a fact that manifested itself in the supposed infertility of biracial offspring. (Indeed, the term "mulatto" is believed to be derived from the Portuguese word for mule, the usually sterile offspring of male donkeys and female horses.) Keith E. Sealing, "Blood Will Tell: Scientific Racism and the Legal Prohibitions against Miscegenation," 5 *Michigan Journal of Race & Law* 559, 562–563 (2000). Fertility concerns remained part of antimiscegenation debates for decades to come. For example, the state of California, in defending its antimiscegenation law sixty years after *Jackson,* claimed that biracial individuals had

low fertility rates. Respondent's Brief in Opposition to Writ of Mandate, Perez v. Sharp, California Supreme Court, No. 20305, October 3, 1948, pp. 64–66.

20. Peggy Pascoe, *What Comes Naturally: Miscegenation Law and the Making of Race in America* (New York: Oxford University Press, 2009), p. 1. The word "miscegenation" was introduced to the American public in 1864 by two Democratic pamphleteers who, pretending to speak for radical Republicans, and hoping to create a backlash against racial equality, argued that science, nature, and religion called for the free intermixture of the races. *Miscegenation: The Theory of the Blending of the Race, Applied to the American White Man and Negro* (New York: H. Dexter, Hamilton & Co., 1864). For a discussion of the pamphlet, see Novkov, *supra* note 2, p. 38; Pascoe, *supra*, p. 28.

21. Pascoe, *supra* note 20, pp. 115–123.

22. For comprehensive explorations of the American eugenic movement, see Mark H. Haller, *Eugenics: Hereditarian Attitudes in American Thought* (New Brunswick: Rutgers University Press, 1984); Daniel J. Kevles, *In the Name of Eugenics: Genetics and the Uses of Human Heredity* (New York: Knopf, 1985); Donald K. Pickens, *Eugenics and the Progressives* (Nashville: Vanderbilt University Press, 1968).

23. Kenneth M. Ludmerer, *Genetics and American Society: A Historical Appraisal* (Baltimore: John Hopkins University Press, 1972), pp. 20–33. For a discussion of the pseudo-scientific bases for the notion that racial mixing led to the creation of physically and psychologically deficient individuals, see Paul Lawrence Farber, *Mixing Races: From Scientific Racism to Modern Evolutionary Ideas* (Baltimore: John Hopkins University Press, 2011), ch. 2.

24. Julie Novkov, "Racial Constructions: The Legal Regulation of Miscegenation in Alabama, 1890–1934," 20 *Law & History Review* 225, 246 (2002).

25. Novkov, *supra* note 24, p. 246.

26. Gregory Michael Dorr, *Segregation's Science: Eugenics and Society in Virginia* (Charlottesville: University of Virginia Press, 2008), ch. 5; Paul A. Lombardo, "Miscegenation, Eugenics, and Racism: Historical Footnotes to *Loving v. Virginia*," 21 *University of California at Davis Law Review* 421 (1988); Richard B. Sherman, "'The Last Stand': The Fight for Racial Integrity in Virginia in the 1920s," 54 *Journal of Southern History* 69 (1988). For an interesting discussion of the role that gender stereotypes and expectations played in the enactment of Virginia's Racial Integrity Act, see Lisa Lindquist Dorr, "Arm in Arm: Gender, Eugenics, and Virginia's Racial Integrity Acts of the 1920s," 11 *Journal of Women's History* 143 (1999). As Dorr and others have noted, it is no coincidence that Virginia enacted a statute authorizing the sterilization of the "feebleminded"—later upheld by the Supreme Court in Buck v. Bell, 274 U.S. 200 (1927)—in the same year it enacted its Racial Integrity Act. Eugenicists viewed both measures as crucial to the promotion of a "pure" and "fit" white race.

27. Starting in 1886, Virginia defined a "colored" person as someone with one-quarter or more of black blood. By the early twentieth century, however, that definition, from a white supremacy perspective, had become insufficiently restrictive because it was perceived to permit too much racial intermixing. In 1910, therefore, the Virginia legislature enacted a statute defining a white person as someone who had less than one-sixteenth African ancestry. The Racial Integrity Act of 1924 went even further by deeming anyone who had *any* trace of black ancestry to be a non-Caucasian. The 1924 law also for the first time prohibited marriages between whites and Asians. Three years later, the Alabama and Georgia legislatures enacted similar "one-drop" laws. Wallenstein, *supra* note 6, pp. 137, 141–142.

28. Dorr, *supra* note 26, p. 145 (quoting John Powell and Earnest Sevier Cox, "Is White America to Become a Negroid Nation?," *Richmond Times-Dispatch*, July 22, 1923).

29. W. A. Plecker, "Virginia's Attempt to Adjust the Color Problem," 15 *American Journal of Public Health* 111, 111 (1925) (emphasis added). Plecker gave another speech in 1924 claiming that "because the mixed breeds are a menace and not an asset, we have them as the greatest problem and most destructive force which confronts the white race and American civilization." W. A. Plecker, *The New Family and Racial Improvement* (Richmond, Va.: Bureau of Vital Statistics, 1928), p. 16.

30. Perez v. Sharp, 198 P.2d 17, 23 (Ca. 1948).

31. Respondent's Brief in Opposition to Writ of Mandate, *supra* note 19, pp. 68, 78.

32. *Perez*, 198 P.2d at 26.

33. *Perez*, 198 P.2d at 22, 26. Three justices, in a dissenting opinion, accepted the state's empirical claims. The dissenters reasoned that "there is authority for the conclusion that the crossing of the primary races leads gradually to retrogression and to eventual extinction of the resultant type unless it is fortified by reunion with the parent stock"; p. 44 (Shenk, J., dissenting). The dissent also accepted the claim that children are harmed by the "social tension" created by interracial unions; p. 45.

34. For a detailed discussion of *Naim*, including the strategic decisions made by the lawyers on both sides, see Gregory Michael Dorr, "Principled Expediency: Eugenics, *Naim v. Naim*, and the Supreme Court," 42 *American Journal of Legal History* 119 (1998).

35. Dorr, *supra* note 34, p. 144 n. 107.

36. Naim v. Naim, 87 S.E.2d 749, 756 (Va. 1955).

37. Naim v. Naim, 350 U.S 985 (1956).

38. Rachel F. Moran, *Interracial Intimacy: The Regulation of Race and Romance* (Chicago: University of Chicago Press, 2001), p. 90.

39. For a discussion of the background and implications of *McLaughlin*, see Ariela R. Dubler, "From *McLaughlin v. Florida* to *Lawrence v. Texas*: Sexual Freedom and the Road to Marriage," 106 *Columbia Law Review* 1165 (2006); Elizabeth H. Pleck, *Not Just Roommates: Cohabitation after the Sexual Revolution* (Chicago: University of Chicago Press, 2012), ch. 1. Although Florida had a statute that criminalized cohabitation regardless of the race of the parties, that statute required proof that sexual intercourse had taken place. The provision prohibiting interracial cohabitation criminalized the sharing of the home but did not require the state to prove that the couple had engaged in sexual intercourse.

40. McLaughlin v. State, 153 So. 2d 1 (Fla. 1963); McLaughlin v. Florida, 377 U.S. 914 (1964) (noting probable jurisdiction).

41. Brief of Appellee, McLaughlin v. Florida, U.S. Supreme Court, No. 11, September 30, 1964, pp. 41–42. As Virginia would later argue in *Loving*, Florida in *McLaughlin* claimed, incongruously and implausibly, that *Brown v. Board of Education* supported its view that preventing the psychological harm supposedly experienced by children of interracial unions justified the enactment of its statutes prohibiting interracial relationships; pp. 41–42.

42. Brief of Appellee, McLaughlin v. Florida, U.S. Supreme Court, No. 11, September 30, 1964, pp. 41–42.

43. McLaughlin v. Florida, 379 U.S. 184, 196 (1964).

44. Albert I. Gordon, *Inter-Marriage: Interfaith, Interracial, Interethnic* (Boston: Beacon Press, 1964).

45. Gordon, *Inter-Marriage*, p. 354 (quoted in Brief of Appellee, Loving v. Virginia, U.S. Supreme Court, No. 395, March 20, 1967, at Appendix B).

46. Gordon, *Inter-Marriage*, p. 370 (quoted in Brief of Appellee, *supra* note 45, at Appendix B). Although Gordon in his book also focused on the well-being of children of interfaith

marriages, he concluded that "the problems which confront the children of Negro-white marriages appear to be even more complex and emotionally frustrating" than those of children raised by married parents of different faiths. Gordon added that "it is my belief that interracially intermarried parents are committing a grave offense against their children that is far more serious and even dangerous to their welfare than they realize"; p. 334.

47. Brown v. Board of Education, 347 U.S. 483 (1954).
48. Brief of Appellee, *supra* note 45, p. 35 (quoting State v. Brown, 108 So. 2d 233, 234 (La. 1959)).
49. Loving v. Virginia, 388 U.S. 1 (1967).
50. Michael Grossberg, "Guarding the Altar: Physiological Restrictions and the Rise of State Intervention in Matrimony," 26 *American Journal of Legal History* 197, 219 (1982).
51. Grossberg, *supra* note 50, p. 219 (quoting from Christopher Tiedeman, *A Treatise on the Limitations of the Police Power* (St. Louis: F. H. Thomas Law Book Co., 1886), p. 536). Grossberg points out that Tiedeman was ideologically opposed to most governmental regulation. The fact that he supported marital restrictions imposed on the mentally disabled was illustrative of how "hereditary alarm became so pervasive" throughout American society in the second half of the nineteenth century; p. 536.
52. Haller, *supra* note 22, p. 45. For the leading, ostensibly scientific, study of feeblemindedness published in the early twentieth century, see Henry H. Goddard, *Feeble-Mindedness: Its Causes and Consequences* (New York: Macmillan, 1914). For a comprehensive discussion of the history of the social and medical responses to individuals with cognitive disabilities during the nineteenth and early twentieth centuries, see James W. Trent, *Inventing the Feeble Mind: A History of Mental Retardation in the United States* (Berkeley: University of California Press, 1994).
53. Kevles, *supra* note 22, p. 79 (quoting Michael Guyer, *Being Well-Born: An Introduction to Genetics* (Indianapolis: Bobbs-Merrill, 1916), pp. 264–265).
54. General Statutes of Connecticut, Revision of 1902, Section 1354 (quoted in Stevenson Smith, Madge W. Wilkinson, and Louisa C. Wagoner, *A Summary of the Laws of the Several States Governing I.—Marriage and Divorce of the Feeble-minded, the Epileptic, and the Insane. II.—Asexualization. III.—Institutional Commitment and Discharge of the Feeble-minded and the Epileptic*, Bulletin of the University of Washington, no. 82 (1914), p. 5).
55. Grossberg, *supra* note 50, p. 221.
56. Edward J. Larson, *Sex, Race, and Science: Eugenics in the Deep South* (Baltimore: Johns Hopkins University Press, 1995), p. 22.
57. J. P. Chamberlain, "Eugenics and Limitations of Marriage," 9 *American Bar Association Journal* 429, 429 (1923).
58. Jessie Spaulding Smith, "Marriage, Sterilization and Commitment Laws Aimed at Decreasing Mental Deficiency," 5 *Journal of the American Institute of Criminal Law and Criminology* 364 (1915).
59. Kevles, *supra* note 22, ch. 7. Charles Davenport, a biologist and leading eugenicist who ran the Eugenics Record Office in Cold Spring Harbor, New York, explained that "the proper action in the case of imbeciles or the gross epileptics who wish to marry is not to decline to give them a marriage license, but to place them in an institution under State care during at least the entire reproductive period. No cheap device of a *law* against marriage will take the place of compulsory segregation of gross defectives." Charles B. Davenport, *State Laws Limiting Marriage Selection Examined in the Light of Eugenics*, Eugenics Record

Office, Bulletin No. 9 (Cold Spring Harbor, N.Y.: Eugenics Record Office, 1913), p. 12. *See also* Edward W. Spencer, "Some Phases of Marriage Law and Legislation from a Sanitary and Eugenic Standpoint," 25 *Yale Law Journal* 58, 69 (1915) (contending that the "feebleminded" were unable to control their sexual urges and that, as a result, "segregation, asexualization and sterilization, rather than prohibition of marriage, are the only effective safeguards to society, so far as such persons are concerned").

60. Buck v. Bell, 274 U.S. 200 (1927).

61. Gould v. Gould, 61 A. 604, 604–605 (Conn. 1905).

62. Spencer, *supra* note 59, p. 64.

63. Jonathan Matloff, "Idiocy, Lunacy, and Matrimony: Exploring Constitutional Challenges to State Restrictions on Marriages of Persons with Mental Disabilities," 17 *American University Journal of Gender, Social Policy & Law* 497 (2009); Brooke Pietrzak, "Marriage Laws and People with Mental Retardation: A Continuing History of Second Class Treatment," 17 *Developments in Mental Health Law* 33 (1997).

64. John Witte, Jr., *The Sins of the Fathers: The Law and Theology of Illegitimacy Reconsidered* (New York: Cambridge University Press, 2009), p. 139.

65. Michael Grossberg, *Governing the Hearth: Law and the Family in Nineteenth-Century America* (Chapel Hill: University of North Carolina Press, 1985), pp. 200–207; Witte, *supra* note 64, pp. 146–148.

66. Grossberg, *supra* note 65, pp. 228–229.

67. Gail Reekie, *Measuring Immorality: Social Inquiry and the Problem of Illegitimacy* (New York: Cambridge University Press, 1998), pp. 120–125.

68. Percy Gamble Kammerer, *The Unmarried Mother: A Study of Five Hundred Cases* (Boston: Little Brown, 1918), p. 292.

69. Kammerer, *supra* note 68, pp. 263, 235, 298. Goddard, in his ostensibly scientific study of feeblemindedness published in 1914, claimed to find a "decided relation between illegitimacy and hereditary feeble-mindedness." Goddard, *supra* note 52, p. 499.

70. *Children of Illegitimate Birth and Measures for Their Protection* (Washington, D.C.: Department of Labor, Children's Bureau, 1926) (Pub. No. 166). *See also* Alberta S. B. Guibord and Ida R. Parker, *What Becomes of the Unmarried Mother? A Study of 82 Cases* (Boston: Research Bureau on Case Work, 1922).

71. Reekie, *supra* note 67, p. 125. Rickie Solinger argues that after World War II, most medical and social work professionals criticized the presumed link between illegitimacy and mental degeneracy in single mothers as being too fatalistic. Under this view, illegitimacy was still explained largely by the mental deficiencies of single mothers, but experts viewed those deficiencies (or neuroses) as treatable through professional psychological guidance. Rickie Solinger, *Wake Up Little Susie: Single Pregnancy and Race Before Roe v. Wade* (New York: Routledge, 1992), p. 16. Solinger adds, however, that the medical and professional view of "illegitimacy as a treatable condition" was largely limited to single white mothers; in contrast, black illegitimacy during the postwar period was understood largely in biologically deterministic ways, that is, as the outgrowth of a "natural" failure among black women to control their sexuality; p. 24.

72. Kammerer, *supra* note 68, p. 308.

73. Kingsley Davis, "Illegitimacy and the Social Structure," 45 *American Journal of Sociology* 215, 215 (1939). For examples of legal briefs filed by marriage equality opponents that rely on a traditional understanding of marriage as articulated in Kingsley Davis, "The Meaning and Significance of Marriage in Contemporary Society," *in Contemporary*

Marriage: Comparative Perspectives on a Changing Institution, Kingsley Davis ed. (New York: Russell Sage Foundation, 1985), p. 1, *see, e.g.,* Brief of Petitioners, Hollingsworth v. Perry, U.S. Supreme Court, No. 12-144, January 22, 2013, pp. 34–35; Brief Amici Curiae of James Q. Wilson, et al., Legal and Family Scholars in Support of Defendants-Appellants, Conaway v. Deane, Maryland Court of Appeals, No. 44, September 8, 2006, p. 10.

74. Davis, "Illegitimacy and the Social Structure," *supra* note 73, p. 219. Davis defended a functional understanding of antiillegitimacy regulations in another article, also published in 1939, in which he sought to schematize different categories of illegitimacy. Kingsley Davis, "The Forms of Illegitimacy," 18 *Social Forces* 77 (1939).

75. Davis, "Illegitimacy and the Social Structure," *supra* note 73, p. 231.

76. Levy v. Louisiana, 192 So. 2d 193 (La. Ct. App. 1966).

77. Brief of Attorney General, State of Louisiana, Levy v. Louisiana, U.S. Supreme Court, No. 508, February 5, 1968, pp. 4–5.

78. Brief of Attorney General, *supra* note 77, pp. 5–8.

79. Levy v. Louisiana, 391 U.S. 68, 71–72 (1968).

80. Brief of Attorney General, *supra* note 77, p. 4.

81. Labine v. Vincent, 401 U.S. 532, 538 (1971). The Court essentially overruled *Labine* six years later in Trimble v. Gordon, 430 U.S. 762 (1977).

82. Weber v. Aetna Casualty & Surety Company, 406 U.S. 164, 173 (1972).

83. *See, e.g.,* Clark v. Jeter, 486 U.S. 456 (1988) (six-year statute of limitations for paternity actions on behalf of nonmarital children, when paternity actions on behalf of marital children are not subject to statute of limitations, violates equal protection guarantees); Jimenez v. Weinberger, 417 U.S. 628 (1974) (Social Security Act provision denying benefits to nonmarital children is unconstitutional); New Jersey Welfare Rights Organization v. Cahill, 411 U.S. 619 (1973) (state law rendering nonmarital children ineligible for welfare benefits violates equal protection clause); Gomez v. Perez, 409 U.S. 535 (1973) (state cannot render nonmarital children ineligible to receive child support from father); Glona v. American Guarantee & Liability Insurance Co., 391 U.S. 73 (1968) (state cannot prohibit mother from suing for wrongful death of nonmarital child). *But see* Lalli v. Lalli, 439 U.S. 259 (1978) (requiring nonmarital child to show proof of parent/child relationship with deceased intestate individual did not violate equal protection principles); Mathews v. Lucas, 427 U.S. 495 (1976) (requiring showing of dependency by nonmarital children to qualify for Social Security survivor benefits did not violate Fifth Amendment). For an illuminating discussion of how the law continues to discriminate against nonmarital children, see Solangel Maldonado, "Illegitimate Harm: Law, Stigma, and Discrimination Against Nonmarital Children," 63 *Florida Law Review* 345 (2011).

84. Martin Ottenheimer, *Forbidden Relatives: The American Myth of Cousin Marriage* (Urbana: University of Illinois Press, 1996), pp. 19–31. The statutes also usually criminalized sexual conduct between the individuals in question regardless of whether they sought to marry.

85. Leigh B. Bienen, "Defining Incest," 92 *Northwestern Law Review* 1501, 1531 (1998); Grossberg, *supra* note 65, p. 111. *See also* Peter Bardaglio, "'An Outrage upon Nature': Incest and the Law in the Nineteenth-Century South," *in In Joy and Sorrow: Women, Family and Marriage in the Victorian South, 1830–1900,* Carol Blesser, ed. (New York: Oxford University Press, 1991), pp. 32, 33 ("incest among members of the nuclear family confused the roles and duties of individuals and eroded the stability of the household, thereby weakening its effectiveness as an institution of social control.").

86. Noah Webster, "Explanation of the Reezons Why Marriage iz Prohibuted between Natural Relations," *in Collection of Essays and Fugitiv Writings on Moral, Historical, Political and Literary Subjects* (Boston: I. Thomas and E. T. Andrews, 1790), p. 324 (quoted in Ottenheimer, *supra* note 84, p. 45).

87. Joel Bishop, *Commentaries on Marriage and Divorce* (Boston: Little Brown, 5th ed., 1872), pp. 273–274 (quoted in Grossberg, *supra* note 65, p. 145).

88. Ottenheimer, *supra* note 84, p. 50. Elsewhere in his book, Ottenheimer explains that "with the acceptance of the Spencerian bioevolutionary view of social interaction…, families [in the latter part of the nineteenth century] were seen as breeding units for a society moving along an evolutionary scale of complexity (and progress)"; p. 8. In explaining why southern legislatures in particular moved, in the second half of the nineteenth century, to enlarge the number of consanguineous relationships covered by the incest marital bans, Peter Bardaglio notes that they were partly motivated by "new concerns about the possibility of transmitting hereditary defects through marriage, concerns that also made themselves evident during this period in laws banning interracial marriages." Bardaglio, *supra* note 85, p. 44.

89. Ottenheimer, *supra* note 84, ch. 4. In the nineteenth century, the only European countries that prohibited cousins from marrying were Austria, Hungary, Russia, and Spain. Today, no European country does so; p. 90.

90. Ottenheimer, *supra* note 84, ch. 6; Denise Grady, "Few Risks Seen to the Children of 1st Cousins," *N.Y. Times*, April 4, 2002, at A1.

91. On contemporary bans of cousin marriages, see Ottenheimer, *supra* note 84, pp. 32–33 (table 2), 37–41. About a dozen states still prohibit affinity marriages, despite the absence of genetic concerns arising from such unions. For an exploration of affinity marriage prohibitions, see Christine McNiece Metteer, "Some 'Incest' Is Harmless Incest: Determining the Fundamental Right to Marry of Adults Related by Affinity Without Resorting to State Incest Statutes," 10 *Kansas Journal of Law & Public Policy* 262 (2000).

92. For a discussion of the studies, see Naomi Cahn, "Accidental Incest: Drawing the Line—or the Curtain?—for Reproductive Technology," 32 *Harvard Journal of Law & Gender* 59, 85–86 (2009).

93. Alan H. Bittles, "Genetic Aspects of Inbreeding and Incest," *in Inbreeding, Incest, and the Incest Taboo: The State of Knowledge at the Turn of the Century*, Arthur P. Wolf and William H. Durham, eds. (Stanford: Stanford University Press, 2005), pp. 38, 49–54.

94. Cahn, *supra* note 92, pp. 92–93. For an argument that bans on incestuous marriages violate the fundamental right to marry, see Carolyn S. Bratt, "Incest Statutes and the Fundamental Right to Marriage: Is Oedipus Free to Marry?," 18 *Family Law Quarterly* 257 (1984).

95 Lowe v. Swanson, 663 F.3d 258, 264 (6th Cir. 2011). *But see* Israel v. Allen, 577 P.2d 762, 764 (Col. 1978) (holding that prohibiting an adopted brother and sister from marrying is unconstitutional and rejecting the argument that the state has a legitimate interest in promoting "family harmony").

96. Sarah Barringer Gordon, *The Mormon Question: Polygamy and Constitutional Conflict in Nineteenth-Century America* (Chapel Hill: University of North Carolina Press, 2002), p. 26; Orma Linford, "The Mormons and the Law: The Polygamy Cases," 9 *Utah Law Review* 308, 308–309 (1964).

97. Edwin B. Firmage and Richard C. Mangrum, *Zion in the Courts: A Legal History of the Church of Jesus Christ of Latter-day Saints, 1830–1900* (Urbana: University of Illinois Press, 1988), pp. 131–132; Gordon, *supra* note 96, p. 58.

98. Gordon, *supra* note 96, ch. 3.
99. On the antipolygamy statutes enacted by Congress in the decades before Utah became a state, see Nancy F. Cott, *Public Vows: A History of Marriage and the Nation* (Cambridge, Mass.: Harvard University Press, 2000), pp. 112–114; 118–120; Firmage and Magnum, *supra* note 97, pp. 130–132, 148–149, 161–162, 198–202; Gordon, *supra* note 96, ch. 5; Linford, *supra* note 96, pp. 314–328; Kelly E. Phipps, "Marriage and Redemption: Mormon Polygamy in the Congressional Imagination, 1862–1887," 95 *Virginia Law Review* 435 (2009).
100. Gordon, *supra* note 96, p. 57.
101. Gordon, *supra* note 96, pp. 47, 52, 137; Carol Weisbrod and Pamela Sheingorn, "*Reynolds v. U.S.*: Nineteenth Century Forms of Marriage and the Status of Women," 10 *Connecticut Law Review* 828, 829 (1978). It is important to note, however, that the concerns raised by antipolygamists about protecting the interests of women were driven by highly paternalistic understandings of the role of women in society, rather than by what we would today categorize as feminist concerns; pp. 829–830. Indeed, while antipolygamists at first supported an 1870 federal law giving Utah women the right to vote, they later changed their minds after Mormon women consistently voted for candidates who supported polygamy. Gordon, *supra* note 96, pp. 167–171; Nancy L. Rosenblum, "Democratic Sex: *Reynolds v. U.S.*, Sexual Relations and Community," *in Sex, Preference, and Family: Essays on Law and Nature*, David M. Estlund and Martha C. Nussbaum, eds. (New York: Oxford University Press, 1997), pp. 63, 76. Since the enfranchisement of women strengthened rather than weakened polygamy, Congress included a provision in the Edmunds-Tucker Act of 1887 rescinding the right of Utah women to vote. Firmage and Mangrum, *supra* note 97, p. 199.
102. Gordon, *supra* note 96, pp. 69–70.
103. Cott, *supra* note 99, pp. 114–115, 117–118; Martha M. Ertman, "Race Treason: The Untold Story of America's Ban on Polygamy," 19 *Columbia Journal of Gender & Law* 287 (2010); Gordon, *supra* note 96, p. 142; Phipps, *supra* note 99, pp. 481–482.
104. Reynolds v. United States, 98 U.S. 145, 164 (1878).
105. *Reynolds*, 98 U. S. at 165. On the background, reasoning, and impact of *Reynolds*, see Gordon, *supra* note 96, ch. 4; Linford, *supra* note 96, pp. 321–341; Rosenblum, *supra* note 101, pp. 71–81. On Lieber's views of political institutions and polygamy, see Maura I. Strassberg, "Distinctions of Form or Substance: Monogamy, Polygamy and Same-Sex Marriage," 75 *North Carolina Law Review* 1501, 1518–1523 (1997). The Supreme Court reiterated the views it expressed in *Reynolds* in later cases upholding antipolygamy legislation. Late Corporation of the Church of Jesus Christ Latter-Day Saints v. U.S., 136 U.S. 1, 49 (1890) (claiming, in upholding the Edmunds-Tucker Act of 1887, that "the organization of a community for the spread and practice of polygamy is, in a measure, a return to barbarism."); Davis v. Beason, 133 U.S. 333, 341 (1890) (claiming, in upholding an Idaho statute denying the vote to those who advocated polygamy, that "bigamy and polygamy...tend to destroy the purity of the marriage relation, to disturb the peace of families, to degrade woman, and to debase man. Few crimes are more pernicious to the best interests of society, and receive more general or more deserved punishment."); Murphy v. Ramsey, 114 U.S. 15, 45 (1885) (claiming, in upholding the Edmunds Act of 1882, that monogamous marriage was "the sure foundation of all that is stable and noble in our civilization [and] the best guaranty of that reverent morality which is the source of all beneficent progress in social and political improvement.").

106. Martha Ertman has noted that some antipolygamy literature, including political cartoons, raised concerns about the supposed physical weaknesses of Mormon offspring. That literature, however, did not contend that the weaknesses were the result of *polygamy* as such; instead, the claim was that the Mormons were an inferior *race*, and in that way analogous to people of Asian and African descent. From this perspective, polygamous marriages contributed to race degeneration. Ertman, *supra* note 103, pp. 313–318. *See also* Christine Talbot, " 'Turkey Is in Our Midst': Orientalism and Contagion in Nineteenth Century Anti-Mormonism," 8 *Journal of Law & Family Studies* 363 (2006). For their part, some Mormons defended the practice of polygamy by making the eugenic claim that the children of polygamous marriages were physically superior. Ertman, *supra* note 103, pp. 323–334; Gordon, *supra* note 96, p. 85.

Chapter 2

1. John M. Finnis, "Law, Morality, and 'Sexual Orientation,' " 69 *Notre Dame Law Review* 1049, 1066 (1994). *See also* Patrick Lee and Robert George, "What Sex Can Be: Self-Alienation, Illusion, or One-Flesh Union," 42 *American Journal of Jurisprudence* 135 (1997). For more recent articulations of similar arguments against the recognition of same-sex marriages, see Sherif Girgis, Ryan T. Anderson, and Robert P. George, *What Is Marriage? Man and Woman: A Defense* (New York: Encounter Books, 2012).
2. Lee and George, *supra* note 1, p. 150.
3. Douglas W. Kmiec, "The Procreative Argument for Proscribing Same-Sex Marriage," 32 *Hastings Constitutional Law Quarterly* 653, 657 (2005).
4. Prepared Statement of Hadley Arkes, H.R. 3396, Defense of Marriage Act, Hearing Before the Subcommittee on the Constitution of the Committee on the Judiciary, U.S. House of Representatives, 104th Congress, May 15, 1996, p. 11.
5. Brief of Apellees, Morrison v. Sadler, Indiana Court of Appeals, No. 49A02-0305-CV-447, October 3, 2003, p. 11.
6. Brief of Family Research Council as Amicus Curiae in Support of Defendants-Respondents, Hernandez v. Robles, New York Court of Appeals, No. 2006-0087, April 20, 2006, p. 49.
7. The historical record did not support the claim, often made by opponents of marriage equality during the 1990s, that no society had ever recognized same-sex marriages. *See, e.g.,* John Boswell, *Same-Sex Unions in Premodern Europe* (New York: Villard, 1994); William N. Eskridge, Jr., "A History of Same-Sex Marriage," 79 *Virginia Law Review* 1419 (1993).
8. Lawrence v. Texas, 539 U.S. 558, 605 (2003) (Scalia, J., dissenting).
9. On mothers' pensions, see Mimi Abramovitz, *Regulating the Lives of Women: Social Welfare Policy from Colonial Times to the Present* (Boston: South End Press, 1996), ch. 6; Linda Gordon, *Pitied but Not Entitled: Single Mothers and the History of Welfare, 1890–1935* (New York: Free Press, 1994), ch. 3; Theda Skocpol, *Protecting Soldiers and Mothers: The Political Origins of Social Policy in the United States* (Cambridge, Mass.: Harvard University Press, 1992), ch. 8. On the enactment of the ADC, see Gordon, *supra*, ch. 9.
10. Abramovitz, *supra* note 9, p. 319; Gwendolyn Mink, *Welfare's End* (Ithaca: Cornell University Press, 1998), p. 46.
11. Mink, *supra* note 10, p. 47.
12. Abramovitz, *supra* note 9, pp. 324–325.
13. Abramovitz, *supra* note 9, p. 321.

14. Angela Onwuachi-Willig, "The Return of the Ring: Welfare Reform's Marriage Cure as the Revival of Post-bellum Control," 93 *California Law Review* 1647 (2005); Susan L. Thomas, "Race, Gender, and Welfare Reform: The Antinatalist Response," 28 *Journal of Black Studies* 419 (1998).

15. Thomas, *supra* note 14, p. 424.

16. Thomas, *supra* note 14, pp. 424–425.

17. Mink, *supra* note 10, pp. 48–49.

18. Mink, *supra* note 10, p. 50; King v. Smith, 392 U.S. 309 (1968).

19. New Jersey Welfare Rights Organization v. Cahill, 411 U.S. 619 (1973).

20. Mink, *supra* note 10, p. 51.

21. Abramovitz, *supra* note 9, pp. 335–336.

22. Abramovitz, *supra* note 9, p. 335.

23. Abramovitz, *supra* note 9, p. 335.

24. U.S. Department of Labor, Office of Policy Planning and Research, *The Negro Family: The Case for National Action* (March 1965), p. 14.

25. On the 1967 amendments, see Abramovitz, *supra* note 9, pp. 337–340; Mink, *supra* note 10, pp. 58–59.

26. Charles A. Murray, *Losing Ground: American Social Policy, 1950–1980* (New York: Basic Books, 1984), ch. 12. *See also* Stuart M. Butler and Anna Kondratas, *Out of the Poverty Trap: A Conservative Strategy for Welfare Reform* (New York: Free Press, 1987), pp. 139–140; George F. Gilder, *Wealth and Poverty* (New York: Basic Books, 1981), pp. 111–112.

27. *The Family: Preserving America's Future, A Report to the President from the White House Working Group on the Family* (1986), p. 6; Leslie Maitland Werner, "Reagan to Name New Domestic Aide," *N.Y. Times*, January 30, 1987, A23.

28. *The Family: Preserving America's Future, supra* note 27, p. 15.

29. *The Family: Preserving America's Future, supra* note 27, p. 23 (quoting Dissenting Views, "Safety Net Programs: Are They Reaching Poor Children?," U.S. House of Representatives Select Committee on Children, Youth and Families, October 3, 1986)).

30. Family Support Act of 1988, Pub. L. No. 100-485. For a discussion of this statute and its implications, see Martha L. Fineman, "Images of Mothers in Poverty Discourses," 1991 *Duke Law Journal* 274.

31. Mink, *supra* note 10, p. 42.

32. Andrew Rosenthal, "After the Riots: Quayle Says Riots Sprang from Lack of Family Values," *N.Y. Times*, May 19, 1992, A1.

33. Barbara Dafoe Whitehead, "Dan Quayle Was Right," *The Atlantic*, April, 1993, p. 47.

34. Charles Murray, "The Coming White Underclass," *Wall Street Journal*, October 29, 1993, A14.

35. Murray, *supra* note 34.

36. David Popenoe, *Life without Father: Compelling New Evidence That Fatherhood and Marriage Are Indispensable for the Good of Children and Society* (New York: Free Press, 1996), ch. 2.

37. David Blankenhorn, *Fatherless America: Confronting Our Most Urgent Social Problem* (New York: Basic Books, 1995).

38. Sara McLanahan and Gary Sandefur, *Growing Up with a Single Parent: What Hurts, What Helps* (Cambridge, Mass.: Harvard University Press, 1994), p. 3.

39. McLanahan and Sandefur, *supra* note 38, pp. 134, 85.

40. On the role of race in the setting of welfare policy, see Onwuachi-Willig, *supra* note 14; Jill S. Quadagno, *The Color of Welfare: How Racism Undermined the War on Poverty* (New York: Oxford University Press, 1994); Thomas, *supra* note 14.

41. Murray, *supra* note 34; "First Lady Assails Orphanage Plan," *N.Y. Times*, December 1, 1994, A28.

42. John R. Hand, "Buying Fertility: The Constitutionality of Welfare Bonuses for Welfare Mothers Who Submit to Norplant Insertion," 46 *Vanderbilt Law Review* 715 (1993); Tamar Lewin, "A Plan to Pay Welfare Mothers for Birth Control," *N.Y. Times*, February 9, 1991, A9. In 1997, the company that made Norplant settled a class-action lawsuit brought by women who claimed that it had not provided adequate notice of the contraceptives' side effects. David J. Morrow, "Maker of Norplant Offers a Settlement in Suit over Effects," *N.Y. Times*, August 27, 1999, A1. A few years later, the manufacturer stopped selling the product in the United States.

43. H.B. 3207, S.C. (1993); S.B. 2895, Miss. (1992).

44. Thomas, *supra* note 14, p. 435.

45. Lucy A. Williams, "Race, Rat Bites and Unfit Mothers: How Media Discourse Informs Welfare Legislation Debates," 22 *Fordham Urban Law Journal* 1159 (1995).

46. April L. Cherry, "Social Contract Theory, Welfare Reform, Race, and the Male Sex-Right," 75 *Oregon Law Review* 1037, 1041 (1996) (citing House Committee on Ways and Means, 103rd Congress, *Overview of Entitlement Programs 1993 Green Book*, pp. 708–709 (table 36)).

47. Mink, *supra* note 10, p. 33.

48. Cherry, *supra* note 46, p. 1092 (citing U.S. Census, "Household and Family Characteristics," March 1994).

49. U.S. General Accounting Office, *Families on Welfare—Sharp Rise in Never-Married Women Reflects Societal Trend* (May 31, 1994); Sam Fulwood, "Out-of-Wedlock Births Rise Sharply among Most Groups," *L.A. Times*, July 14, 1993, A1.

50. Abramovitz, *supra* note 9, p. 365.

51. Note, "Dethroning the Welfare Queen: The Rhetoric of Reform," 107 *Harvard Law Review* 2013, 2026 n. 81 (1994).

52. Abramovitz, *supra* note 9, p. 365 (citing Press Release, "Researchers Dispute Contention That Welfare Is a Major Cause of Out of Wedlock Births," June 23, 1994). *See also* Barbara Vobeja, "Gauging Welfare's Role in Motherhood: Sociologists Question Whether 'Family Caps' Are a Legitimate Solution," *Wash. Post*, June 2, 1994, A1; Gregory Acs, *The Impact of AFDC on Young Women's Childbearing Decisions* (Washington, D.C.: The Urban Institute, 1994). For studies showing a lack of association between receiving welfare benefits and higher out-of-wedlock childbirths, *see, e.g.,* Greg J. Duncan and Saul D. Hoffman, "Welfare Benefits, Economic Opportunities, and Out-of-Wedlock Births among Black Teenage Girls," 27 *Demography* 519 (1990); David Ellwood and Mary Jo Bane, "The Impact of AFDC on Family Structure and Living Arrangements," *in Research in Labor Economics* (vol. 7), Ronald Ehrenberg, ed. (Greenwich, Conn.: JAI Press, 1985), p. 137; Mark R. Rank, "Fertility among Women on Welfare: Incidence and Determinants," 54 *American Sociological Review* 296 (1989).

53. Ed Gillispie and Bob Schellhas, eds., *Contract with America: The Bold Plan by Rep. Newt Gingrich, Rep. Dick Armey and the House Republicans to Change the Nation* (New York: Times Books, 1994), p. 66. For a comprehensive analysis and trenchant critique of the role that procreative considerations played in welfare reform debates in the early 1990s, see Linda C. McClain, " 'Irresponsible' Procreation," 47 *Hastings Law Journal* 339 (1996).

54. Personal Responsibility and Work Opportunity Reconciliation Act of 1996, Pub. L. No. 104-193, § 408(a)(4), (5).

55. Personal Responsibility and Work Opportunity Reconciliation Act of 1996, *supra* note 54, § 103(a)(1).

56. Personal Responsibility and Work Opportunity Reconciliation Act of 1996, *supra* note 54, § 103(a)(1); §402(a)(1)(v); § 403(a)(2).

57. Personal Responsibility and Work Opportunity Reconciliation Act of 1996, *supra* note 54, § 912.

58. Personal Responsibility and Work Opportunity Reconciliation Act of 1996, *supra* note 54, § 101(1), (2), (3).

59. Report 104–664, Defense of Marriage Act, Committee on the Judiciary, U.S. House of Representatives, July 9, 1996, p. 13.

60. McClain, *supra* note 53, p. 347.

61. Cheryl Wetzstein, "Abortion Tops 'Family Cap' Debate; Policy Feared as Coercion to End Pregnancy," *Washington Times*, May 1, 1995, A6.

62. Michael J. Camasso, "Isolating the Family Cap Effect on Fertility Behavior: Evidence from New Jersey's Family Development Program Experiment," 22 *Contemporary Economic Policy* 453 (2004). On welfare reform and the promotion of abortion, see Susan Frelich Appleton, "When Welfare Reforms Promote Abortion: 'Personal Responsibility,' 'Family Values,' and the Right to Choose," 85 *Georgetown Law Journal* 155 (1996).

63. William J. Bennett, "…But Not a Very Good Idea, Either," *Wash. Post*, May 21, 1996, A19.

64. William J. Bennett, *The Broken Hearth: Reversing the Moral Collapse of the American Family* (New York: Doubleday, 2001), p. 115.

65. Brief of Appellees, State v. Baker, Vermont Supreme Court, No. 98-32, April 30, 1998, p. 43.

66. Brief of Amici Curiae Massachusetts Family Institute, Goodridge v. Department of Public Health, Massachusetts Supreme Judicial Court, No. SJC-08860, December 20, 2002, pp. 4–5.

67. *See, e.g.*, Blankenhorn, *supra* note 37, pp. 2–3; Gilder, *supra* note 26, p. 122; Popenoe, *supra* note 36, p. 4; Institute for American Values & Institute for Marriage & Public Policy, *Marriage and the Law: A Statement of Principles* 15 (New York: Institute for American Values, 2006).

68. Trial Testimony of Kyle Pruett, Baehr v. Miike, Hawai'i Circuit Court, Civ. No. 91-1394-05, September 10, 1996.

69. Trial Testimony of David Blankenhorn, Perry v. Schwarzenegger, U.S. District Court, Northern District of California, No. C 09-2292-VRW, January 26 & 27, 2010.

70. Lynn D. Wardle, "'Multiply and Replenish': Considering Same-Sex Marriage in Light of State Interests in Marital Procreation," 24 *Harvard Journal of Law & Public Policy* 771, 798 (2001).

71. Wardle, *supra* note 70, p. 799.

72. Brief Amicus Curiae of the Family Institute of Connecticut in Support of the Defendants-Appellees, Kerrigan v. Commissioner of Public Health, Connecticut Supreme Court, No. 17716, April 25, 2007, p. 11.

73. *See, e.g.*, Kerry Adams and Peter Brooks, "Marriage as a Message: Same-Sex Couples and the Rhetoric of Accidental Procreation," 21 *Yale Journal of Law & Humanities* 1 (2009); Julie A. Nice, "The Descent of Responsible Procreation: A Genealogy of an Ideology," 45 *Loyola of Los Angeles Law Review* 781 (2012); Edward Stein, "The 'Accidental Procreation' Argument for Withholding Legal Recognition for Same-Sex Relationships," 84 *Chicago Kent Law Review* 403 (2009).

74. Abrams and Brooks, *supra* note 73, pp. 3–4; Stein, *supra* note 73, pp. 416.

75. Goodridge v. Department of Public Health, 798 N.E.2d 941, 995 (Mass. 2003) (Cordy, J., dissenting).

76. Morrison v. Sadler, 821 N.E.2d 15, 24 (Ct. App. Ind. 2005).

77. Hernandez v. Robles, 855 N.E.2d 1, 7 (N.Y. 2006).

78. Abrams and Brooks, *supra* note 73, p. 24; Kenji Yoshino, "Too Good for Marriage," *N.Y. Times*, July 14, 2006, A19.

79. For an argument that the changes in the procreative and child-based claims raised by same-sex marriage opponents should lead courts to approach them with skepticism, see Courtney G. Joslin, "Searching for Harm: Same-Sex Marriage and the Well-Being of Children," 46 *Harvard Civil Rights–Civil Liberties Law Review* 81 (2011).

80. Nancy F. Cott, *Public Vows: A History of Marriage and the Nation* (Cambridge, Mass.: Harvard University Press, 2000), p. 124.

81. Mary Ware Dennett, *Birth Control Laws: Shall We Keep Them, Change Them or Abolish Them?* (New York: Grafton Press, 1926), pp. 10–14; Note, "Some Legislative Aspects of the Birth-Control Problem," 45 *Harvard Law Review* 723 (1932).

82. For the history of the birth control movement in the United States, see Peter C. Engelman, *A History of the Birth Control Movement in America* (Santa Barbara, Calif.: Praeger, 2011); Linda Gordon, *Moral Property of Women: A History of Birth Control Politics in America* (Urbana: University of Illinois Press, 2002): Carole R. McCann, *Birth Control Politics in the United States, 1916–1945* (Ithaca: Cornell University Press, 1994).

83. United States v. One Package of Japanese Pessaries, 86 F.2d 737 (2nd Cir. 1936).

84. Elaine Tyler May, *America and the Pill: A History of Promise, Peril, and Liberation* (New York: Basic Books, 2010), p. 20.

85. Griswold v. Connecticut, 381 U.S. 479 (1965).

86. Eisenstadt v. Baird, 405 U.S. 438 (1972).

87. Carey v. Population Services International, 431 U.S. 678 (1977).

88. May, *supra* note 84, p. 168.

89. Donal E. J. MacNamara and Edward Sagarin, *Sex, Crime, and the Law* (New York: Free Press, 1977), p. 187.

90. On the history of sodomy statutes in the United States, see William N. Eskridge, *Dishonorable Passions: Sodomy Laws in America, 1861–2003* (New York: Viking, 2008).

91. Eskridge, *supra* note 90, pp. 76–88, 96–99.

92. Louis B. Schwartz, "Morals Offenses and the Model Penal Code," 63 *Columbia Law Review* 669 (1962).

93. Roe v. Wade, 410 U.S. 113 (1973); Eisenstadt v. Baird, 405 U.S. 438 (1972); Griswold v. Connecticut, 381 U.S. 479 (1965).

94. Lawrence v. Texas, 539 U.S. 558 (2003).

95. Cynthia Grant Bowman, *Unmarried Couples, Law, and Public Policy* (New York: Oxford University Press, 2010), p. 13.

96. Note, "Fornication, Cohabitation, and the Constitution," 77 *Michigan Law Review* 252, 254 (1977). By 2009, the number of states that criminalized cohabitation was down to seven (Idaho, Illinois, Massachusetts, Minnesota, South Carolina, Utah, and West Virginia). Bowman, *supra* note 95, p. 16.

97. Marvin v. Marvin, 557 P.2d 106 (Cal. 1976).

98. For discussions of the law's treatment of cohabiting couples, see Bowman, *supra* note 95, ch. 2; Joanna L. Grossman and Lawrence M. Friedman, *Inside the Castle: Law and the Family in 20th Century America* (Princeton: Princeton University Press, 2011), pp. 127–141; Elizabeth H. Pleck, *Not Just Roommates: Cohabitation after the Sexual Revolution* (Chicago: University of Chicago Press, 2012).

99. U.S. Census Bureau, *Married-Couple and Unmarried-Partner Households: 2000* (February 2003), p. 1.

100. Pamela J. Smock, "Cohabitation in the United States: An Appraisal of Research Themes, Findings, and Implications," 26 *Annual Review of Sociology* 1, 3 (2000).

101. J. Herbie Difonzo and Ruth C. Stern, "The Winding Road from Form to Function: A Brief History of Contemporary Marriage," 21 *Journal of the American Academy of Matrimonial Lawyers* 1, 24 (2008).

102. U.S. Census Bureau, *America's Families and Living Arrangements: 2000* (June 2001), p. 9.

103. U.S. Census, "Unmarried Partners of the Opposite Sex by Presence of Children (1960– 2012)," November 2012, available at www.census.gov/hhes/families/files/ucl.xls, accessed January 2014.

104. U.S. Census, *supra* note 99, p. 3.

105. U.S. Census, *supra* note 99, p. 13.

106. Larry Bumpass and Hsien-Hen Lu, "Trends in Cohabitation and Implications for Children's Family Contexts in the United States," 54 *Population Studies* 29, 29 (2000).

107. Lawrence M. Friedman, "A Dead Language: Divorce Law and Practice before No-Fault," 86 *Virginia Law Review* 1497, 1503 (2000).

108. Herbert Jacob, *Silent Revolution: The Transformation of Divorce Law in the United States* (Chicago: University of Chicago Press, 1988).

109. Difonzo and Stern, *supra* note 101, p. 24.

110. U.S. Census, *supra* note 102, p. 7.

111. Wendy Sigle-Rushton and Sara McLanahan, "Father Absence and Child Well-Being: A Critical Review," *in The Future of the Family*, Daniel P. Moynihan, Timothy M. Smeeding, and Lee Rainwater, eds. (New York: Russell Sage Foundation, 2004), p. 117.

112. Sigle-Rushton and McLanahan, *supra* note 111, p. 119.

113. Joyce A. Martin, Melissa M. Park, and Paul D. Sutton, National Center for Health Statistics, *Births: Preliminary Data for 2001*, National Vital Statistics Reports, vol. 50, no. 10 (Hyattsville, Md.: National Center for Health Statistics, 2002).

114. Only three states (Arizona, Arkansas, and Louisiana) have adopted covenant marriage laws. Naomi Cahn and June Carbone, *Red Families v. Blue Families: Legal Polarization and the Creation of Culture* (New York: Oxford University Press, 2010), p. 125. And only a tiny percentage (less than 2 percent) of couples in those three states have chosen to enter into covenant marriages. Andrew J. Cherlin, *The Marriage-Go-Round: The State of Marriage and the Family in America Today* (New York: Knopf, 2009), p. 4; Grossman and Friedman, *supra* note 98, pp. 187–188.

115. The marriage rate in Massachusetts increased sharply (by 16 percent) between 2003 (5.6 per one thousand residents) and 2004 (6.5 per one thousand residents). This was likely the result of the pent-up demand of same-sex couples, many of whom had been waiting for years for the opportunity to marry. By 2009, the Massachusetts marriage rate was back down to where it was in 2003.

116. Law professor Linda Bowen has also found that the enactment of constitutional amendments and statutes banning same-sex marriages is not associated with either higher marriage rates or lower divorce rates when compared to states that have failed to enact such laws. Dierdre M. Bowen, "I Wanna Marry You: An Empirical Analysis of the Irrelevance and Distraction of DOMAs," available at the website of the Social Science Research Network, http://papers.ssrn.com/sol3/papers.cfm?abstract_id=2209593, accessed Janary 2014.

117. M.V. Lee Badgett, *When Gay People Get Married: What Happens When Societies Legalize Same-Sex Marriage* (New York: New York University Press, 2009); ch. 4; William N. Eskridge, Jr., and Darren R. Spedale, *Gay Marriage: For Better or for Worse? What We've Learned from the Empirical Evidence* (New York: Oxford University Press, 2006), ch. 5. Badgett and Eskridge/Spedale refuted claims made by conservative journalist Stanley Kurtz about the supposed negative impact that the recognition of same-sex relationships had on the marriages and relationships of heterosexuals in Scandinavian countries. Stanley Kurtz, "The End of Marriage in Scandinavia," *The Weekly Standard*, February 2, 2004, 26.

118. Cahn and Carbone, *supra* note 114, pp. 1–2.

119. Jodi Levin-Epstein, Center for Law and Social Policy, *Lifting the Lid off the Family Cap* (Washington, D.C.: Center for Law and Social Policy, December 2003).

120. *Arkansas Welfare Waiver Demonstration Project* (University of Arkansas at Little Rock School of Social Work, 1997); Wendy Tanisha Dyer and Robert W. Fairlie, "Do Family Caps Reduce Out-of-Wedlock Births? Evidence from Arkansas, Georgia, Indiana, New Jersey and Virginia," 23 *Population Research and Policy Review* 441 (2004); Ted Joyce, Robert Kaestner, Sanders Korenman, and Stanley Henshaw, National Bureau of Economic Research, *Family Cap Provisions and Changes in Births and Abortions*, Working Paper 10214 (January 2004); Neeraj Kaushal and Robert Kaestner, "From Welfare to Work: Has Welfare Reform Worked?," 20 *Journal of Policy Analysis and Management* 699 (2001); Melissa Schettini Kearney, "Is There an Effect of Incremental Welfare Benefits on Fertility Behavior? A Look at the Family Cap," 34 *Journal of Human Resources* 295 (2004); Phillip B. Levine, "The Impact of Social Policy and Economic Activity throughout the Fertility Decision Tree," National Bureau of Economic Research, Working Paper 9021 (June 2002); Suzanne Ryan, Jennifer Manlove, and Sandra L. Hofferth, "State-Level Welfare Policies and Nonmarital Subsequent Childbearing," 25 *Population Research Policy Review* 103 (2006); Geoffrey L. Wallace, "The Effects of Family Caps on the Subsequent Fertility Decisions of Never-Married Women," 26 *Journal of Population Research* 73 (2009). A study of the New Jersey family cap program found that it was associated with lower fertility rates, but only among black women and short-term users of welfare. The study also found, quite disturbingly, that the family cap program was associated with an increase in the abortion rates among these two groups of women. Camasso, *supra* note 62.

Chapter 3

1. Sara McLanahan and Gary Sandefur, *Growing Up with a Single Parent: What Hurts, What Helps* (Cambridge, Mass.: Harvard University Press, 1994), p. 3.

2. *See, e.g.*, Maggie Gallagher, "What Is Marriage For? The Public Purposes of Marriage Law," 62 *Louisiana Law Review* 773 (2002); Lynn D. Wardle, "Considering the Impacts on Children and Society of 'Lesbigay' Parenting," 23 *Quinnipiac Law Review* 541 (2004); Brief of Appellant King County, Andersen v. King County, Washington Supreme Court, No. 75934-1, October 15, 2004.

3. This point has been recognized by several courts. *See, e.g.*, Perry v. Brown, 671 F.3d 1052, 1089 (9th Cir. 2012); Goodridge v. Department of Public Health, 798 N.E.2d 941, 963 (Mass. 2003).

4. *See, e.g.*, Greg J. Duncan, Pamela A. Morris, and Chris Rodrigues, "Does Money Really Matter? Estimating Impacts of Family Income on Young Children's Achievement with Data from Random-Assignment Experiments," 47 *Developmental Psychology* 1263 (2011).

5. *See, e.g.,* Pamela E. Davis-Kean, "The Influence of Parent Education and Family Income on Child Achievement: The Indirect Role of Parental Expectations and the Home Environment," 19 *Journal of Family Psychology* 294 (2005).

6. *See, e.g.,* Michael E. Lamb, "Mothers, Fathers, Families, and Circumstances: Factors Affecting Children's Adjustment," 16 *Applied Developmental Science* 98 (2012).

7. Michael S. Wald, "Adults' Sexual Orientation and State Determinations Regarding Placement of Children," 40 *Family Law Quarterly* 381 (2006).

8. For a summary of studies showing that children raised by married couples have generally better outcomes than those raised by single parents, see Paul R. Amato, "The Impact of Family Formation Change on the Cognitive, Social, and Emotional Well-Being of the Next Generation," 15 *The Future of Children* 75 (2005).

9. Michael J. Rosenfeld, "Nontraditional Families and Childhood Progress through School," 47 *Demography* 755, 755 (2010).

10. Lamb, *supra* note 6, p. 102 (emphasis added).

11. Claire Crawford, Alissa Goodman, Ellen Greaves and Rob Joyce, "Cohabitation, Marriage and Child Outcomes: An Empirical Analysis of the Relationship between Marital Status and Cohabitation in the United Kingdom Using the Millennium Cohort Study," 4 *Child and Family Law Quarterly* 176, 196 (2012). *See also* Alissa Goodman and Ellen Greaves, *Cohabitation, Marriage and Child Outcomes* (London: Institute for Fiscal Studies, 2010).

12. *See, e.g.,* Nadia Garnefski and Rene F. W. Diekstra, "Adolescents from One Parent, Stepparent and Intact Families: Emotional Problems and Suicidal Attempts," 20 *Journal of Adolescence* 201 (1997) (studying "adolescents living in intact families" without distinguishing between biological and adoptive parents); Elizabeth Thomson, Thomas L. Hanson, and Sara S. McLanahan, "Family Structure and Child Well-Being: Economic Resources vs. Parental Behaviors," 73 *Social Forces* 221, 225 (1994) (noting that for purposes of the study, "family structure was determined by the relationship of each parent to children younger than 19 in the household" and that "original two-parent families are married-couple families in which all children younger than 19 in the household *were born to or adopted by the couple*") (emphasis added). Both of these studies were cited in Brief of Amicus Curiae Alliance for Marriage, Inc., in Support of Appellants-Intervenors, Andersen v. King County, Washington Supreme Court, No. 75934-1, October 18, 2004, pp. 8–11. Michael Lamb has noted that "the term 'biological' has been used misleadingly in some of the research to identify children raised by the same parents from birth, whether or not they were biological or adoptive parents." Lamb, *supra* note 6, p. 105.

13. Amato, *supra* note 8, at 80. *See also* Andrew J. Cherlin, *The Marriage-Go-Round: The State of Marriage and the Family in America Today* (New York: Knopf, 2009), p. 22. For examples of briefs filed by defenders of same-sex marriage bans that cite Amato's work, see Brief of the American College of Pediatricians in Support of Appellants, Perry v. Brown, U.S. Court of Appeals for the Ninth Circuit, No. 10-16696, September 24, 2010, p. 6; Brief of Family Research Council as Amicus Curiae in Support of Defendants-Appellants, Conaway v. Deane, Maryland Court of Appeals, No. 44, September 8, 2006, p. 32 n.18.

14. For examples of efforts by marriage equality opponents to analogize between same-sex couple parent households and stepparent households, see e.g., Douglas W. Kmiec, "The Procreative Argument for Proscribing Same-Sex Marriage," 32 *Hastings Constitutional Law Quarterly* 653, 659 (2005); Brief of the American College of Pediatricians in Support of Appellants, *supra* note 13, pp. 10–11.

15. Carlos A. Ball, *The Right to be Parents: LGBT Families and the Transformation of Parenthood* (New York: New York University Press, 2012), ch. 3; Carlos A. Ball, "Rendering Children Illegitimate in Former Partner Parenting Cases: Hiding Behind the Facade of Certainty," 20 *American University Journal of Gender, Social Policy & Law* 623 (2012).

16. Amato, *supra* note 8, pp. 80–81.

17. Susan Golombok, Fiona MacCallum, Emma Goodman, and Michael Rutter, "Families with Children Conceived by Donor Insemination: A Follow-Up at Age Twelve," 73 *Child Development* 952 (2002); Susan Golombok, Clare Murray, Vasanti Jadva, Emma Lycett, Fiona MacCallum, and John Rust, "Non-genetic and Non-gestational Parenthood: Consequences for Parent-Child Relationships and the Psychological Well-Being of Mothers, Fathers and Children at Age 3," 21 *Human Reproduction* 1918 (2006); Susan Golombok, Jennifer Readings, Lucy Blake, Polly Casey, Alex Marks, and Vasanti Jadva, "Families Created through Surrogacy: Mother-Child Relationships and Children's Psychological Adjustment at Age 7," 47 *Developmental Psychology* 1579 (2001); Fiona MacCallum, Susan Golombok, and Peter Brinsden, "Parenting and Child Development in Families with a Child Conceived through Embryo Donation," 21 *Journal of Family Psychology* 278 (2007); Fiona MacCallum and Sarah Keeley, "Embryo Donation Families: A Follow-Up in Middle Childhood," 22 *Journal of Family Psychology* 799 (2008); Lucy Owen and Susan Golombok, "Families Created by Assisted Reproduction: Parent-Child Relationships in Late Adolescence," 32 *Journal of Adolescence* 835 (2009).

18. Trial Testimony of David Blankenhorn, Perry v. Schwarzenegger, No. C 09-2292-VRW Northern District of California, January 26, 2010, p. 2795.

19. Laura Hamilton, Simon Cheng, and Brian Powell, "Adoptive Parents, Adaptive Parents: Evaluating the Importance of Biological Ties for Parental Investment," 72 *American Sociological Review* 95, 96 (2007).

20. *See, e.g.*, L. DiAnne Borders, Lynda K. Black, and B. Kay Pasley, "Are Adopted Children and Their Parents at Greater Risk for Negative Outcomes?," 47 *Family Relations* 237 (1998); Femmie Juffer and Marinus H. van IJzendoorn, "Adoptees Do Not Lack Self-Esteem: A Meta-analysis of Studies on Self-Esteem of Transracial, International, and Domestic Adoptees," 133 *Psychological Bulletin* 1067 (2007); Elizabeth Raleigh and Grace Kao, "Is There a (Transracial) Adoption Achievement Gap? A National Longitudinal Analysis of Adopted Children's Educational Performance," 35 *Children & Youth Services Review* 142 (2013); Marinus H. van IJzendoorn, Femmie Juffer, and Caroline W. Klein Poelhuis, "Adoption and Cognitive Development: A Meta-analytic Comparison of Adopted and Nonadopted Children's IQ and School Performance," 131 *Psychological Bulletin* 301 (2005).

21. *See, e.g.*, Femmie Juffer and Marinus H. van IJzendoorn, "Behavior Problems and Mental Health Referrals of International Adoptees," 293 *Journal of the American Medical Association* 2501 (May 25, 2005); Brent C. Miller, Xitao Fan, Matthew Christensen, Harold D. Grotevant, and Manfred van Dulmen, "Comparisons of Adopted and Nonadopted Adolescents in a Large, Nationally Representative Sample," 71 *Child Development* 1458 (2000). For reviews of the literature on the children of adoptive parents, see, e.g., Steven Nickman et al., "Children in Adoptive Families: Overview and Update," 44 *Journal of the American Academy Child & Adolescent Psychiatry* 987 (2005); Jesus Palacios and David Brodzinsky, "Adoption Research: Trends, Topics, Outcomes," 34 *International Journal of Behavioral Development* 270 (2010).

22. Marinus H. van IJzendoorn and Femmie Juffer, "Adoption as Intervention: Meta-analytic Evidence for Massive Catch-up and Plasticity in Physical, Socio-Emotional, and Cognitive Development," 47 *Journal of Child Psychology and Psychiatry* 1228 (2006).

23. Lamb, *supra* note 6; Timothy J. Biblarz and Judith Stacey, "How Does the Gender of Parents Matter?," 72 *Journal of Marriage and Family* 3 (2010).

24. *See, e.g.*, Kevin MacDonald and Ross D. Parke, "Bridging the Gap: Parent-Child Play Interaction and Peer Interactive Competence," 55 *Child Development* 1265 (1984); K. Alison Clark-Stewart, "And Daddy Makes Three: The Father's Impact on Mother and Young Child," 49 *Child Development* 466 (1978).

25. For example, a brief filed by a conservative association of pediatricians with the federal Court of Appeals in the Proposition 8 litigation relied on studies that used convenience (i.e., nonrandom) sampling to defend its view that men and women parent in different ways. Brief of the American College of Pediatricians in Support of Appellants, *supra* note 13, pp. 21–22. The brief cited one study whose child subjects all attended two private schools in Houston. Thomas G. Power, Marianne P. McGrath, Sheryl O. Hughes, and Sarah H. Manire, "Compliance and Self-Assertion: Young Children's Responses to Mothers versus Fathers," 30 *Developmental Psychology* 980 (1994). Another study cited in the same brief identified parent subjects by placing advertisements in Montreal neighborhood newspapers. Daniel Paquette and Mark Bigras, "The Risky Situation: A Procedure for Assessing the Father-Child Activation Relationship," 180 *Early Child Development & Care* 33 (2010).

26. Michael E. Lamb, "How Do Fathers Influence Children's Development? Let Me Count the Ways," *in The Role of the Father in Child Development*, Michael E. Lamb, ed. (New York: Wiley, 5th ed., 2010), p. 3.

27. Catherine S. Tamis-LeMonda, "Conceptualizing Fathers' Roles: Playmates and More," 47 *Human Development* 220, 223 (2004). A review of studies on the differences between men and women found that both genders overlapped considerably in attributes and that there was little evidence of categorical differences between the two. Bobbi J. Carothers and Harry T. Reis, "Men and Women Are from Earth: Examining the Latent Structure of Gender," 104 *Journal of Personality and Social Psychology* 385 (2013).

28. Lamb, *supra* note 6, p. 101.

29. For a critique of a socioevolutionary understanding of parenting that links it to biological determinism, see Tamis-LeMonda, *supra* note 27. For an analysis of historical changes in the understanding of fatherhood in the United States, see Elizabeth H. Pleck, "Two Dimensions of Fatherhood: A History of the Good Dad–Bad Dad Complex," *in The Role of the Father in Child Development*, Michael E. Lamb, ed. (New York: Wiley, 4th ed., 2004), p. 32; Elizabeth H. Pleck and Joseph H. Pleck, "Fatherhood Ideals in the United States: Historical Dimensions," *in The Role of the Father in Child Development*, Michael E. Lamb, ed. (New York: Wiley, 3rd ed., 1997), p. 33.

30. Brief on the Merits for Respondent the Bipartisan Legal Advisory Group of the U.S. House of Representatives, United States v. Windsor, U.S. Supreme Court, No.12-307, January 13, 2013, p. 48.

31. Amici Curiae Brief of Social Science Professors in Support of Hollingsworth and Bipartisan Legal Advisory Group Addressing the Merits and Supporting Reversal, Hollingsworth v. Perry and Windsor v. United States, U.S. Supreme Court, Nos. 12-144 & 12-307, January 29, 2013, pp. 7–8.

32. *See, e.g.*, National Institute of Child Health and Human Development Early Child Care Research Network, "Mothers' and Fathers' Support for Child Autonomy and Early School Achievement," 44 *Developmental Psychology* 895 (2008); Michelle L. Kelley, Tammy S. Smith, Arlene P. Green, Andrea E. Berndt, and Melissa C. Rogers, "Importance of Fathers' Parenting to African-American Toddlers' Social and Cognitive Development," 21 *Infant Behavior & Development* 733 (1988); Jacqueline D. Shannon, Catherine S. Tamis-LeMonda,

Kevin London, and Natasha Cabrera, "Beyond Rough and Tumble: Low-Income Fathers' Interactions and Children's Cognitive Development at 24 Months," 2 *Parenting: Science and Practice* 77 (2002).

33. Anne Martin, Rebecca M. Ryan, and Jeanne Brooks-Gunn, "The Joint Influence of Mother and Father Parenting on Child Cognitive Outcomes at Age 5," 22 *Early Childhood Research Quarterly* 423 (2007); Rebecca M. Ryan, Anne Martin, and Jeanne Brooks-Gunn, "Is One Good Parent Good Enough? Patterns of Mother and Father Parenting and Child Cognitive Outcomes at 24 and 36 Months," 6 *Parenting: Science and Practice* 211 (2006).

34. *See, e.g.*, Catherine S. Tamis-LeMonda, Jacqueline D. Shannon, Natasha J. Cabrera, and Michael E. Lamb, "Fathers and Mothers at Play with Their 2- and 3-Year-Olds: Contributions to Language and Cognitive Development," 75 *Child Development* 1806 (2004); National Institute of Child Health and Human Development Early Child Care Research Network, "Fathers' and Mothers' Parenting Behavior and Beliefs as Predictors of Children's Social Adjustment in the Transition to School," 18 *Journal of Family Psychology* 628 (2004).

35. Joseph H. Pleck, "Fatherhood and Masculinity," *in The Role of the Father in Child Development*, Michael E. Lamb, ed. (New York: Wiley, 5th ed., 2010), p. 44.

36. Lamb, *supra* note 26, pp. 4–5.

37. Brian Powell and Douglas B. Downey, "Living in Single-Parent Households: An Investigation of the Same-Sex Hypothesis," 62 *American Sociological Review* 521 (1997).

38. Powell and Douglas B. Downey, *supra* note 37, pp. 530, 537.

39. *See, e.g.*, Defendant-Intervenors-Appellants Opening Brief, Perry v. Brown, U.S. Court of Appeals for the Ninth Circuit, No. 10-16696, September 17, 2010, p. 89 (criticizing trial court for rejecting the "instinctive, commonsense belief" that children do best when raised by married heterosexual couples who are biologically related to their children). *See also* Hernandez v. Robles, 855 N.E.2d 1, 7 (N.Y. 2006) ("Intuition and experience suggest that a child benefits from having before his or her eyes, every day, living models of what both a man and a woman are like.").

Chapter 4

1. *See, e.g.*, S v. S, 608 S.W.2d 64 (Ky. Ct. App. 1980); S.E.G. v. R.A.G., 735 S.W.2d 164 (Mo. Ct. App. 1987); M.J.P. v. J.G.P., 640 P.2d 966 (Ok. 1982); Dailey v. Dailey, 635 S.W.2d 391 (Tenn. Ct. App. 1981).

2. *See, e.g.*, Hassenstab v. Hassenstab, 570 N.W.2d 368 (Neb. Ct. App. 1997); Inscoe v. Inscoe, 700 N.E.2d 70 (Ohio Ct. App. 1997); Van Driel v. Van Driel, 525 N.W.2d 37 (S.D. 1994).

3. Clifford J. Rosky, "Fear of the Queer Child," 61 *Buffalo Law Review* 607 (2013).

4. Dudley Clendinen and Adam Nagourney, *Out for Good: The Struggle to Build a Gay Rights Movement in America* (New York: Simon & Schuster, 1999), pp. 303–304.

5. *See, e.g.*, Perry v. Schwarzenegger, 704 F. Supp. 2d 921, 980 (N.D. Cal. 2010); Gill v. Office of Personnel Management, 699 F. Supp. 2d 374, 388 (D. Mass. 2010). *See also* Florida Department of Children and Families v. Matter of Adoption of X.X.G., 45 So.3d 79, 87 (Fla. Dist. Ct. App. 2010).

6. Hernandez v. Robles, 855 N.E.2d 1, 8 (N.Y. 2006) ("commonsense premise[s]"); Lofton v. Secretary of Department of Children & Family Services, 358 F.3d 804, 819 (11th Cir. 2004) ("unprovable assumptions").

7. *See, e.g., Hernandez*, 855 N.E.2d at 7–8; *Lofton*, 358 F.3d at 826; Jackson v. Abercrombie, 884 F. Supp. 2d 1065, 1115 (D. Ct. Haw. 2012); Andersen v. King County, 138 P.3d 963, 983 (Wash. 2006).

8. *See, e.g.*, SmithKline Corp. v. Abbott Laboratories, 740 F.3d 471 (9th Cir. 2014); Kerrigan v. Commissioner of Public Health, 957 A.2d 407, 432 (Conn. 2008); Varnum v. Brien, 763 N.W.2d 862, 895–896 (Iowa 2009).

9. *See, e.g., Lofton*, 358 F.3d at 817–818; Conaway v. Deane, 932 A.2d 571, 608 (Md. 2006); *Andersen*, 138 P.3d at 975–976.

10. FCC v. Beach Communications, Inc., 508 U.S. 307, 313 (1993).

11. *Beach Communications*, 508 U.S. at 313; Ginsberg v. New York, 390 U.S. 629, 642–643 (1968).

12. Heller v. Doe, 509 U.S. 312, 321 (1993).

13. *See, e.g.*, Kimel v. Florida Board of Regents, 528 U.S. 62, 83–84 (2009). A third limitation imposed by the rational basis test is that there must be a rational relationship between the government's ends and the means it has chosen to achieve them. *See, e.g.*, Nordlinger v. Hahn, 505 U.S. 1, 10 (1992).

14. *See, e.g.*, Romer v. Evans, 517 U.S. 620, 633–636 (1996); City of Cleburne v. Cleburne Living Center, 473 U.S. 432, 448–450 (1985); Department of Agriculture v. Moreno, 413 U.S. 528, 534–535 (1973).

15. *See, e.g.*, Massachusetts v. Department of Health & Human Services, 682 F.3d 1, 10 (1st Cir. 2012); Robert C. Farrell, "The Two Versions of Rational-Basis Review and Same-Sex Relationships," 86 *Washington Law Review* 281, 306–328 (2011).

16. Mark Regnerus, "How Different Are the Adult Children of Parents Who Have Same-Sex Relationships? Findings from the New Family Structures Study," 41 *Social Science Research* 752 (2012).

17. Martha Kirkpatrick, Catherine Smith, and Ron Roy, "Lesbian Mothers and Their Children: A Comparative Survey," 51 *American Journal of Orthopsychiatry* 545 (1981); Susan Golombok, Ann Spencer, and Michael Rutter, "Children in Lesbian and Single-Parent Households: Psychosexual and Psychiatric Appraisal," 24 *Journal of Child Psychology & Psychiatry* 551 (1983); Sharon L. Huggins, "A Comparative Study of Self-Esteem of Adolescent Children of Divorced Lesbian Mothers and Divorced Heterosexual Mothers," 18 *Journal of Homosexuality* 123 (1989). A follow-up to the study led by Susan Golombok conducted more than a decade later, when the children in question were young adults, found no differences between the children of lesbian mothers and children of heterosexual mothers in levels of anxiety and depression. Fiona Tasker and Susan Golombok, "Adults Raised as Children in Lesbian Families," 65 *American Journal of Orthopsychiatry* 203 (1995).

18. *See, e.g., Lofton*, 358 F.3d at 825; Goodridge v. Department of Public Health, 798 N.E.2d 941, 999 (Mass. 2003) (Cordy, J., dissenting).

19. Michael S. Wald, "Adults' Sexual Orientation and State Determinations Regarding Placement of Children," 40 *Family Law Quarterly* 381, 409 (2006).

20. The studies, in chronological order, include: David K. Flaks, Ilda Ficher, Frank Masterpasqua, and Gregory Joseph, "Lesbians Choosing Motherhood: A Comparative Study of Lesbian and Heterosexual Parents and Their Children," 31 *Developmental Psychology* 105 (1995); Anne Brewaeys, Ingrid Ponjaert, E. V. Van Hall, and Susan Golombok, "Donor Insemination: Child Development and Family Functioning in Lesbian Mother Families," 12 *Human Reproduction* 1349 (1997); Susan Golombok, Fiona Tasker, and Clare Murray, "Children Raised in Fatherless Families from Infancy: Family Relationships and the Socioemotional Development of Children of Lesbian and Single Heterosexual Mothers," 38 *Journal of Child Psychology & Psychiatry* 783 (1997); Raymond W. Chan, Barbara Raboy, and Charlotte J. Patterson, "Psychosocial Adjustment among Children Conceived via Donor Insemination by Lesbian and Heterosexual Mothers," 69 *Child Development* 443 (1998); Katrien Vanfraussen, Ingrid

Pojaert-Kristoffersen, and Anne Brewaeys, "What Does It Mean for Youngsters to Grow Up in a Lesbian Family Created by Means of Donor Insemination?," 20 *Journal of Reproductive and Infant Psychology* 237 (2002); Susan Golombok, Beth Perry, Amanda Burston, Clare Murray, Julie Mooney-Somers, Madeleine Stevens, and Jean Golding, "Children with Lesbian Parents: A Community Study," 39 *Developmental Psychology* 20 (2003); Fiona MacCallum and Susan Golombok, "Children Raised in Fatherless Families from Infancy: A Follow-Up of Children of Lesbian and Single Heterosexual Mothers at Early Adolescence," 45 *Journal of Child Psychology & Psychiatry* 1407 (2004); Beth Perry, Amanda Burston, Madeleine Stevens, Howard Steele, Jean Golding, and Susan Golombok, "Children's Play Narratives: What They Tell Us about Lesbian-Mother Families," 74 *American Journal of Orthopsychiatry* 467 (2004); Nanette Gartrell, Amalia Deck, Carla Rodas, Hedi Peyser, and Amy Banks, "The National Lesbian Family Study: 4. Interviews with the 10-Year-Old Children," 75 *American Journal of Orthopsychiatry* 518 (2005); Henny M. W. Bos, Frank van Balen, and Dymphna C. van den Boom, "Child Adjustment and Parenting in Planned Lesbian-Parent Families," 77 *American Journal of Orthopsychiatry* 38 (2007); Henny M. W. Bos and Frank van Balen, "Children in Planned Lesbian Families: Stigmatisation, Psychological Adjustment and Protective Factors," 10 *Culture, Health & Sexuality* 221 (2008); Susan Golombok and Shirlene Badger, "Children Raised in Mother-Headed Families from Infancy: A Follow-Up of Children of Lesbian and Single Heterosexual Mothers, at Early Adulthood," 25 *Human Reproduction* 150 (2010); Nanette Gartrell and Henny Bos, "US National Longitudinal Lesbian Family Study: Psychological Adjustment of 17-Year-Old Adolescents," 126 *Pediatrics* 28 (2010); Loes van Gelderen, Henny M. W. Bos, Nanette Gartrell, Jo Hermanns, and Ellen C. Perrin, "Quality of Life of Adolescents Raised from Birth by Lesbian Mothers: The US National Longitudinal Family Study," 33 *Journal of Developmental & Behavioral Pediatrics* 1 (2012); Henry Bos, Nanette Gartrell, and Loes van Gelderen, "Adolescents in Lesbian Families, *DSM*-Oriented Scale Scores and Stigmatization," 25 *Journal of Gay & Lesbian Social Services* 121 (2013).

21. Brewaeys et al., *supra* note 20.

22. Chan et al., *supra* note 20.

23. For studies that have partly relied on data gathered from third parties, see, e.g., Chan et al., *supra* note 20; Flaks et al., *supra* note 20; Golombok et al. (2003), *supra* note 20; MacCallum and Golombok, *supra* note 20; Vanfraussen et al., *supra* note 20.

24. Nanette Gartrell, Amy Banks, Nancy Reed, Jean Hamilton, Carla Rodas, and Amalia Deck, "The National Lesbian Family Study: 3. Interviews with Mothers of Five-Year-Olds," 70 *American Journal of Orthopsychiatry* 542 (2000).

25. Golombok et al. (2003), *supra* note 20.

26. Golombok et al. (2003), *supra* note 20, p. 30.

27. Jennifer L. Wainwright, Stephen T. Russell, and Charlotte J. Paterson, "Psychosocial Adjustment, School Outcomes, and Romantic Relationships of Adolescents with Same-Sex Parents," 75 *Child Development* 1886 (2004).

28. Jennifer L. Wainright and Charlotte J. Patterson, "Delinquency, Victimization, and Substance Use among Adolescents with Female Same-Sex Parents," 20 *Journal of Family Psychology* 526 (2006).

29. Jennifer L. Wainright and Charlotte J. Patterson, "Peer Relations among Adolescents with Female Same-Sex Parents," 44 *Developmental Psychology* 117 (2008).

30. Ian Rivers, Paul Poteat, and Nathalie Noret, "Victimization, Social Support, and Psychosocial Functioning among Children of Same-Sex and Opposite-Sex Couples in the United Kingdom," 44 *Developmental Psychology* 127 (2008).

31. Michael J. Rosenfeld, "Nontraditional Families and Childhood Progress through School," 47 *Demography* 755 (2010).

32. Daniel Potter, "Same-Sex Parent Families and Children's Academic Achievement," 74 *Journal of Marriage and Family* 556 (2012).

33. *Lofton*, 358 F.3d at 825; *Goodridge*, 798 N.E.2d at 980 (Sosman, J., dissenting).

34. Tasker and Golombok, *supra* note 20.

35. Tamar D. Gershon, Jeanne M. Tschann, and John M. Jemerin, "Stigmatization, Self-Esteem, and Coping among the Adolescent Children of Lesbian Mothers," 24 *Journal of Adolescent Health* 437 (1999); Vanfraussen et al., *supra* note 20.

36. Wainwright et al., *supra* note 27; Wainwright and Patterson, *supra* note 28; Wainwright and Patterson, *supra* note 29.

37. Rivers et al., *supra* note 30; Stephen Erich, Heather Kanenberg, Kim Case, Theresa Allen, and Takis Bogdanos, "An Empirical Analysis of Factors Affecting Adolescent Attachment in Adoptive Families with Homosexual and Straight Parents," 31 *Children & Youth Services Review* 398 (2009).

38. Bos et al. (2013), *supra* note 20; Gartrell and Bos, *supra* note 20; Golombok and Badger, *supra* note 20; van Gelderen et al., *supra* note 20.

39. *Lofton*, 358 F.3d at 826.

40. *Hernandez*, 855 N.E.2d at 8.

41. Gartrell and Bos, *supra* note 20; Golombok and Badger, *supra* note 20.

42. Stephen Erich, Patrick Leung, Peter Kindle, and Sharon Carter, "Gay and Lesbian Adoptive Families: An Exploratory Study of Family Functioning, Adoptive Child's Behavior, and Familial Support Networks," 9 *Journal of Family Social Work* 17, 27 (2005). *See also* Paige Averett, Blace Nalavany, and Scott Ryan, "An Evaluation of Gay/Lesbian and Heterosexual Adoption," 12 *Adoption Quarterly* 129 (2009) (cross-sectional study of adopted children between the ages of one and eighteen raised by gay, lesbian, and heterosexual couples found no association between parental sexual orientation and the children's psychological adjustment); Tony Xing Tan and Jennifer Baggerly, "Behavioral Adjustment of Adopted Chinese Girls in Single-Mother, Lesbian Couple, and Heterosexual-Couple Households," 12 *Adoption Quarterly* 171 (2009) (study comparing adopted Chinese girls raised in single-mother, lesbian-couple, and heterosexual-couple households found no significant differences in behavioral adjustment as a function of family type).

43. Erich et al., *supra* note 37, p. 401.

44. Rachel H. Farr, Stephen L. Forssell, and Charlotte J. Patterson, "Parenting and Child Development in Adoptive Families: Does Parental Sexual Orientation Matter?," 14 *Applied Developmental Science* 164 (2010).

45 Rachel H. Farr and Charlotte J. Patterson, "Coparenting among Lesbian, Gay, and Heterosexual Couples: Associations with Adopted Children's Outcomes," 84 *Child Development* 1226 (2013).

46. Justin A. Lavner, Jill Waterman, and Letitia Ann Peplau, "Can Gay and Lesbian Parents Promote Healthy Development in High-Risk Children Adopted from Foster Care?," 82 *American Journal of Orthopsychiatry* 465, 470 (2012). Another study also suggests that lesbian and gay couples adopt transracially more often than heterosexual couples. Rachel H. Farr and Charlotte J. Patterson, "Transracial Adoption by Lesbian, Gay, and Heterosexual Couples: Who Completes Transracial Adoptions and With What Results?," 12 *Adoption Quarterly* 187 (2009).

47. Abbie E. Goldberg and JuliAnna Z. Smith, "Predictors of Psychological Adjustment in Early Placed Adopted Children with Lesbian, Gay, and Heterosexual Parents," 27 *Journal of Family Psychology* 431 (2013).

48. Regnerus, *supra* note 16, pp. 761–762.

49. The problematic way Regnerus identified "lesbian mothers" and "gay fathers" is also reflected in how he dealt with respondents who reported that *both* their mother and father participated in at least one same-sex relationship. Regnerus, in order to increase the number of "gay fathers" in his study, arbitrarily determined that those children should be deemed to have been raised by gay fathers rather than by lesbian mothers; Regnerus, *supra* note 16, p. 758.

50. Regnerus, *supra* note 16, p. 757.

51. Regnerus, *supra* note 16, p. 757.

52. Cynthia Osborne, "Further Comments on the Papers by Marks and Regnerus," 41 *Social Science Research* 779, 780 (2012).

53. *See, e.g.*, Lawrence A. Kurdek, Mark A. Fine, and Ronald J. Sinclair, "School Adjustment in Sixth Graders: Parenting Transitions, Family Climate, and Peer Norm Effects," 66 *Child Development* 430 (1995); Lawrence L. Wu and Brian C. Martinson, "Family Structure and the Risk of a Premarital Birth," 16 *American Sociological Review* 210 (1993).

54. American Psychological Association, *Lesbian and Gay Parenting* (Washington, D.C.: American Psychological Association, 2005); Committee on Psychosocial Aspects of Child and Family Health of the American Academy of Pediatrics, "Promoting the Well-Being of Children Whose Parents Are Gay or Lesbian," 131 *Pediatrics* 827 (2013).

55. *See, e.g.*, Henny Bos and Theo G. M. Sandfort, "Children's Gender Identity in Lesbian and Heterosexual Two-Parent Families," 62 *Sex Roles* 114 (2010); Golombok et al., *supra* note 17; Richard Green, Jane Barclay Mandel, Mary E. Hotvedt, James Gray, and Laurel Smith, "Lesbian Mothers and Their Children: A Comparison with Solo Parent Heterosexual Mothers and Their Children," 15 *Archives of Sexual Behavior* 167 (1986).

56. Golombok et al. (2003), *supra* note 20, p. 28.

57. Abbie E. Goldberg, *Lesbian and Gay Parents and Their Children: Research on the Family Life Cycle* (Washington, D.C.: American Psychological Association, 2010), p. 129.

58. Beverly Hoeffer, "Children's Acquisition of Sex-Role Behavior in Lesbian-Mother Families," 51 *American Journal of Orthopsychiatry* 536 (1981); Kirkpatrick et al., *supra* note 17; Golombok et al., *supra* note 17.

59. Green et al., *supra* note 55.

60. Judith Stacey and Timothy J. Biblarz, "(How) Does the Sexual Orientation of Parents Matter?," 66 *American Sociological Review* 159, 177–178 (2001).

61. Abbie E. Goldberg, Deborah A. Kashy, and JuliAnna Z. Smith, "Gender-Typed Play Behavior in Early Childhood: Adopted Children with Lesbian, Gay, and Heterosexual Parents," 67 *Sex Roles* 503 (2012).

62. Bos and Sandfort, *supra* note 55.

63. Brewaeys et al., *supra* note 20; Farr et al., *supra* note 44; Megan Fulcher, Erin L. Sutfin, and Charlotte J. Patterson, "Individual Differences in Gender Development: Associations with Parental Sexual Orientation, Attitudes, and Division of Labor," 58 *Sex Roles* 330 (2008); MacCallum and Golombok, *supra* note 20; Erin L. Sutfin, Megan Fulcher, Ryan P. Bowles, and Charlotte J. Patterson, "How Lesbian and Heterosexual Parents Convey Attitudes about Gender to Their Children: The Role of Gendered Environments," 58 *Sex Roles* 501 (2008). The Fulcher study did find one difference: "Children with lesbian parents found

gender transgressions committed by boys to be less serious than did children of heterosexual parents." Fulcher et al., *supra*, p. 336. Gender transgression was measured by showing children pictures of other children engaged in gender-atypical conduct, such as a "boy with fingernail polish and [a] girl playing football," and then asking them how they felt about the pictures; p. 334.

64. Weinberger v. Wiesenfeld, 420 U.S. 636, 648, 650 (1975).

65. *Wiesenfeld*, 420 U.S. at 652.

66. Stanton v. Stanton, 421 U.S. 7, 10 (1975).

67. *Stanton*, 421 U.S. at 14–15.

68. Orr v. Orr, 440 U.S. 268, 279–280 (1979).

69. Mississippi Univ. for Women v. Hogan, 458 U.S. 718, 729–730 (1982).

70. United States v. Virginia, 518 U.S. 515, 522, 541 (1996).

71. *See, e.g., Orr*, 440 U.S. at 279 (holding that the state's purpose of "allocat[ing] ... family responsibilities under which the wife plays a dependent role" is constitutionally impermissible); *Wiesenfeld*, 420 U.S. at 648 (noting that Congress's purpose behind the statutory provision under challenge was to allow widows to take care of children without having to work).

72. *Stanton*, 421 U.S. at 14, 17 (1975).

73. Edward O. Laumann, Jonathan H. Gagnon, Robert T. Michael, and Stuart Michaels, *The Social Organization of Sexuality* (Chicago: University of Chicago Press, 1994), p. 290.

74. Gary J. Gates, "How Many People Are Lesbian, Gay, Bisexual, and Transgender?," Williams Institute (2011), p. 2, available at http://williamsinstitute.law.ucla.edu/wp-content/uploads/Gates-How-Many-People-LGBT-Apr-2011.pdf, accessed January 2014.

75. *See, e.g.*, J. Michael Bailey, Michael P. Dunne, and Nicholas G. Martin, "Genetic and Environmental Influences on Sexual Orientation and Its Correlates in an Australian Twin Sample," 78 *Journal of Personality & Social Psychology* 524 (2000); Niklas Langström, Qazi Rahman, Eva Carlström, and Paul Lichtenstein, "Genetic and Environmental Effects on Same-Sex Sexual Behavior: A Population Study of Twins in Sweden," 39 *Archives of Sexual Behavior* 75 (2010).

76. *See, e.g.*, Ralf W. Dittman, M. E. Kappes, and M. H. Kappes, "Sexual Behavior in Adolescent and Adult Females with Congenital Adrenal Hyperplasia," 17 *Psychoneuroendroconology* 153 (1992); Melissa Hines, Charles Brook, and Gerard S. Conway, "Androgen and Psychosexual Development: Core Gender Identity, Sexual Orientation, and Recalled Childhood Gender Role Behavior in Women and Men with Congenital Adrenal Hyperplasia (CAH)," 41 *Journal of Sex Research* 75 (2004).

77. "Answers to Your Questions: For a Better Understanding of Sexual Orientation and Homosexuality," American Psychological Association (2008), p. 2, available at www.apa.org/topics/sexuality/sorientation.pdf, accessed January 2014.

78. Almost all of the published studies in this area have investigated the sexual orientation of the daughters of lesbian mothers. One exception is a 1995 study that reported on the sexual orientation of eighty-two adult sons of gay men. J. Michael Bailey, David Bobrow, Marilyn Wolfe, and Sarah Mikach, "Sexual Orientation of Adult Sons of Gay Fathers," 31 *Developmental Psychology* 124 (1995). The researchers, who did not use a control group composed of children of heterosexual parents, found that "of sons whose sexual orientation could be rated with confidence ... 91% were heterosexual," while the remaining 9 percent were gay; p. 126. Richard Green published a study in 1978 that also did not utilize a control group of children of heterosexual parents. Most of the children

in the study were not yet adolescents. The primary purpose of the study was to assess the gender attitudes and preferences of the children rather than their sexual orientation. However, Green reported that all of the (small number of) teenagers and young adults in the study had a heterosexual sexual orientation. Richard Green, "Sexual Identity of 37 Children Raised by Homosexual or Transsexual Parents," 135 *American Journal of Psychiatry* 692 (1978). An unpublished study of young adult children of twenty-four gay men in the United Kingdom that compared their sexual orientation to the young adult children of twenty-four straight men found that "the children of gay fathers were more likely than the children of heterosexual fathers to have been attracted to someone of the same gender and to have a sexual relationship with someone of the same gender." Susan Golombok and Fiona Tasker, "Gay Fathers," *in The Role of the Father in Child Development*, Michael E. Lamb, ed. (New York: Wiley, 5th ed., 2010), pp. 319, 332 (describing Fiona Tasker and Helen Barrett, "The Sexual Identity of Young Adult Sons and Daughters of Gay Fathers," paper presented at the 7th Conference of the European Federation of Sexology, Brighton, United Kingdom, May 12–16 (2004)). The study also found that while none of the children of the heterosexual fathers identified as lesbian, gay, or bisexual, six of the children of the gay fathers did. "Of these, two sons identified as gay, one daughter identified as lesbian, and two sons and one daughter identified as bisexual"; p. 332.

79. Golombok and Tasker, *supra* note 20.
80. Bos and Sandfort, *supra* note 55, pp. 118–119.
81. Golombok and Badger, *supra* note 20.
82. Nanette K. Gartrell, Henny M. W. Bos, and Naomi G. Goldberg, "Adolescents of the U.S. National Longitudinal Lesbian Family Study: Sexual Orientation, Sexual Behavior, and Sexual Risk Exposure," 40 *Archives of Sexual Behavior* 1199 (2011).
83. Gartrell et al., *supra* note 82, p. 1205.
84. For a summary of these surveys, see Gates, *supra* note 74.
85. Gartrell et al., *supra* note 82, pp. 1202–1204.
86. Nanette K. Gartrell, Henny M. W. Bos, and Naomi G. Goldberg, "New Trends in Same-Sex Sexual Contact for American Adolescents?," 41 *Archives of Sexual Behavior* 5 (2012).
87. Bowers v. Hardwick, 478 U.S. 186 (1986).
88. Romer v. Evans, 517 U.S. 620, 633 (1996).
89. Cass R. Sunstein, "The Supreme Court 1995 Term—Forward: Leaving Things Undecided," 110 *Harvard Law Review* 4, 62 (1996).
90. Clifford J. Rosky, "No Promo Hetero: Children's Right to Be Queer," 35 *Cardozo Law Review* 425, 450 (2013).
91. Lawrence v. Texas, 539 U.S. 558 (2003).
92. Christian Legal Society v. Martinez, 130 S.Ct. 2971, 2990 (2010).
93. United States v. Windsor, 133 S.Ct. 2675, 2693 (2013).
94. Carey v. Population Services International, 431 U.S. 678, 694 n. 17 (1977) (plurality opinion) ("In the area of sexual mores, as in other areas, the scope of permissible state regulation is broader as to minors than as to adults."). It bears noting that the plurality in *Carey* recognized that adolescents enjoy a constitutional right to privacy that limits the ability of the state to regulate in matters related to procreation.
95. Supplemental Brief of Appellee, State v. Limon, Kansas Supreme Court, No. 00-85898-AS, June 18, 2004, pp. 8–9.
96. State v. Limon, 122 P.3d 22, 30–35 (Kan. 2005).

Chapter 5

1. In re Marriage Cases, 183 P.2d 384 (Ca. 2008).

2. Ellen Ann Andersen, *Out of the Closets & Into the Courts: Legal Opportunity Structure and Gay Rights Litigation* (Ann Arbor: University of Michigan Press, 2005), p. 144. One study found that nearly 60 percent of all state and local ballot initiatives relating to civil rights in the period 1959–1993 concerned the rights of lesbians and gay men. Barbara S. Gamble, "Putting Civil Rights to a Popular Vote," 41 *American Journal of Political Science* 245 (1997).

3. Romer v. Evans, 517 U.S. 620 (1996). For an exploration of the background, reasoning, and impact of *Romer*, see Carlos A. Ball, *From the Closet to the Courtroom: Five LGBT Rights Lawsuits That Have Changed Our Nation* (Boston: Beacon, 2010), ch. 3.

4. The amendment to the Hawai'i constitution granted the legislature the authority to limit marriage to one man and one woman. For an exploration of the events leading up to the adoption of that amendment, see Ball, *supra* note 3, pp. 178–185.

5. Although California voters had previously approved a statute banning same-sex marriage, the 2008 vote was more momentous because it addressed the issue of whether the state constitution should be amended to deny same-sex couples the opportunity to marry.

6. Arizona voters in 2006 rejected a measure that would have banned same-sex marriages and civil unions. Two years later, voters approved a narrower measure banning same-sex marriages only.

7. Frank Schubert and Jeff Flint, "Passing Prop 8," *Politics* (February 2009), p. 45.

8. It's Already Happened, Yes on Proposition 8 Campaign, available at www.youtube.com/watch?v=0PgjcgqFYP4, accessed January 2014. For an extensive analysis of the political campaign on behalf of Proposition 8, including the use of television and Internet advertisement, see Melissa Murray, "Marriage Rights and Parental Rights: Parents, the State, and Proposition 8," 5 *Stanford Journal of Civil Rights & Civil Liberties* 357 (2009).

9. David Fleischer, *The Prop 8 Report: What Defeat in California Can Teach Us about Winning Future Ballot Measures on Same-Sex Marriage* (2010), pp. 32–35, available at the website of the LGBT Mentoring Project, http://prop8report.lgbtmentoring.org/, accessed January 2014.

10. Official ballot pamphlet from Proposition 8, available in William B. Rubenstein, Carlos A. Ball, and Jane Schacter, *Cases and Materials on Sexual Orientation* (St. Paul, Minn.: West, 4th ed., 2011), p. 641. A similar campaign based on the purported need to protect children from being "exposed" to same-sex marriage in the schools was waged in Maine in 2009 as part of a successful effort to persuade voters to repeal a statute allowing same-sex couples to marry. Abby Goodnough, "Focus of Gay-Marriage Fight Is Maine," *N.Y. Times*, October 28, 2009, A18.

11. Brief for Respondents, Romer v. Evans, U.S. Supreme Court, No. 94-1039, June 19, 1995, p. 48.

12. Everything to Do With Schools, Yes on Proposition 8 Campaign, available at www.youtube.com/watch?v=7352ZVMKBQM, accessed January 2014. The mother who appears in this ad had sued unsuccessfully to have materials presenting gay people in a positive light kept out of her young daughter's classroom in Massachusetts. Parker v. Hurley, 514 F.3d 87 (1st Cir. 2008).

13. *Perry*, 704 F. Supp. 2d 921, 988 (N.D. Cal. 2010).

14. *Perry*, 704 F. Supp. 2d at 931.

15. Trial Testimony of David Blankenhorn, Perry v. Schwarzenegger, No. C 09-2292-VRW U.S. District Court, Northern District of California, January 26, 2010, pp. 2767–2768.

16. Trial Testimony of David Blankenhorn, *supra* note 15, pp. 2794, 2797–2798.

17. Trial Testimony of David Blankenhorn, *supra* note 15, pp. 2744, 2776.

18. For an articulation of this view, see Patrick Lee, Robert P. George, and Gerard V. Bradley, "Marriage and Procreation: Avoiding Bad Arguments," *Public Discourse* (March 30, 2011), available at www.thepublicdiscourse.com/2011/03/2637/, accessed January 2014. Blankenhorn alluded to this point when he claimed during his trial testimony that "marriage predates law. Marriage is not a creature of law." Trial Testimony of David Blankenhorn, *supra* note 15, p. 2790.

19. Trial Testimony of Nancy Cott, Perry v. Schwarzenegger, No. C 09-2292-VRW, U.S. District Court, Northern District of California, January 12, 2010, pp. 226, 222; Nancy F. Cott, *Public Vows: A History of Marriage and the Nation* (Cambridge, Mass.: Harvard University Press, 2000).

20. Stephanie Coontz, *Marriage, a History: How Love Conquered Marriage* (New York: Penguin Books, 2005).

21. Andrew J. Cherlin, "The Deinstitutionalization of American Marriage," 66 *Journal of Marriage and Family* 848 (2004).

22. Cherlin, *supra* note 21, pp. 851–852. Cherlin elaborates on this point in Andrew J. Cherlin, *The Marriage-Go-Round: The State of Marriage and the Family in America Today* (New York: Knopf, 2009), ch. 4. *See also* Paul R. Amato, Alan Booth, David R. Johnson, and Stacy J. Rogers, *Alone Together: How Marriage in America Is Changing* (Cambridge, Mass.: Harvard University Press, 2007).

23. *Perry*, 704 F. Supp. 2d at 980.

24. David Blankenhorn, "How My View on Gay Marriage Changed," *N.Y. Times*, June 22, 2012, A27.

25. Perry v. Brown, 671 F.3d 1052 (9th Cir. 2012).

26. Brief of Petitioners, Hollingsworth v. Perry, U.S. Supreme Court, No. 12-144, January 22, 2013, pp. 28, 32.

27. For an earlier challenge to DOMA, see Wilson v. Ake, 354 F. Supp. 2d 1298 (M.D. Fla. 2005).

28. Gill v. Office of Personnel Management, 699 F. Supp. 2d 374, 390 (D. Mass. 2010).

29. Letter of Eric H. Holder, Jr., U.S. Attorney General, to John H. Boehner, Speaker of the U.S. House of Representatives, February 23, 2011, available in Rubenstein et al., *supra* note 10, p. 684. For arguments that it was appropriate for the Obama administration to cease defending DOMA in the courts, see Carlos A. Ball; "When May a President Refuse to Defend a Statute? The Obama Administration and DOMA," 106 *Northwestern University Law Review Colloquy* 77 (2011); Dawn Johnsen, "The Obama Administration's Decision to Defend Constitutional Equality Rather Than the Defense of Marriage Act," 81 *Fordham Law Review* 599 (2012).

30. Windsor v. United States, 833 F. Supp. 2d 394 (S.D.N.Y. 2012).

31. Windsor v. United States, 699 F.3d 169 (2nd Cir. 2012).

32. Brief on the Merits for Respondent the Bipartisan Legal Advisory Group of the U.S. House of Representatives, United States v. Windsor, U.S. Supreme Court, No.12-307, January 13, 2013, p. 44.

33. Brief on the Merits for Respondent, *supra* note 32, pp. 47–48.

34. *Perry*, 704 F. Supp. 2d at 973.

35. Trial Testimony of David Blankenhorn, *supra* note 15, p. 2803.

36. Hollingsworth v. Perry, 133 S. Ct. 2652 (2013).

37. United States v. Windsor, 133 S. Ct. 2675 (2013).

38. *Windsor*, 133 S. Ct. at 2693.

39. *Windsor*, 133 S. Ct. at 2694, 2696.

40. Committee on Psychosocial Aspects of Child and Family Health of the American Academy of Pediatrics, "Promoting the Well-Being of Children Whose Parents Are Gay or Lesbian," 131 *Pediatrics* 827 (2013).

41. Douglas B. Mogul, "In Supporting Gay Marriages, AAP Reaches Correct Conclusion, Wrong Process," March 23, 2013, available at the website of Pediatrics, http://pediatrics. aappublications.org/content/early/2013/03/18/peds.2013-0376.abstract/reply#pediatrics_el_55419, accessed January 2014.

42. Mogul, *supra* note 41.

43. Brief of Leon R. Kass, Harvey C. Mansfield, and the Institute for Marriage and Public Policy as Amici Curiae in Support of Petitioners, Hollingsworth v. Perry, U.S. Supreme Court, No. 12-144, January 29, 2013, p. 2.

44. Brief of Leon R. Kass, Harvey C. Mansfield, and the Institute for Marriage and Public Policy, *supra* note 43, pp. 3, 31.

45. Virginia's brief warned that "if this Court...should undertake an inquiry [about the wisdom of antimiscegenation laws], it would quickly find itself mired in a veritable Serbonian bog of conflicting scientific opinion upon the effects of interracial marriage, and the desirability of preventing such alliances, from the physical, biological, genetic, anthropological, cultural, psychological and sociological point of view." Brief of Appellee, Loving v. Virginia, U.S. Supreme Court, No. 395, March 20, 1967, p. 41.

46. Loving v. Virginia, 388 U.S. 1 (1967).

47. *See, e.g.*, Levy v. Louisiana, 391 U.S. 68 (1968); Weber v. Aetna Casualty & Surety Company, 406 U.S. 164 (1972).

Conclusion

1. In addition, as Courtney Joslin has shown, Congress has traditionally extended family-based benefits to children regardless of whether they are biologically related to the adults who serve as their parents. Courtney G. Joslin, "Marriage, Biology, and Federal Benefits," 98 *Iowa Law Review* 1467 (2013).

2. Kathryn Edin and Maria Kefalas, *Promises I Can Keep: Why Poor Women Put Motherhood before Marriage* (Berkeley: University of California Press, 2005); Pamela J. Smock, Wendy D. Manning, and Meredith Porter, " 'Everything's There Except Money': How Money Shapes Decisions to Marry among Cohabitors," 67 *Journal of Marriage and Family* 680 (2005).

3. Stanton v. Stanton, 421 U.S. 7, 14 (1975).

INDEX

abortion, 49, 57

accidental procreation, 51–54, 67–68, 119.
  See also responsible procreation

Add Health, 90, 92

adoption, 2, 3, 40, 52, 53, 67, 71, 131
  bans, 83, 85, 87, 121
  and social science studies, 73, 75, 92–94,
    98, 114, 134
  transracial, 88, 93

adultery, 21, 55–56, 57, 58, 59, 61, 62

Aid to Dependent Children, 40–41. *See
  also* Aid to Families with Dependent
  Children

Aid to Families with Dependent Children,
  42–43, 44, 46, 47, 49

Alabama, 42, 101

Alito, Samuel, 92

alternative insemination. *See* reproductive
  technologies

American Academy of Pediatrics, 96, 125

American Law Institute, 56

American Medical Association, 55

American Psychiatric Association, 83

American Psychological Association, 96,
  103

antimiscegenation laws. *See* interracial
  marriages

Arkansas, 15, 63, 64, 65

Arkes, Hadley, 39–40

assisted reproduction. *See* reproductive
  technologies

Avon Longitudinal Study of Parents and
  Children, 90

Badger, Shirlene, 104

Badgett, M.V. Lee, 65–66

Baker, Jack, 1–2

ballot box measures, 84, 111, 113

Barr, Bob, 3

Barwick, Paul, 2

Bauer, Gary, 43, 48

Bennett, William, 48–49

Biblarz, Timothy, 98, 99

biological parents,
  and child outcomes, 6, 7, 19, 50, 69,
    73–76, 114, 134
  and family optimality, 30, 81, 118,
    119–120, 130–131
  lesbian mothers who are, 92–93
  and link to marriage, 3, 5, 37, 39–40, 117

Bipartisan Legal Advisory Group to the U.S.
  House of Representatives, 78, 118–120,
  122, 123

birth control. *See* contraception

Bishop, Joel, 32

Blackstone, William, 118

Blankenhorn, David, 45, 50. 75, 114–115,
  116–117, 121

Bos, Henry, 104

Bowers v. Hardwick, 106–107

Brown v. Board of Education, 19, 20, 22

Bryant, Anita, 84

Buck v. Bell, 24

Bush, George W., 122

Cahn, Naomi, 66

California, 18–19, 43, 59, 89, 111–112, 113.
  See also Proposition 8

Canada, 119

Canady, Charles, 3

Carbone, June, 66

Cherlin, Andrew, 116

children of lesbians and gay men,
  gender role development of, 7, 85–86,
    96–99, 110, 134
  harm to, 5, 68, 84, 121, 123–124, 127
  psychological adjustment and social
    functioning of, 7, 85–86, 87–96, 110,
    134, 135
  sexual orientation of, 7, 85–86, 102–106,
    110, 134
Civil Rights Act of 1866, 15
Civil Rights Act of 1964, 116
civil unions, 111, 130
Clinton, Bill, 46
Clement, Paul, 122
cohabitation, 55, 60, 61,132
  and children, 58, 72, 80, 127, 133
  interracial, 20–21, 22
  laws against, 57–58, 62
  and polygamy, 34
  and welfare reform, 41
Colorado, 107, 111, 113
Colorado for Family Values, 113
Comstock Act, 54–55
Connecticut, 118
  and contraception ban, 54, 55
  and disability marriage ban, 23,
    24, 51
  and same-sex marriage, 51, 64, 65
contraception, 38, 46, 54–55, 57, 61
Coontz, Stephanie, 116
Cooper, Charles, 120–121
Cordy, Robert, 52
Cott, Nancy, 115–116
coverture, 115, 136
custody, 3, 56, 71, 83, 88, 131

Darwin, Charles, 17
Davis, Kingsley, 26–27
Davis, Sylvester, 18
Defense of Marriage Act. *See also*
    United States v. Windsor
  constitutional challenge of, 78, 118–120,
    122, 123–124
  legislative history of, 3–4, 39–40, 123
  and Supreme Court, 6, 8, 68, 85, 108, 112,
    122, 123–124
  and welfare reform, 48

disability marriage bans, 6, 11, 22–24, 32,
    35, 70, 129
  and same-sex marriage bans, 29–31
divorce, 21, 38, 41, 43, 49, 132
  no-fault, 49, 59–60
  rates of, 59–60, 61, 62, 64, 65, 66
DOMA. *See* Defense of Marriage Act
domestic partnerships, 93, 111, 121, 130
donor insemination. *See* reproductive
    technologies
dual-gender parenting, 51, 76–80, 120,
    135–136. *See also* fatherhood;
    motherhood

Early Childhood Longitudinal
    Study–Kindergarten Cohort, 91
Eichor, Rick, 3–4
equal protection, 85, 100, 107, 109, 128
  and nonmarital children, 28
  and same-sex marriage, 117, 118, 123
Erich, Stephen, 92
Eskridge, Bill, 65
eugenics,
  and disability marriage bans, 23, 24,
    143n59
  and interracial marriage bans, 12, 17–18,
    18–19, 20, 22
  and nonmarital children, 25, 26
  and polygamy, 148n106

family caps, 47, 49, 66–67, 132
family optimality, 5, 7, 129
  and adoptive parents, 75
  and antimiscegenation laws, 17, 18, 21, 22
  and biological parents, 73–76, 130–131
  and dual-gender parents, 76–80, 131
  inappropriateness of standard, 69–71,
    74, 75
  and married parents, 69, 71–72
  and nonmarital children, 28
  raised during Proposition 8 litigation,
    114, 117, 118, 122
  and single parents, 69, 71–72
  and stepparents, 73–74
Family Research Council, 40, 48
Family Support Act, 44
Farr, Rachel, 93

fatherhood, 45, 47, 49–50, 52, 80, 135–136.
  See also fathers
fathers. *See also* gay fathers
  absence of, 3, 6, 44, 49–50, 89
  acknowledgment of paternity by, 25
  and dual-gender parenting, 76–80, 88
  inheriting from, 25, 26–27, 28
  and parental responsibility, 47–48, 52
  single, 60
  and welfare reform, 43, 44–45
Fight Repression of Erotic Expression, 1
Florida, 20, 83, 84, 113
fornication, 12–13, 21, 55–56, 57, 58, 61, 62
foster care, 3, 71, 85, 87, 93, 95
Fourteenth Amendment, 15, 20. *See also*
  equal protection.
Friedman, Lawrence, 59
Full Faith and Credit Clause, 4

Galton, Francis, 17
gay fathers, 93–94, 98–99. *See also* children
  of lesbians and gay men
gender. *See also* dual-gender parenting
  and constitutional review, 4, 85
  and government policies, 99–102, 131,
    135–136
  role development, 7–8, 84, 85, 86, 87,
    96–99, 110, 134
  and same-sex marriage, 11, 29, 37, 51,
    118, 119, 127, 128
  and sodomy laws, 56
  and stereotyping 100–103
Georgia, 63, 65, 106
Gingrich, Newt, 46
Glass, David, 42
Goldberg, Abbie, 93, 98
Golombok, Susan, 90, 104, 105
Gordon, Albert, 21
Gordon, Sarah Barringer, 34
Grossberg, Michael, 22

Hawai'i, 3, 4, 50, 62, 111, 118
Head Start, 79
heightened judicial scrutiny, 85, 86, 101,
  118, 119
Hoffman, Connie, 20
Holland, 66, 89

Hollingsworth v. Perry, 120, 122–123, 125,
  128. *See also* Proposition 8

Iceland, 60
illegitimacy. *See* nonmarital children
incest, 11, 31–33
Indiana, 15, 40, 52–53
infertility, 16, 39, 40
Institute for American Values, 45, 50,
  114–115
Institute for Marriage and Public Policy,
  125, 128
interracial marriages, 6, 11, 35, 129
  and biology, 17, 19
  and child psychological development,
    21–22, 126, 127
  and eugenics, 17–18
  and post-Civil War litigation, 15–16
  and post-World War II litigation, 18–22,
    126–128
  prohibitions of in California, 18–19
  prohibitions of in Florida, 20
  prohibitions of in Maryland, 14–15
  prohibitions of in Massachusetts, 15
  prohibitions of in Pennsylvania, 15
  prohibitions of in Virginia, 12–14, 19–20,
    21–22
  and same-sex marriages, 11–12, 29–31
  and sterility, 16, 140n19
  and slavery, 12–13
  and weak progeny, 16, 19
Iowa, 64, 65

Jolly, Wilbur, 42

Kammerer, Percy, 24–25
Kansas, 23, 109
Kennedy, Anthony, 121, 123
Kentucky, 63, 64, 65
Kmiec, Douglas, 39

Labine v. Vincent, 28
Lamb, Michael, 72, 77
Lamberth, Ruth, 19
Lavner, Justin, 93
Lawrence v. Texas, 57, 107–108, 123
Leiber, Francis, 34

lesbian mothers. *See also* children of lesbians and gay men
    following dissolution of heterosexual relationships, 87–88
    in planned lesbian families, 3, 89–90, 91, 104
Levy v. Louisiana, 27–28
Locke, John, 118
Long, Russell, 43
Longitudinal Study of Adolescent Health. *See* Add Health
Louisiana, 27, 28, 30, 42, 63, 65
Loving v. Virginia, 13, 19, 20, 21–22, 27, 126, 127, 128

marriage. *See also* disability marriage bans; interracial marriages; nonmarital children; same-sex marriage
    of affinity, 32–33
    common law, 20, 25
    of cousins, 32
    covenant, 61
    deinstitutionalization of, 114–115, 117
    different understandings of, 115–117
    and parenting, 25, 69, 71–72, 75–76, 80
    polygamous, 31–35
    and procreation, 3–5, 7, 38, 48–53, 55, 117
    rates of, 58, 62–64, 65
    state versus federal regulation of, 119, 122, 123, 140n14
married parents,
    compared to single parents, 45, 69, 71–72, 75–76, 80
    as optimal parents, 3, 5, 7, 30, 84, 114, 126–127, 133–134
Massachusetts, 15, 25, 55, 62–63, 64, 112
McConnell, Michael, 1–2
McLanahan, Sara, 45, 69
McLaughlin, Dewey, 20
McLaughlin v. Florida, 20–21, 22
Mendel, Gregor, 17
Michigan, 23, 63, 64, 65
Minnesota, 1–2
Mississippi, 42, 46, 63, 64, 65, 101
Missouri, 15, 63, 64, 65
Model Penal Code, 56

Mogul, Douglas, 125, 126, 127
Montana, 63, 64, 65
Montesquieu, Baron de, 118
Morrison v. Sadler, 52–53
motherhood, 47, 49–50, 80, 135–136. *See also* mothers
mothers. *See also* lesbian mothers
    and dual-gender parenting, 76–80, 88
    and interracial marriage bans, 12–14
    and nonmarital children, 25–26, 27
    and parental responsibility, 6, 66
    single, 7, 38, 50, 60, 133
    and welfare reform, 41–47, 61, 62
Moynihan, Patrick, 43, 44
Murray, Charles, 43, 44–45, 46

Naim, Ham, 19–20
National Longitudinal Lesbian Family Study, 92, 104–106
National Survey of Family Growth, 105
natural law, 39, 40, 140n15
Nebraska, 23
New Jersey, 23, 42, 49
New York, 118, 119, 123
nexus test, 83
no-fault divorce. *See* divorce
nonmarital children, 6, 11, 35, 129, 132
    and economic factors, 45–46, 132–133
    and government benefits, 25–28, 68
    historical explanations of, 25–26, 144n71
    and interracial unions, 14
    rates of, 60, 62, 64–65, 66, 133
    and same-sex marriage bans, 29–31, 51
    and Supreme Court cases, 27–28, 60, 126–127, 128
    and welfare reform, 41–47, 48–49, 61, 67
North Carolina, 19, 42
North Dakota, 63
Novkov, Julie, 17

Obama administration, 118
Ohio, 46, 63, 64, 65
Old Age Insurance Program, 41
optimality. *See* family optimality
Oregon, 63, 64, 65
Ottenheimer, Martin, 32

Pascoe, Peggy, 16
Patterson, Charlotte, 90
Pediatrics, 125, 127
Perez, Andrea, 18
Perez v. Sharp, 19, 21
Personal Responsibility and Work
    Opportunity Reconciliation Act,
    47–48, 66
Pleck, Joseph, 79
Plecker, Walter, 18
polygamy, 33–35
Popenoe, David, 45
Potter, Daniel, 91
procreation. *See also* accidental procreation;
    responsible procreation
    and biological facts, 3, 38–40, 130–131
    and birth control, 54–55
    and disability marriage bans, 23–24
    and incest, 31–33
    and interracial marriages, 14, 16, 21
    and nonmarital children, 26–27
    and polygamy, 34–35
    and sex, 56–57
Proposition 8. *See also Hollingsworth*
    v. Perry
    constitutional litigation of, 6, 8, 50, 75, 78,
    114, 125–126, 128
    passage of, 111–112
    political campaign in favor of, 112–118
    and Supreme Court, 85, 92, 120–123, 135
Pruett, Kyle, 50

Quayle, Dan, 44

rational basis test, 101–102, 107, 119, 121
    explained, 85–86
    and social science studies, 7, 87, 96, 97,
    99, 103, 106, 109–110
Reagan administration, 43–44, 48, 120
Reagan, Ronald, 43, 48
Regnerus, Mark, 87, 94–96
reproductive technologies, 3, 52–53, 67,
    74–75, 89, 131
responsible procreation. *See also* accidental
    procreation
    compared to accidental procreation,
    51–52

and economic factors, 132–133
no quick fixes in promotion of, 8,
    131–133
and same-sex marriage, 5, 7, 29, 37–38,
    40, 48–51, 61–62, 68, 118, 123
and welfare reform, 7, 40–48, 66
Reynolds v. United States, 34
Romer v. Evans, 107, 108
Rosenfeld, Michael, 71, 91, 94
Rosky, Clifford, 107

same-sex marriage. *See also* Defense of
    Marriage Act; Proposition 8
    constitutional analysis of bans, 1–2, 4, 6,
    7, 11, 52–53, 84–85, 97–99, 123–124
    litigation, 2, 3, 4, 40, 49, 50, 52–53
    objections to, 3–7, 28–31, 37–40, 48–53,
    71–81, 112–115, 117–118, 119–120
Sandefur, Gary, 45, 69
Sandfort, Theo, 104
Sanger, Margaret, 54
Save Our Children, 84, 113
Scalia, Antonin, 40, 121
Scandinavian countries, 65
sexual orientation. *See also* children of
    lesbians and gay men; social science
    studies
    of children 102–106, 108–109, 113,
    163n78
    and conduct versus status, 107
    determination of, 95, 102–103
    legal classification of, 85–86, 118, 119, 120
    as a state interest, 106–110
Singer, John, 2
single parents. *See also* nonmarital children
    compared to married parents, 69, 71–72,
    75–76, 80, 89
    and family optimality, 30
    rates of, 60.
    and welfare reform, 41–47
Smith, JuliAnna, 93
social science studies,
    and children of adoptive parents, 75,
    92–95
    and children of cohabiting parents,
    72, 80
    and children of dual-gender parents, 76–81

social science studies (*Cont.*)
  and children of lesbians and gay men,
    7–8, 76, 80, 86–99, 102–106, 110, 117,
    134, 135, 163n78
  and children of married parents, 76, 80
  and children of single parents, 45, 69, 76,
    79, 80
  and children of stepparents, 69, 73–74,
    75, 80
  and convenience samples, 88, 89
  criticisms of, 5, 6, 88, 91–92
  and family instability, 95, 96
  and parental education, 70
  and parental income, 70
  and reproductive technologies, 74–75
Social Security Act, 41
sodomy laws, 3, 56–57, 61, 62, 106, 107
Sotomayor, Sonia, 120
South Carolina, 46, 59
South Dakota, 23
Spedale, Darren, 65
Spyer, Thea, 119
Stacey, Judith, 98, 99
Stanton v. Stanton, 100, 102
Stearns, Cliff, 4
stepparents, 33, 44, 69, 73–74, 75, 80, 127
sterilization, 24, 42, 46, 141n26,
    143n59
Stonewall riots, 3

Sunstein, Cass, 107
Texas, 15, 57

United Kingdom, 72, 74, 90
United States v. Virginia, 101
United States v. Windsor, 8, 108, 119–120,
    122, 123–124, 125
U.S. Department of Health and Human
    Services, 105
Utah, 33–34, 63, 64, 65, 100

Vermont, 49, 118
Virginia, 12–14, 15, 21, 30, 126
    and Racial Integrity Act, 18, 19–20
visitation, 3, 83, 88, 131

Wald, Michael, 88
Walker, Vaughn, 114, 117
Wardle, Lynn, 5, 50–51, 52
Weber v. Aetna Casualty & Surety Company, 28
Webster, Noah, 32
Weinberger v. Wiesenfeld, 100
welfare reform, 7, 40–48, 49, 50, 61–62, 66,
    133. *See also* family cap
Whitehead, Barbara Dafoe, 44
Windsor, Edith, 119, 120
widowers, 60, 100
widows, 41, 42, 60, 100, 120
Wisconsin, 23